Billion Doll   ay

Arizona Interstate 19

Memoirs Of

INSPECTOR R S DAVIS

Acknowledgements

Many thanks to all the dedicated employees of the U.S. Geological Survey Earth Resources Observation and Science Center (EROS) and U.S. Selective Service System for their assistance and contributions in the production of this book.

Many thanks also to the fellow Inspectors, Customs Agents and Border Patrol Agents who day in and day out endured the hardship of life and death on the border. Everyday is a new challenge and not all of us made it home at the end of the day. Those whose names are on the Law Enforcement Memorial attest to the challenges and mission of Border Security. We are frequently under staffed, outnumbered by our adversaries and most definitely out funded by the drug cartels and other international criminal organizations who do not have to battle conflicting political parties for day to day survival. Politicians hurl words and insult each other when rocks, bricks and lead are all too common on the Mexican Border. Be safe my working family, I pray for you every night.

Lastly but nearest to my heart I greatly owe everything to my family who endured the long hours, days, months and yes even years that I was away from home for the job. You were at my side for the good times, the bad times and sometimes the terrifying times that all law enforcement families must survive. You were there with moral support and on occasion as nurses and therapists during recovery periods. Thank you, Miki, Matt, Toby, Ricky and Ryan, for the patience, support and advice you offered me over the years.

BILLION $ DOLLAR $ HIGHWAY

Table of Contents

BILLION $ DOLLAR $ HIGHWAY

Introduction

Interstate 19 is the main route from Nogales, Mexico through Nogales, Arizona to the two largest narcotics transship cities in Arizona: Tucson and Phoenix. I-19 is the only interstate freeway in the United States that is marked in kilometers rather than miles. This is the first red flag as to who runs southern Arizona. As far back as prohibition and probably before that Tucson and Phoenix have been hub cities for illegal alcohol, drugs and other illicit contraband entering the United States from Mexico. The actual value of the illicit contraband that traveled north on Interstate 19 (Billion Dollar Highway) into the United States has never been recorded but I venture to say it is easily in the billions of dollars. There are as many mediums to smuggle the illegal wares as the human mind can imagine. Some of these conduits are:

Tunnels - When I first arrived in Nogales as a new Customs Inspector, I learned that there remained tunnels from the bootlegging of booze during prohibition. These early tunnels usually ran from residences in Mexico to residences in the United States. Some of the tunnels were abandoned however some are still in use today for the illegal movement of contraband northbound and southbound. For the most part the tunnels are now used for smuggling drugs and humans north into the United States and weapons and money south into Mexico. In present times the only change is that today's new tunnels are generally much more sophisticated sometimes with wheeled carts making the tunnels resemble mine shafts. They have also expanded from mainly residence to residence to any location on one side to any location on the other. Many run from business to business, parking lot to parking lot or a combination thereof.

Wheeled conveyance – Cars, trucks, trains and even hand carts. These conveyances, much like the tunnels, are only limited by the imagination. If one can look at a wheeled conveyance and imagine a good location to hide contraband, it can be done. This can be accomplished by using natural voids or constructing voids that we generally refer to as compartments. I have heard the term "false compartment" used many times but I prefer the more accurate terms natural, factory or man-made. I have only seen one false compartment and that was on a watermelon truck where the outline of a compartment was visible from the outside of the cargo area but once the watermelons were removed, the compartment was no longer there, only the outline. Your will see many of these concealment methods in the following chapters.

Air conveyances – Fixed wing, rotary wing and catapults – catapults? Yep, even catapults. Air smuggling is still a problem today though nothing like it was in the 1980's and 1990's with the Amado Carrillo Fuentes Drug Trafficking Organization (DTO). In Mexico it is common that members of DTO's including the Drug Kingpins have at least one nickname or moniker. Carrillo Fuentes was affectionately known as Lord of the Sky's due to his use of aircraft for smuggling. The U.S. government's deployment and use of radar along the borders has curtailed traditional aircraft smuggling to a large degree. Recently with the easy acquisition and use of ultra-light aircraft there has been a resurgence in air smuggling. Once again, I will use the statement 'there are as many mediums to smuggle the illegal wares as the human mind can imagine'. Catapults are a prime example. I have seen catapults resembling the ones seen in movies tossing boulders at castles where packages of dope replace the boulders, air operated cannon catapults used to *shoot* large packages of dope across the border and simple slingshot catapults quickly constructed by stringing rubber strips connected to posts or trees essentially making over-sized slingshots. And that is enough on that subject.

Feet and hooves – Human overland backpacking and horse or mule caravans. Backpacking is the most common overland method used. Backpacking when you take a step back and just look at the accomplishment without looking at the illegal activity is quite impressive. The human mules will carry large packages of drugs in burlap bags with shoulder straps across the border and they will journey as much as 60 miles. The average weight of most backpacks usually falls somewhere in the area between 50 to 80 pounds. The trek is across some of the worst terrain in the world. The terrain is from high mountainous desert to canyons and gullies. Of course, there are miles and miles of flatland also and along most of the southwest border water is scarce to say the least. With temperatures as high as 120° Fahrenheit (49° Celsius) dehydration and deaths are commonplace in the vast uninhabited wastelands where dope and human traffickers operate. As I mentioned above, backpackers have been apprehended as far north as 60 miles from the border and have been reported even further north than that.

Billion Dollar Highway is an insight into a small portion of the overall picture, but it will open some eyes, make you laugh and at times maybe make you cry. These are true stories as they occurred when U. S. Customs was my way of life.

Dedication

In memory of my wife Miki
1956 - 2017

My wife was born in Fukuoka, Japan, came to America when she was very young and became an American citizen through naturalization. She, in her words, was an American Japanese. I am an American Indian of the Choctaw Nation and like her; I am an American Indian with American first. She would say that African Americans, Italian Americans, Mexican Americans and all others who put anything in front of American are not true Americans.

I met Miki at, of all places, an automobile accident. Neither one of us were involved in the accident, just bystanders but some 40 years later I lost her on February 2, 2017 when she lost her battle with cancer.

I love her beautiful smile and her sharp witticism. When I dream, I see her laughing and hear her singing her Japanese songs. Silly little songs but made beautiful by her. I still see her as I laid her down on February 2nd after holding her when her last moments of life passed away. Mostly I see her eyes the last time she was able to speak, and she said simply "I love you Rick" - nothing more and nothing more needed.

This book is dedicated to Miki – my best friend, my lifelong companion, my wife, my life.

ベイビー、愛してるよ
I love you Baby

BILLION $ DOLLAR $ HIGHWAY
Pain In The Ass
November 4, 1989
171 Pounds Marijuana

The sun had just risen in the East. Its brilliance creeping up Ephraim Canyon until finally it's warmth, instantaneous with the arrival of its rays, began to displace the early morning chill at the Mariposa Port of Entry on the west side of Nogales. It was 6:58 AM. I am manning Lane #1, the only lane open this lazy Saturday morning.

Traffic is very light (Mariposa was fairly new and unknown in 1989). My rotation on the Lane is 06:30 to 07:00. Two more minutes and its coffee time. Immigration will be relieving me, and they are perpetually late relievers. As my mind is on coffee and how good the morning sun feels I look south and see a car approaching.

As the car pulled up to me and stopped, I noted that it had four occupants. The driver and front seat passenger were both males in their mid to late forties. The driver appeared to be the older of the two. The back seat was occupied by two females. The gal closest to me is in her early twenties and the other, mid-teens. The vehicle is a mid-sized Chrysler station wagon.

"Good day, Sir. Where are you coming from?" I asked the driver in Spanish as he handed me four Mexican Passports.

"Hermosillo." he quickly replied. My antennae went up.

"Where are you going, Sir?" was my next question.

"Tucson." he replied. 'Nervous, very nervous.' I observed.

As I checked each passport, I studied its owner. Front seat passenger: the empty road ahead had him mesmerized. Back seat across the way: eyes transfixed on the back of front seat passengers head. Back seat near me: hands clasped together in her lap, intently studying her manicure.

"What are you bringing from Mexico?" I ask as I reach up and tap the front fender with my knuckle, SOLID.

"Nothing." The driver replied, now also intently scrutinizing the road in front of him.

"Good, open your hood, please." I said to him hopefully making it sound routine.

The driver popped the hood latch and stepped out. I step back towards the rear of the vehicle ensuring that if the car is loaded (with narcotics), he can't flee to Mexico. Mr. Hermosilloite proceeded to the front of the vehicle and begins fiddling with the hood safety catch. I moved on up to the hood area and, using my flashlight, feinted looking for the safety catch. I was actually searching for any gap in the grill/headlight area which might afford a glimpse behind the

5

fender.

I found what I was searching for almost immediately. I shined my flashlight in the gap where I should have seen a wide-open fender well. Pitch black? I'm looking at pitch black using a three cell Mag light. All I have is light reflecting off pitch black PACKAGES! I quickly move my light over and locate the safety catch. "Aqiu esta (here it is)."

As Mr. Smuggler opened the hood my mind was going over what I had. I knew that at least the driver side front fender was loaded. A quick glance at the fender bolts confirmed that they have been recently tampered with. Another quick glance at the passenger side fender bolts and they also have been recently worked. I have three occupants and the driver of the vehicle that (by their demeanor) also know. What I do not know is if they saw me, read me and now know that I know. For me to know how to proceed from here, I must answer this last question.

If these folks know that they are burned I have two options. I can hand cuff the driver here at the hood of the car, escort him to the booth and call for back-up, i.e. take the whole deal down on the lane. Option two is tell him to get back in the car and drive to secondary for a secondary inspection. Option two is, no doubt, the safest but it will afford Mr. Smuggler and his co-conspirators the opportunity to drive through secondary, where they could cut over to the southbound lanes and return to Mexico. The only little hitch with option one is if any of his cronies are armed, the whole damn thing might get interesting. That leaves only option one in my book. I am not letting this one get back to Mexico.

If these folks didn't catch me sneaking a peak and they don't know that I know they are loaded, I could still take the seizure down on the line as in option one above, I could refer them to secondary in hopes that they will suspect no more than a baggage check, or I could refer them to the "Permisso" parking area since they must get permisso's (a permit to proceed) anyhow. Unfortunately, the permisso parking area is a good distance beyond secondary. The only purpose for a permisso parking referral at this point would be for a CCD (Cold Controlled Delivery).

It is time to test the waters and see where I stand. Standing there next to Señor Smuggler I shined my light around the engine compartment. "O. K. close the hood." I said. As nonchalantly as I can I scrutinized the Smuggler's demeanor. Close study wasn't necessary; he openly exhaled and visibly relaxed. His body screamed what his mind thought, 'He doesn't suspect!'.

I came up with one more option, combine options two and three: "Park your car in Secondary Lane #1, then come back here for your Permisso's. There's no traffic so I'll allow you to use Secondary for Permisso parking today." I'm such a nice guy. "I'll hold your passports here for Immigration." Just a little insurance.

I will attempt to initiate a CCD, but I really don't want the load car in the distant permisso parking area. The guy almost broke into tears with relief as he returned to the driver seat and started the car. 'We may be able to pull this off.' I thought at his not too well concealed elation.

6

A CCD is a technique where Customs Special Agents attempt to covertly follow a load of narcotics to its destination. There, hopefully, we can nab some of the upper echelon smugglers along with the mules. The hard part is finding Special Agents that are available on a moment's notice. Their response time must be, generally, ten minutes or less. If no agent can respond in that time frame, we usually take the load down just as the suspects are re-entering their vehicle to depart secondary.

Normally, at 7:00 AM on a Saturday morning, I wouldn't even have considered such a ridiculous idea, but as circumstances dictated on this day, this should be a breeze. Just before I had gone to the line at 6:30, I happened to see OE (Office of Enforcement) Special Agent Jackson Paws. I had inquired as to why an Agent was hanging around Mariposa and had been told that *they*, apparently I missed a few additional agents, were waiting for some event to occur in the trade zone just west of our location. I had further been informed that it was all for naught as their informant had not shown and that they were going to wait until seven o'clock for him to show. Tailor made tail away.

As the vehicle began to pull away from primary on its way to secondary, I put the phone on speaker, hit intercom and called the Supervisors office.

"Supervisor's Office." It was Senior Inspector Soldier Buffalino.

"Soldier, there is a white wagon with wood grain trim in secondary lane one. It's loaded and the occupants are going to come back here for permisso's." I said, looking due south rather than at the phone just in case the smugglers were watching me. I knew that from their vantage point they would not be able to detect that I was talking into the phone on the counter in front of me.

"O.K." Buffalino replied "I'll check it out. Where is it loaded?"

"The left front fender for sure." I said as the load vehicle came to a stop in secondary. The occupants were in no hurry now that they had "cleared" primary. They got out and stretched a bit, shook the long drive from Hermosillo out of their joints and then headed my way. I noticed the two girls disembark very stiffly and massaged their back sides. I added "I think the back seat is also loaded. They think they are only getting pemisso's so you should let OE know this one is ripe for a CCD."

Great! This is going like clockwork. The party was now on their way to me for their passports, then to Immigration. I should only have to stall the party for a couple of minutes while Buffalino verifies the load and then gives me the signal to send them to Immigration.

I can see the vehicle sitting in secondary. If Buffalino hurries he can check the load and give the signal before the party even reaches me. 'Let's go Buffalino, get out there and check it' I am silently screaming in my mind only. The party reaches me, now all smiles and in cheerful conversation among themselves. Still no Buffalino. It's 7:05; no Immigration relief in sight and Buffalino still has not made it to secondary. Now coffee is no longer on my mind, *'Don't come yet Immigration*' has replaced any thought of coffee. The now relaxed smugglers came over to me and I start the stall, "Sorry folks but immigration said that they just arrived and that they will open the doors soon." This stall should work as long as Immigration is late on their relief. I know that they have actually been there since 6:00 AM.

I am now watching the load vehicle out of the corner of my eye. It sure looks lonely sitting there *all by itself*. Finally, I see a K-9 team (Narcotics Detector Dog and handler) pull into secondary.

"Good Morning, Rory." I yelled motioning the handler over "Did you hear about the fight at the basketball game last night?" That B.S. just jumped into my mind out of desperation.

Rory strolled over and said, "What game?"

I now said, under my breath and in English "That car in lane one is loaded. The left front fender for sure. A bunch of OE Agents are inside hanging out for something that didn't materialize so let them know this one is tailor made for a CCD."

Rory retreated back to secondary and just as he neared the entrance to the Supervisors Office, he encountered Inspector Velo Raptor. I saw him say something to Velo and they headed to the car. Velo checked the fender and headed straight toward me.

"It's loaded!" he whispered into my ear, "Where is the driver?"

"Sitting there on that bench with the other occupants." I motioned with my eyes. "They are waiting for Immigration to open, they think. Get inside and let OE know this is set for a CCD."

"Is it loaded?" there's Buffalino, standing halfway to secondary (about twenty-five yards away) yelling. "Well, is it loaded?"

"Yes!" Velo and I yell back.

"Where's the driver?" Buffalino is now close enough that he doesn't have to yell.

"Sitting there on the bench." I said

"Well, handcuff them and put them into the holding cell." the Senior Inspector replied.

Velo and I handcuff the two males and escorted the group in the east door on route to the holding cells. As our little group walked down the hall past the waiting area, we pass OE Agent Jackson and he abruptly fell in behind us where he followed us to the holding cell. We separated the males in separate holding cells after the pat-downs. The females were placed in separate waiting areas. After everyone was secured and comfy in their respective segregated areas, Jackson asked, "What's going on?"

"They're loaded." I said shrugging my shoulders and shaking my head, "The left front fender for sure and probably both fenders as well as the back seat, judging by how stiff the girls appeared when they got out. I tried to get Buffalino going on a CCD, but, well what can I say. I don't think he's ever nabbed a load. Inexperience, you know."

"You sure about the left front fender?" he asked.

"Yea, Jackson, I saw the packages." was my totally disappointed reply.

"Look Rick, go out there and check it out really quick. Let me know if it is loaded anywhere else. I am going to try for a CCD anyhow. Hell, we're all here, might as well try!" Jackson said in despair knowing that a perfect opportunity had, more than likely, been wasted.

Velo and I quickly proceeded to the load vehicle. There was Rory, running his dog. "Whatcha got Rory?" Velo asked.

"Nothing, dog says no." Rory responded with disappointment in his voice.

Velo and I look at each other. "Bull shit, let's check it out." I said.

I immediately checked the left front fender again. By forcing a screwdriver between the fender well cover and the fender a gap is created. Packages are clearly visible with a flashlight. I probed a package with the screwdriver, pulled the screwdriver out and took a sniff.

"Smells like weed to me Velo." I said irritated. Even the damn dog didn't want to co-operate on this one. Velo, with his upper torso in the back seat of the vehicle, looked through the window of the open back door and said, "You're right about the sore butt's. The back seat feels like a concrete bench. Poor girls, maybe they could use a massage!"

Ol' Velo was single at the time and never missed a chance at assisting a female in need. "I don't think OE would appreciate that. Check the door and I'll get the rear quarter panels and tailgate." After less than a minute Velo and I were back in with Jackson, "It's loaded everywhere, rear seat, doors, fenders, quarter panels and the tailgate." I announced.

"We're going to go ahead with a CCD." Jackson advised us, "Go ahead and release the lot and we'll see what happens."

"Before I do, do you have the southbound lanes blocked?" Legally these felons are in my custody and I really would not relish allowing four criminals to go from secure holding areas to Mexico.

"Yea, Southbound is covered." Jackson assured me.

Reluctantly I get Velo and we go open the cells, reunite the group and tell them they can go. I am sure that unless these people are brain dead, there is no way that this whole deal is going to work. As it turned out, I was right. Not ten minutes later the OE convoy returned.

The smugglers left the POE and proceeded to a parking lot about five miles down the road. There the driver got out, opened the hood, closed it, re-entered the vehicle and headed back to Mexico. Opening the hood was, more than likely, a signal to the owners of the load or to the northbound escort. At any rate, as soon as the party headed back to Mexico, OE made a felony stop and returned to the POE.

Illustration 1: Fender well with lining partially removed.
Painted package is difficult to see.

Illustration 2: Enhancing the photo makes the package a bit easier to see.

Velo, myself and of course the, now, all knowledgeable Buffalino dismantled the vehicle to recover 171 Pounds of Marijuana. As reported to OE, there were packages concealed in both front fenders, three of the four doors (the drivers being the exception), the back seat, rear side panels and the tailgate. The smugglers had painted the packages black everywhere that one might get a peek between panels. This method of concealment looks very impressive to the smugglers. To Velo and me, it looked like packages of narcotics painted black.

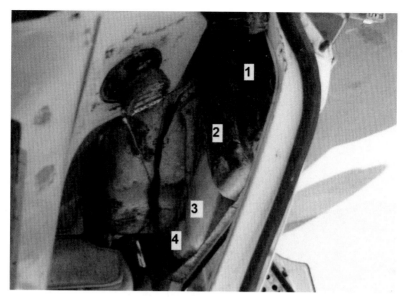

Illustration 3: Side Panel with 4 packages. Top two painted black.

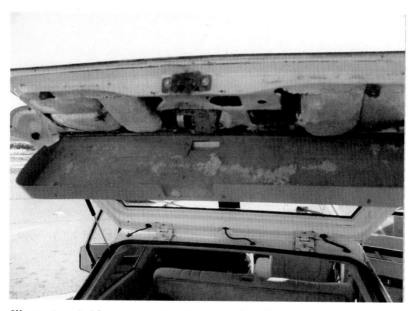

Illustration 4: I have no explanation as to how the packages defied gravity in this shot and yes that is the author starting on the back seat.

Illustration 5: This weed is on its way to the furnace, not the high school.

BILLION $ DOLLAR $ HIGHWAY

Until Death Do Us Part
December 12, 1989
129 Pounds Marijuana

Tuesday, December 12, 1989, a dozen more shopping days to Christmas. I am at the Mariposa POE. The traffic is heavy for Mariposa. It is 10:22 A.M., on the downhill slide for the 6:00 A.M. to 2:00 P.M. shift. There is a new Walmart on Mariposa Road at Interstate 19 which has a lot to do with the increase in traffic. Mariposa in no more, nor will it ever again be, the vacation spot for Nogales Customs. The sleepy little, relatively unknown, United States Port of Entry (POE) is now an adolescent POE thanks to the Industrial Revolution of West Mariposa Road.

I am working Lane #1. Sitting just outside my booth is Customs Inspector Feller Amado. Amado is a journeyman Customs Inspector with many years of service. I will be a journeyman in about a year. Not counting ZT (Zero Tolerance), I have one load of narcotics under my belt. To the best of my knowledge that is one more than Amado has in his career.

Some Inspectors go an entire career and retire without ever intercepting a load of dope. The concealment methods used by smugglers are sometimes mystifying. An inspector must be mentally alert and focused continuously during his/her tour or the one loaded vehicle out of the ten thousand vehicles that he or she processes will be missed.

Illustration 6: Nogales as it looked in the 80's and 90's. Both ports, just a couple of miles as the crow flies. Imagery courtesy of the U.S. Geological Survey. Visit the USGS at https://usgs.gov.

I remember how overwhelmed I felt the first time that I walked out to the Line (the Border) at the Grand Avenue POE and looked down the queue of vehicles waiting to cross into the United States. At that time Grand Avenue was only four lanes and Mariposa had only two lanes. Still, I was looking at four lines of vehicles that stretched as far as the eye could see. Any one of those vehicles may contain millions of dollars' worth of narcotics expertly concealed somewhere in it or on it. My job is to find it. My thoughts were, 'Yeah, Right!!! You have got to be kidding!'

Actually, overwhelming is an understatement. Every known type of privately-owned land vehicle from half of a million dollars' worth of customized recreational vehicle to bicycles pass through these lanes.

Still, not a month ago, I got my career load. At least that is what everyone told me. I was of a different opinion. I figured, if there is one out there, there must be another. I was told it was beginners' luck to get one so quick. 'We'll see.' I thought.

Inspector Amado is sitting there talking about his Navy days to anyone who will listen, which at present is no one. Everybody else had found some pressing task that needed attending. I am totally focused on processing my lane of traffic. A 1988 Chevrolet pick-up truck has just pulled up and stopped. It is occupied by a female in her early to mid-thirties and a teenage male.

"Hello. Where are you coming from?" I asked.

"Nogales (Sonora, MX.). I live there." she replied.

"Where are you going?" as I checked their documents.

Breaking into a big smile she answered, "To Walmart, we're going to do Christmas shopping."

No hesitation, excited about Christmas shopping. I thought 'she's O.K., a quick check of the vehicle and she's DTR (Down the Road)'. As I looked the vehicle over, I started with a visual inspection of the interior of the cab and then a check of the undercarriage. As I checked the under carriage, I noticed that the gas tanks (the vehicle was equipped with duel tanks) looked odd. The film of dirt on them did not match the dirt elsewhere under the vehicle.

I turned to Inspector Amado and said, "Feller, take this one down and check the tanks. They look like they may have been tampered with."

Amado got up, strolled over and looked under the vehicle. "They look O.K. to me." he said as he waived his hand dismissing any chance of him walking the vehicle to secondary and giving it a good inspection.

"I don't know, I don't like them. I'm going to send it down (to Secondary) anyhow." I replied.

"Why don't you walk it down and check it yourself. I'm up (on the Lane) at ten-thirty anyhow. I will take it for you now." Inspector Amado successfully skirted my referral.

Still in possession of the occupants Passports, I told the driver to park in Secondary lane one, two or three. She chose Lane 1. I followed the vehicle to secondary and instructed both occupants to step out of the vehicle and wait inside the office. I escorted them to the waiting area outside the Supervisors office and advised Supervisory Customs Inspector (SCI) Mustang Corners of their presence and told him that I would be checking the gas tanks on their vehicle. As I headed to the vehicle, I noticed that the driver remained calm; however, the teenage rider was on the nervous side. I returned to the vehicle and began the inspection.

Chevrolet saddle tanks are mounted on the vehicle between the frame and outer wall, just in front of the rear tires. The best way to check them is to lay down on one's back, crawl (or slither) under the vehicle and using a small mirror and flashlight, look for trap doors cut into the tank. The trap doors are usually sealed with bondo. Depending upon the sophistication of the builder, the trap door may by visible on top of the tank or it may be concealed. Gas tanks are, in a nutshell, a "Bitch" to check, and saddle tanks are the "Bitch" of gas tanks.

15

I cleaned, scratched, tapped, checked and cleaned, scratched, and tapped again. Nothing! At least three other Inspectors also checked, and all agreed: nothing. We ran a Narcotics Detector Dog, Nothing.

Everything indicated that I was barking up the wrong tree. Still, I just did not like the way that the dirt appeared. I decided to drop (remove) one of the tanks to get a look inside. Against everyone's advice I commenced with the difficult task of removing the driver side tank.

I was on my own and I knew that if I was wrong, I would be paying in extremely hard work to reinstall the tank. One person can get the damn things down, with difficulty and a lot of work, but it is almost impossible for one person to put them back. To this day, I feel let down by those fellow Inspectors who walked away from me.

When I had the tank about half way down, two guys from the Contraband Enforcement Team (CET) pulled into Secondary. Ramrod and Doublea pulled up and asked me what I was doing.

"I am trying to drop this tank." I said still under the vehicle.

"Is it loaded?" one of them asked.

"I don't know, I don't like the looks of it, and I have to see in it before I let it go." I said, wishing they would go away. I didn't know either one of these guys at the time, but I had heard that the CET Team was very arrogant and were a direct line to the District Director.

"What does it sound like?" asked Ramrod.

"It sounds a little dull." I tried to justify what I was doing.

"Did you run a dog?" Ramrod, now on his knees looking under the vehicle.

"Yeah, he didn't hit." Ouch strike one.

"Do you see a trap door or bondo or something?" now Ramrod is looking me in the eye, and I loosen number five of the eight mounting bolts.

"No, actually, I just don't feel right about the way the dirt is distributed under here. The tanks seem to have different dirt than the rest of the undercarriage." Damn, that sounds ridiculous even to me and it is coming out of my face. Strike two.

"Where the hell is the rest of your team?" Ramrod said looking around the empty secondary area. "This should be a team effort."

"They all looked and they decided that there's nothing here." I squirmed out from under the vehicle. I think that was a foul ball. At least it wasn't strike three.

"I'm Ulysis and this is Burt. Is it O.K. if I take a look?" Ramrod asked and to my surprise sounded quite sincere.

"Sure, I need a break." I replied as I lit a cigarette. I walked a safe distance away for the cigarette and more for my own discomfort.

"I don't see anything at all, Burt." Ulysis squirmed out. "And it sounds O.K. to me."

I finished the cigarette and walked back over. "Nothing?"

"Well we don't see anything." Doublea finally breaks his silence. "You don't feel right letting this one go?"

"No, I just don't like the dirt." I feel stupid. Another foul ball.

"Good, never let one go that you don't feel right about. Never!" Doublea said very seriously. "These guys should be helping you. To hell with them, we'll give you a hand."

These two gentlemen were light years from arrogant. They were genuinely there to help me, the new guy. Over the years we became close friends and some 28 years later I was fortunate and honored to work with Doubleas' daughter. She, like her father, is good, good people. I am honored to call them friends.

At the time I was shocked that they were there for me. My team, well that is another story. Finally, I felt like I at least had ball one! Way out of the strike zone. Those two guys dropped down, squirmed under the truck and five minutes later the tank was on the ground. As we pulled the tank out into the light, my heart sank. There lay a naked tank, naked of truck and naked of trap doors.

Illustration 7: The grounded gas tank.

Burt bent down and with a few taps removed the sending unit. The sending unit is where the float and the gas lines which send gas to the engine hook up. It is a round piece which connects to the top of the tank. When removed it reveals an opening approximately three inches in diameter through which the interior of the tank can be checked. Looking in my tank the view was blocked by a metal box, quite non-factory.

"I'll be damned." Ramrod said, "The damn thing *is* loaded."

Loaded!!! Home Run!!!

The method of concealment used on the tanks was a first. To my knowledge and to everyone including EPIC it had never been seen before. It has been seen quite extensively along the southwest border after Nogales published and distributed a document concerning it that also stated, "never before seen". Grand Slam home run!

The tanks are cut in half. A metal box containing the narcotics is suspended in the tank. The tanks are then welded back together and the weld is concealed under the mounting straps. No bondo is used in the process.

Illustration 8: Tank separated to remove the inner compartment containing the drugs.

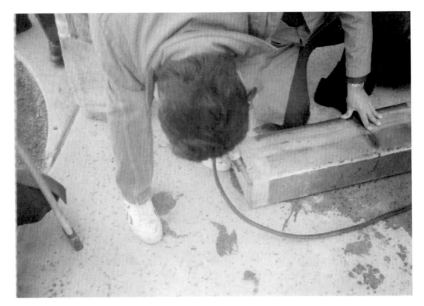

Illustration 9: Opening the compartment with an air chisel.

Illustration 10: Dope visible through the partially open compartment.

Illustration 11: Thar she be, tightly compressed marijuana.

Illustration 12: You could drive a nail in the bricks.

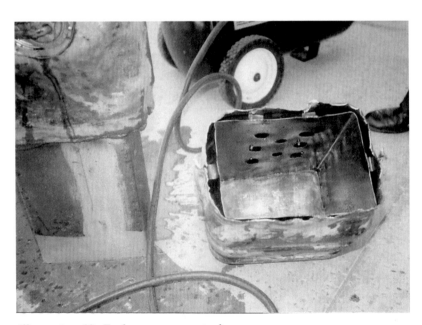

Illustration 13: Tank two same as tank one.

One hundred and twenty-nine pounds of Marijuana were secreted within the two tanks in this seizure. One of the most interesting facts about this method of concealment is how tightly the Marijuana is packed. As one Inspector put it "You could build a house with these bricks." To prove his point, we drove a nail into one and a hammer was needed to pull it out.

In very few cases are the drivers not aware of what they are carrying. It was now time to see what the driver knew. As soon as we had seen the box through the sending unit, both occupants had been moved from the waiting area outside of the Supervisors Office to the holding cells. The passenger was sixteen years old, a juvenile. We could not even interview him without his parents' consent. Too bad, he was nervous and more likely to break.

The driver exhibited no signs of nervousness when she was referred and none when she was moved to the holding cell. It was now time to see just how cool she really is.

We entered her holding cell and there she sat, cool as she could be. As her rights were read to her, she showed the first signs of uneasiness. She was asked if she knew why she was being detained. She stated that she did not.

"Whose vehicle is that?" she was asked

"It is my fiancés. He let me use it to go buy Christmas presents." Some concern in her voice.

"Who is the guy with you? Is he your son?" was the next question.

"No. He's my fiancés nephew. My fiancé sent him along with me." she said now beginning to get worried.

"Why did your fiancé send his nephew with you?"

"I don't know. My fiancé asked me what I was going to get my children for Christmas. I told him that I couldn't afford to buy them anything. He gave me some money and told me to take (the juvenile), go to Walmart and buy them bicycles." Her story sounded good.

"How many bicycles were you going to buy?" I asked.

"Three, one for each of my children" was her response.

"Where is the money?"

Without hesitation the lady dug into her left front jean pocket and produced two one hundred-dollar bills and two fifty-dollar bills. She held them out and we examined them. Her eyes remained riveted on the four bills. She gave the impression that it was the most money she had ever held at one time. The four bills were placed on a counter, side by side, within her view.

Either this gal was an expert liar and an accomplished actress, or she was another grim casualty of the coldhearted and ruthless drug war.

"The vehicle belongs to whom?" she was asked again.

"My fiancé. He has had it ever since I have known him." A frown appeared on her forehead. "He lets me drive it sometimes."

"Madam, does your fiancé always send his nephew with you when you drive the truck?" I asked studying her physical answer as much as her verbal response.

"No." Deep thought, her wheels were beginning to turn. "No, I have never seen (the juvenile) before today."

"How long have you known your fiancé?" again studying her response.

"Four months. I met him at church." She smiled.

"Ma'am, the truck has Marijuana in it." This time no studying was needed.

"Oh no, he told me he didn't do drugs. I have never seen him use it." She seemed genuinely upset.

"I'm not talking about personal use Marijuana." I revealed. "There is a lot of Marijuana, more than one hundred pounds of Marijuana hidden in the vehicle."

The first thing out of her mouth after this revelation was a very pained "We're going to be married. Why would he do that to me? He's my fiancé, why would he do this to me? I don't believe it. I just don't believe it." Now in tears.

This was essentially the end of the interview. She gave us a few faceless names of possible accomplices in Mexico. The juvenile was never interviewed due to his age. Everyone who was involved with the interview believed the lady and believed that she had been used by her fiancé. The United States Attorney declined prosecution. Both the lady and the juvenile were released. The lady was given her Christmas money back. I never found out if she made it to Walmart for the bicycles, I hope she did.

The drug game is an unforgiving game with cold, cruel players that will go to any means to accomplish their mission. A mistake in their game will find the party at fault terminated by one of any number of means leading to horrible endings. Using an unsuspecting persons innermost feelings and a promise of love and marriage is a minor infraction to the inhumane traffickers. They may sit in church every Sunday but, money is their God.

Thanks Doublea and Ramrod, you know who you are!!!

I have never forgotten!!!

BILLION $ DOLLAR $ HIGHWAY

Oops Missed That One
January 8, 1990
14.5 Pounds Marijuana

January 8, 1990, eight days into the new decade. It's a cold day, so cold that I have broken out the heavy artillery. I am wearing my hip length heavy coat, cumbersome but warm. I am manning vehicle lane one and traffic is just enough to ensure the primary booth door remains open. At three o'clock I'll be off the primary lane and have thirty minutes in secondary before returning to the lanes. What's the significance? The lanes are in the shadow of the office, secondary is open to the sun. The significance is an element of comfort. The Arizona sun, even on a cold day, has a very warming effect. In the summer you avoid it. In the winter you're like a turtle on a log, you hang out in it and enjoy the rays.

Three o'clock and my relief finally arrives and I head to Secondary. As I arrive in the Secondary inspection area, I see that there is only one vehicle parked there. Since there are only two lanes and I was manning Customs lane one I know it must have entered through lane two manned by Immigration. I walked over to the window and checked for a referral slip. Ah, my lucky day, no referral slip. Referral slips are placed on the windshield under the wiper blade on the driver side. Since there is no referral slip present that indicates that another inspector is performing the inspection. Since there are no other referrals in secondary, I'm headed for the sunny side of secondary to await the next referral. On my way I get hailed by the resident K-9 (Dog) handler, Cratchit. "Did you look at that LTD by any chance?"

"No, I just got off the line and was headed over to hang out in the sun for a while." I advised. "Why, did you get an alert?"

Cratchit and his dog were both new arrivals straight out of the Academy. "Yeah, he hit on the front fender, I think."

'I think?' I thought, either he alerted, or he didn't. I would hope that a dog handler would know one from the other even if he is straight out of the academy.

"Where is the driver?" I reluctantly asked.

Narcotics smuggling is like most legitimate businesses. Its players come with all degrees of experience, some are rookies like my K-9 handler, and some are All-Pros. A rookie may stand there and watch an inspection, not realizing that a dog is alerting to his illegal wares. A pro is going to be watching every move we make. He will be paying particular attention to a narcotics detector dog and the advantage is in his corner. He knows where the load is, so he knows *when* to be watching for an alert. If he thinks that he has been had, he'll head for Mexico as fast as he can run. One more caveat, an All-Pro will have studied every Inspector that works the line. He will know us better than we know ourselves. He will know our abilities and even our sub-

24

conscience reactions. He will wait until he knows he's been had, and then the foot race will be on. Since I haven't seen the driver, he may already be in Mexico knocking down a beer. Cratchit may not know if the dog hit or not but an all pro smuggler would not miss an alert. If this is the case, I'm probably looking at my third load. I'm almost hoping to hear, 'I don't know, he was standing right there.'

"He's inside." No such luck. "Velo Raptor escorted him in when the dog first hit."

I should have known, Raptor is a good Inspector, a damn good Inspector. He is not going to allow a smuggler the opportunity to escape on the chance that the vehicle is loaded. Better yet I am confident that the driver is sitting in a holding cell behind lock and key.

"Has Raptor checked the car yet?" I asked having no desire to jump in on another Inspectors examination before he has had a chance to return from the escort and patdown of a potential smuggler.

"Yes, he has already checked it and he just went back inside to release the driver. I asked him to wait a few minutes to let me run the dog again. I was going to discipline the dog for a false alert, but he gave such a strong alert I don't think he's false alerting. There *must* be odor there." now Cratchit was convinced. Two minutes ago he wasn't sure if the dog had alerted. The situation is really beginning to smell to high heaven.

"Well, let me take a look. Four eyes are better than two." I said, my hopes somewhat diminished with the knowledge that Raptor had already gone over the car and Cratchit can't make up his mind on an alert or not.

I walked over to where the car sat with its hood and trunk still open. I went straight to the engine compartment and looked at the front fender mounting bolts. Nothing, they had never been removed. Opening the passengers' door and using my flashlight I looked into the cavity behind the front fender that is visible when the door is open. Empty, nothing indicating that the area had ever been used. Had the area been used in the recent past, residual odor would be present thus the dog alert.

Still kneeling on the pavement at the front passenger side door, I checked up in the uppermost recesses of the dash. Seeing nothing unusual there I was leaning to the idea that the dog was seeking a reward more than he was seeking dope. That or someone might need some remedial training; and it is not the dog. Just as I was about to pull out I noticed slats on the kick panel. The kick panel is the area inside the car just to the front of the door. The slats, I realized, were the area that the fresh air entered the vehicle when the operator had his air conditioner/heater in "vent".

Not knowing what I should see I shined my light up into the slats and saw that the vent appeared to be closed. There was a metal plate just behind the slats. I had no idea if this was normal or not. Being the dead of winter and cold however, I did not find it unusual that the vent would be closed. Still I shined my light around the edge of the plate/door and saw small bolts.

Now this did seem a bit unusual as I have opened and closed many air vents and have never had to dismantle the car to do so.

I removed the plastic cover (a chore in itself as it covers the entire kick plate area) and exposed the vent plate/door. Looking at the bolts, there were obvious signs of recent tampering. I looked under the passenger seat and low and behold, there sat a socket driver with a socket attached. I picked up the driver and tried the socket on the bolts, perfect fit. I began removing the first bolt, there were six, and the driver's door opened. I looked up and there was the driver getting in the car.

"Hey, what are you doing?" I asked.

"I'm leaving. The other Inspector told me I could go." he responded.

I had forgotten that according to Cratchit, Raptor had gone in to release the guy.

I immediately stood up and looking over the roof of the car I said, "Sorry, but I'm not finished checking your car yet."

On the far Southwest side of secondary there was a bench. "Go sit on that bench until I finish my inspection." I told the subject. I watched him proceed to the bench as instructed and sit down. His demeanor said, 'Go ahead, I've got all day.'

I noticed that three or four inspectors were now standing between me and the bench, soaking up the sun. One of those inspectors was Raptor. As I continued to remove bolts Raptor came over and opened the drivers' door.

"What do you have on this one? The dog hit the fender and I didn't see anything." Raptor asked.

"I don't know, I was checking out the dash and I noticed this plate. I don't know if it is factory or not, but I thought I would take it off and see what is behind it." I was now on the forth bolt.

"I didn't even know that area existed." Raptor said.

"Me either. I just accidentally saw it as I was trying to wiggle out from under the dash." I said as I started to remove the last bolt.

Raptor leaned in on his side and looked at the kick plate on the drivers' side. "There is one on this side too. Up here behind the emergency brake pedal."

I looked over and saw the slats, "Is there a plate over that one?"

Raptor shined his flashlight up and in between the slats. "Yes, yes there is. I'll tell you what though; someone has been messing with it pretty recently. Like about today."

Just as Raptor made his deduction I got the last bolt out. I tapped the plate and it fell to the floor with a clang. There in the open cavity sat the packages we were seeking. It was loaded! I looked at Raptor and he looked at me. We read each other's mind. Our driver was sitting twenty yards away, watching everything we were doing.

I stood up and looked to where our guy had so nonchalantly plopped down. Our guy was no longer sitting nonchalantly or any other chalantly, he had stood up and was slowly walking backwards toward Mexico. Etched on his face was a touch of uncertainty but also determination. As I came fully erect our eyes met and the uncertainty was replaced with full blown knowledge. He knew I had found his illicit cargo. The smuggler smiled, waved, turned and ran.

I yelled at the group of Inspectors "Get him! Get him! He's loaded!" as I broke into a foot pursuit. I was by the group of Inspectors before they realized what was happening.

The smuggler had about a twenty-five-yard head start on me, but I had about half a mile to catch him. About thirty yards into the chase I realized that I was not gaining on the runner. I couldn't get up to speed. I slowed down and wiggled my way out of the hip length coat. Once out of the confining, weighty beast I began to make-up the distance. Unfortunately, in shedding the coat, I had given him another ten yards. He reached the border about five yards in front of me. All I could do was hang on to the border fence, gasp for breath and watch him jog his way past Mexican Customs to freedom. He won the foot race but, we got his dope and his car. Still I feel as if we lost.

As I walked the half mile or so back to the Port I was joined by Raptor carrying my coat. "I thought you had him." Raptor said. "If it weren't for the coat, you would have had him. That or if you had another quarter of a mile."

"If there had been another quarter mile, I would need an ambulance." I said not all together joking. Cold weather and I are not compatible. Sucking in that cold air kicks my bronchitis into full attack. I knew I would be sleeping under the vaporizer that night. If you want to call sitting up all night sleeping.

As we got back to the load vehicle there was quite a stir of course. The area had been secured by the Supervisor Lacky Goose. "The rabbit get away?" he asked.

"Yes, he beat me by about five yards." I said holding the coat. "These sure weren't designed for the half mile sprint."

"No, I guess not." Goose said. "Where is the load?"

"In the air vent area. There's an area between the door and the firewall where the air circulates into the car." I replied.

"Let's see what you got." Goose directed as he motioned to the vehicle.

It turned out that both sides were loaded. Raptor did the honors on the drivers' side, but he refused to write the load. He said that he had missed it and had released the smuggler so he shouldn't be the one to write it. Raptor was and still is one of the best Inspectors at the Port, full of class and one of my best friends. Together we retrieved twelve packages of Marijuana that weighed in at fourteen and a half pounds.

I was lucky to find the air vent area. I had no idea what I was looking for when I found the compartment. I had no idea that the area even existed before I opened it up, much less how much room was involved.

Illustration 14: The dope on the bench where the smuggler sat.

Fourteen- and one-half pounds of Marijuana isn't anywhere near a mega load. It is, however, quite substantial if you figure the mule crossed three to four times a week. That's 43.5 to 58 pounds per week. Over a year we're talking 2,262 to 3,016 pounds. At roughly eight hundred dollars per pound that's $1,809,600 to $2,412,800 per year. Not a mega load, but I'll take it. By the way, Cratchit ran his K-9 Rob again and Rob got his well-deserved reward.

Illustration 15: Dope on the scale.

Hindsight being 20/20, that night lying in bed I thought about this entire ordeal and as I reconstructed the seizure, I came to the conclusion that I had made some assumptions and missed a few critical flags.

I was so unsure of Cratchit's ability to read his dog and knowing that the vehicle had already been searched by Raptor I started my search thinking it was going to be negative. That conclusion resulted with the driver sitting on a bench with his documents and the ability to rabbit back to Mexico with all his documents. My failure to at least secure his documents removed any chance to identify the smuggler. This oversight therefore prevented us from identifying him for a warrant. Lesson learned and never forgotten.

The tools under the seat and the fresh marks on the bolts made the case that the driver was complicit in tampering with the air vent yet there he sat watching the inspection.

The hood and trunk on the vehicle were open when I started my examination and when the driver returned to the vehicle, he opened the driver's door. Most people don't drive with the hood and trunk open. Flag three, yep I should have heard the hood and trunk close before the driver opened his door. The reason he opened the door before closing the hood and trunk was to see if I was hot or cold regarding the location of the dope.

Obviously, he saw that I was within minutes of finding his marijuana so when his butt hit that bench, he was already planning his escape.

He was no longer as interested in me as he was in not alerting the other Inspectors standing within his capture zone. I will give him this he masterfully managed to get up and begin inching his way to Mexico. He worked on his head start without attracting attention until he

29

knew that I had discovered his stash.

Yep, this guy was an all pro but in the smuggler's business they have to be successful every time and I am sure he had some explaining to do when he got back to mother Mexico.

Many loads are guaranteed by the smuggler's life. In this case with a small load of marijuana probably not but it is very possible that the organization he worked for would want to know why he was in our office for so long. Also, what did he tell us. They almost always have someone watching and timing the load vehicle. Therefore, I would guess that their concern with his time in the office would be whether or not we able to flip him. Was he now working for us and if not, how did he just walk away. Informants in Mexico do not have a long life expectancy. We will never know but I would not want to be in his shoes when they started asking questions.

BILLION $ DOLLAR $ HIGHWAY

Malo. Muy Malo Hombre
January 19, 1990
88 Pounds Marijuana

I look at my watch, almost 6:30 A. M., I'm running late. I work 65 miles away in Nogales, AZ. I live in a modest apartment complex on the Southwest side of Tucson, AZ. with my wife of fifteen plus years and our three children. We moved to Tucson one year ago due to medical reasons for our youngest son. He had been in and out of hospitals for six of his eight years. In Tucson, at the University Medical Center, we finally found a Pediatric Neurologist that seemed capable of diagnosing and hopefully finding a cure to his problem. I can't remember the number of doctors we had taken him to. I can certainly tell you this though; they had managed to keep us just above the poverty level.

I ran out and jumped in the better of our two cars, a 1982 Ford Escort. I got it to start, but it will never make it all the way to Nogales. I walked back into the apartment and called work.

"U.S. Customs, Grand Avenue." it was Supervisory Customs Inspector Selok Montana. "Mr. Montana, this is Inspector Davis. I'm having some car problems and I need to let the day shift Supervisor know that I'll be late." I reported to him.

Selok came back with " O.K. I'll let him know but I'm going to tell him that you promised to get him a 'Load' for being late."

After spending the morning and a hundred dollars we couldn't afford at a local mechanic I head south on I-19 with the Escort and its new 'module'. I pulled into the Secondary parking area at noon, four hours late. As I am walking by the secondary office a voice rings from within, "Why don't you get that referral? We've been busting our butts all morning while you slept in."

I looked in and there sits three of the biggest skates in the port. With that crew, one thing was certain, there was no "butt busting" going on this morning. The voice was that of an Inspector that was well noted as a Romeo. I can remember only one narcotic load that Inspector Ira interdicted in his career, but I couldn't count the number of phone numbers he nabbed.

I proceed to the secondary inspection area and one car, an '81 Cutlass Supreme, is parked in the third lane. Denny Chen, an Inspector for the U. S. Department of Agriculture (Aggie for short), is standing just to the front of the vehicle. "It's yours (meaning a Customs referral)." Denny advised.

The car is occupied by a female driver (early twenties) and two young children. The youngest, approximately two years old, in the front passenger seat. The older child, approximately three years old, is lying on the back seat scarcely visible due to a large Piñata atop him. The Piñata dominates the seat as it stretches from side to side and, due to its size, is actually wedged in.

31

"Hello, where in Mexico are you coming from?" I asked.

"Just here in Nogales." She answers with a beaming smile.

"What are you bringing from Mexico?" I continued with the Secondary Declaration.

Partially turning to her left and pointing with her left hand over the seat she declares "Only this Piñata and a bag of Mexican candy in the trunk."

Most people when pointing or reaching to the back seat turn the opposite way and use their right hand. This allows much more room to maneuver. The only reason I could deduce for such an awkward move was to display some cleavage, and it worked. Oh man did it ever work. She must have worn that top specifically for this occasion. Inspector Ira would have been impressed. His apathy and laziness cost him quite a show and the show went all the way to her belly button. Nope, no navel rings.

My thoughts at this point were not on anatomy but on reality; 'This girl is way too nice and showing way too much. I've never seen this girl before and will probably never see her again, so why is she advertising?'

"That's it? Just the Piñata and the candy?" I queried quite professionally. My lack of interest did not deter her mock interest in me one iota.

"Yes, that's all. We are going to have a party." she winked as she spoke.

"Where do you live?" I'm quite sure she's not a local crosser.

"Tucson." she replies still auditioning for the Miss America pageant.

"OK Step out and open the hood and the trunk." I directed.

"Sure." she says as she reaches down to pop the hood release then slides out of the car and opens the trunk. Still beaming and displaying, she leans over and, once again revealing her breasts, points to a clear plastic bag obviously containing candy. "See, just the candy."

"Yes Ma'am, looks like Piñata candy to me. Now I need you to have the children step out of the car and the three of you wait at the table over there." I directed pointing to one of the agriculture inspection tables.

"The Children? Not the baby in the back, he's asleep! Can't he stay?" The pageant must be over as her demeanor instantly changed to something close to panic.

"No, I can't inspect your car with the children in it. For their safety they must get out of the car" I replied.

"Malo. Muy malo hombre." (Bad. Very bad man.) I guess that her infatuation for me has passed. There seems to be pure hatred in her voice now.

As my ex-admirer worked to get the children out on the passenger side I quickly reached in the car from the driver's side and pressed on the area of her greatest concern. The back seat was as hard as a park bench.

When the young mother finally extracted her children form the vehicle, she stood there at the passenger's side door mumbling pleasantries as to her new formed opinion of me.

After my quick check of the back seat that gave me reason to believe it was loaded with more than Piñata candy I directed her to the secondary office rather than the Aggie table where she and her children could be more "comfortable" rather than wait in secondary where it was much colder.

The Secondary Office was divided into two sections. The first section was an office where only Inspectors had access. The second section was set-up as a holding area. It had benches and a door which could be opened only from the outside. The two sections were separated by a counter four feet high and two feet wide.

I escorted the trio into the holding area and told them to wait there for the completion of the inspection. The three skates hadn't moved one iota until I sat the trio. Then Inspector Ira was on his feet and at the counter almost mystically.

I returned to the vehicle, opened the passenger's side door, reached under the back seat and felt a package. I closed the door and advised the Aggie Inspector, who was still standing in front of the car, not to let anyone near the car as it was loaded. Denny gave me the thumbs up and I headed to the Supervisors office.

I entered the Supervisors office and told the Supervisory Customs Inspector (SCI) Johnny Climbs that I had a load and was going to call the Office of Enforcement Duty Agent. SCI Climbs looked at me with a very puzzled look on his face.

"Where do you have a load?" he asked.

"In secondary. The car there in lane three has a seat load." I replied. I proceeded to call the duty agent and apprised him of the situation.

"Does she know that you know?" the agent asked.

"No, I don't think so. I checked and verified pretty quickly so I don't think so. I think this one is set-up pretty good for a tail away." I informed him.

"Let me check on that. I'll see if there are enough agents available. I'll call you back in a couple of minutes and let you know." The Special Agent hung up.

I looked at SCI Climbs who was staring at me with an odd look on his face. "He's checking on a tail away, but he didn't sound too sincere." I said.

"I would like to hear how you nabbed a load, placed the occupants in the secondary holding area and verified the load when, to the best of my knowledge, you were still in Tucson having your car worked on." he said with a puzzled look on his face.

I had forgotten that I had yet to check in with Mr. Climbs. I explained to him how I had just arrived and was walking across Secondary to report in when the load went down.

Always looking on the bright side I added: "Well, look at the bright side Mr. Climbs. Had I reported in first, you would have just finished adding me to the roster, changing the rotation and then you would just have to change it back again so I can work the load. Look at how much work I saved you."

Mr. Climbs just turned and walked away shaking his head and mumbled something about something or someone being full of it. I didn't quite get what he was referring to.

The Special Agent called back and advised that a tail away was out of the picture. I can't say that I was surprised considering that most of the Special Agents were tied up between 11 AM and 1 PM every day. They never missed lunch.

"A tail away is out." I advised Climbs. "I'm going to go ahead and bring the driver here and put her in the lock up. She has a couple of very young kids, so they will have to remain with her. We need to get a female Inspector to pat her down so I'll leave the door (to the lock up) open and have the female Inspector stand-by and guard the lot."

I returned to the Secondary office and my suspect is now standing, leaning on the counter, deeply conversing with Inspector Ira who is practically lying on the counter. I notice that she is leaning with both elbows on the counter and both shoulders pulled forward. She was still showing what she's made of.

"Ma'am, get your things and come with me, I am going to bring you to the Supervisors office." I informed her.

"Why?" asked Inspector Ira. Now she hesitated and looked at her knight in shining armor as she reached out and put her hand on Ira's forearm.

"Get your purse and come with me." I told her matter-of-factually, ignoring Inspector Ira.

As she gathered her purse and her children Inspector Ira looked at me and said, "She's not . . .?"

He didn't finish the question, but I knew exactly what he was asking.

I nod my head in the affirmative and Inspector Ira almost fell backward, reached into his shirt pocket and removed a single piece of paper. He proceeded to tear it into many little pieces, but I saw the name and phone number before he got to it. Ira's dating game bit him on the butt. I had to laugh. As much as I tried to stay professional with this experienced smuggler, I could not help from letting an itty-bitty laugh sneak out.

As we walked to the supervisor's office through secondary past her car the girl asked, "Why do I have to go to this other office? Did you find something in the car? I don't know nothing about it!"

Illustration 16: Picture taken from the door of the supervisor's office. Arrow points to the secondary office.

I told her, "I just need for you to wait in this office." as we entered the door. My thoughts, however, were 'Well, well. That's an admission of guilt.'

Inspector Ira had asked, "She's not?", not "It's not?". Had she not known about the load in the car, Miss Tucson should have been thinking in the lines of 'she's not: wanted? . . .illegal? . . . in trouble?'. Why did she assume that we were talking about the car?

As we arrived at the Supervisors office two female inspectors were waiting. One took charge of the children and the other escorted the suspect to the lock-up area out of eyesight of the

35

children for the patdown. After the patdown the children were re-united with their mother.

While this was going on, I returned to the car. Denny advised me that no one had disturbed the car. The three skates had, however, taken up a position near Denny. There were times when my co-workers embarrassed me. This was one of those times; I have an unarmed Aggie watching a load of dope while three armed Inspectors sit on their duff in the secondary office.

Now that stealth was no longer required for an O.E. operation, I checked to make sure that the packages I had felt were indeed narcotics. I disengaged the back seat and lifted it. "Looks like Marijuana to me." I announced. Taking a small knife, I made a small cut in one of the packages and removed a small portion, placed it in a Marijuana Test ampule and received a positive test for Marijuana.

When the Office of Enforcement Special Agent arrived and did his thing with the vehicle, I removed and seized fourteen packages of Marijuana from the back seat and the back seat back rest. I transported the evil weed to the Supervisors office where it weighed in at eighty-eight pounds.

Illustration 17: Not quite personal use!

I started on the seemingly endless paperwork that accompanies a seizure and the Special Agent came out of the Interview Room where he had been conducting his interview with the suspect. He took my statement and I relayed in detail her demeanor, her actions and emphasized that when she was being moved to the Supervisors office she practically incriminated herself.

Agent Werfargo strolled over to the phone and called the U.S. Attorney. I couldn't help but hear his side of the conversation. In a nut shell he told the U.S. Attorney that we didn't have a case against the suspect as it was not her car and she claimed no knowledge of its contents. Of course the U.S. Attorney declined prosecution.

I was rather irritated at the Special Agent and asked him what he was doing. He stated that he believed the suspects story. Irritating, really irritating! Oh well, I had done my job. The load of dope didn't get through. Sometimes you just have to bite your tongue and let it go at that.

I did however, get the last laugh. After the suspect was released, she requested the use of the phone to call for a ride home (the load vehicle was seized). She placed a call to her brother in Tucson. Her end of the conversation, again, was self- incriminating.

"I need a ride from the Customs office in Nogales." she said and then a pause while she listened to the voice on the other end.

"They found the pot in the car." as she again incriminated herself. Another pause.

"No, NO. I didn't tell them nothing. Nothing. Just come and get me." she said not even a bit of hesitation knowing we could hear her end of the conversation.

As the young mother and her children departed the office to wait outside, I looked at the Special Agent. I said nothing, just shook my head. I realized this poor agent's dilemma, an arrest and prosecution meant that *he* would have to actually get off his duff and put in some actual work.

BILLION $ DOLLAR $ HIGHWAY

TROLL Team
Passenger Processing Team
February 1990 - June 1990

In mid-February 1990 I was accepted for an opening on the Passenger Processing special narcotics interdiction team which had been established by the Chief of Passenger Processing some three months earlier. The mission of the team, as stated, was to *protect the interests of the United States Customs Service Passenger Processing*. Basically, stop narcotics that were being smuggled through the vehicle and pedestrian lanes. Legitimate commercial goods, immigration inspections, agriculture issues and the dozen or so other agencies whose laws Customs enforced were not our concern. Our concern was strictly narcotics enforcement. To accomplish this, we were removed from the regular rotation and given free reign of the vehicle and pedestrian lanes.

The team consisted of one Supervisor, one Senior and three Inspectors. The Senior made the schedule as to which port we were to work. In Nogales there are two Ports; Grand Avenue Port of Entry now renamed the Deconcini Port of Entry and the Mariposa Port of Entry.

This assignment was a chance that I had been waiting for. When I came to work for Customs, I had one thing in mind: dope. My idea of Customs was that it was an elite agency whose main concern was interdicting loads of Narcotics. I had worked for the Federal Government from age nineteen; I was now thirty-seven. At the time, Customs was deemed as the lead agency in narcotics interdiction under Commissioner William Von Rob who was Commissioner until 1989. The country, thanks to the Reagan administration, was in a "Zero Tolerance" frame of mind. Drugs, drug users and particularly drug suppliers were not to be tolerated. This country was moving away from the 'Timothy Leary Era' of widely accepted drug abuse.

When I was in high school there were a few "Dopers", but they were the oddballs who associated only with each other and hung out in a remote corner of the campus. My family and I had moved to Las Cruces, New Mexico in the summer and I had just started my junior year at Las Cruces High. I can remember the first time I saw the "Pot Heads" gathered quite a distance from the building, bunched up under the bleachers at the football field smoking away. Cigarettes were accepted in high school back then and there was a smoking area with ash trays and the works, so I asked one of the local students what they were doing way out there on the north end of the campus. I was shocked when I found out they were smoking dope.

When I graduated from High School the "Draft" was alive and well.

Illustration 18: 1969 Vietnam Draft
Photo courtesy of U.S. Selective Service System

Everyone's thoughts were on Vietnam so almost all the males that I graduated with (including me) started college the first summer session (college deferment). Here the percentage of drug abusers rose. It was in college that I, for the first time, smelled Marijuana being burned (smoked).

I noticed that the "Dopers" were all basically the same. You could pick them out in class, at the Student Union Building (SUB), anywhere. They all had the burned out, sallow faced I don't know who I am or where I am look about them.

Two of these no-mind people I knew. Four guys that I had graduated with and I had a Western Civilization class at 7:30 AM on Monday's, Wednesday's and Friday's. We all met at the SUB for breakfast and/or coffee at 7:00 AM on those Western Civilization days. About the third week of the session, two of the guys started slacking off and coming late or not showing at all. They changed from friends and fellow students seeking a degree to bitter, numb minded strangers. Everything was bad. The school was bad, the war was bad, the country was bad and the three of us who had not turned to dope were bad. Everything and everyone were bad except dope and fellow dopers.

By the second summer session they had distanced themselves from us, from their families and I guess from reality. I saw those two only a few times after that first summer session. Each time I saw them they looked worse. When one of them was found floating in a local motel swimming pool I didn't even go to his funeral. No one that I knew did.

Eventually, due to lack of funds, I had to lay off college in my second year. My job, where I had worked since my junior year of high school, had taken a nose dive. The draft still loomed in the background like a monster waiting to pluck you out, or in. Things, in general, were not well. In June, a friend of mine who's funds had also run short for college, came over to the house and showed me his draft notice. I felt that mine was in the mail. The previous two years of college had not been wasted. I studied my situation and came up with the best way around the draft.

SELECTIVE SERVICE SYSTEM
1971 RANDOM SELECTION SEQUENCE, BY MONTH AND DAY

	Jan	Feb	Mar	Apr	May	Jun	Jul	Aug	Sep	Oct	Nov	Dec
1		335	014	224	179	065	104	326	283	306	243	347
2	195	354	077	216	096	304	322	102	161	191	205	321
3	336	186	207	297	171	135	030	279	183	134	294	110
4	099	094	117	037	240	042	059	300	231	266	039	305
5	033	097	299	124	301	233	287	064	295	166	286	027
6	285	016	296	312	268	153	164	251	021	078	245	198
7	159	025	141	142	029	169	365	263	265	131	072	162
8	116	127	079	267	105	007	106	049	108	045	119	323
9	053	187	278	223	357	352	001	125	313	302	176	114
10	101	046	150	165	146	076	158	359	130	160	063	204
11	144	227	317	178	293	355	174	230	288	084	123	073
12	152	262	024	089	210	051	257	320	314	070	255	019
13	330	013	241	143	353	342	349	058	238	092	272	151
14	071	260	012	202	040	363	156	103	247	115	011	348
15	075	201	157	182	344	276	273	270	291	310	362	087
16	136	334	258	031	175	229	284	329	139	034	197	041
17	054	345	220	264	212	289	341	343	200	290	006	315
18	185	337	319	138	180	214	090	109	333	340	280	208
19	188	331	189	062	155	163	316	083	228	074	252	249
20	211	020	170	118	242	043	120	069	261	196	098	218
21	129	213	246	008	225	113	356	050	068	005	035	181
22	132	271	269	256	199	307	282	250	088	036	253	194
23	048	351	281	292	222	044	172	010	206	339	193	219
24	177	226	203	244	022	236	360	274	237	149	081	002
25	057	325	298	328	026	327	003	364	107	017	023	361
26	140	086	121	137	148	308	047	091	093	184	052	080
27	173	066	254	235	122	055	085	232	338	318	168	239
28	346	234	095	082	009	215	190	248	309	028	324	128
29	277	----	147	111	061	154	004	032	303	259	100	145
30	112	----	056	358	209	217	015	167	018	332	067	192
31	060	----	038	----	350	----	221	275	----	311	----	126

Illustration 19: #1 Draft Pick - July 9

Photo courtesy of U.S. Selective Service System

If I were drafted the Military would place me where they wanted me, probably the Infantry. If I joined the military, I could pick my job. I entered the U.S. Army in July as an Electronics Technician.

Most of the Soldiers that I served with for the first couple of years were draftees. They were there because they had been forced into service by law. The general attitude during that time by the American public, at least that of our peers and that which the press relayed, was not very favorable towards the GI. Vietnam was not a "*popular*" war, and the press made sure we, the men and women in uniform, were the targets. I suppose that if one were looking for excuses to do dope there were certainly plenty of them. I know that I heard them by the gobs. I saw it first hand when my ex-fiancée dumped me before I got out of boot camp. When I came home on a short leave after completing both boot camp and advanced individual training (AIT) and just before going overseas I sought out my ex-fiancée (I didn't know that she was an ex at the time, just that she had not written me once). I found her at her place of work stocking shelves in a store. I walked over and said, "Hi Linda" and she ignored me. I asked if she remembered me and she told me that she wouldn't talk to a baby killer much less marry one. Oooook? She must not have known that there were no babies in boot camp or AIT and if there was a baby killing session, I must have missed it. I was probably in the; don't zig when you should zag, keep from getting your ass shot off training. At any rate, drug use in the military overseas was astounding. The encounter with my ex-fiancée surely could have qualified as an excuse to hit the smack but I had already accepted that she was gone; I just had to see for myself. I wanted nothing to do with drugs myself nor would I want to shame my parents and siblings by becoming a user.

My college exposure to dopers did not prepare me for what I would encounter in the Army. I do not know how many people I saw come in as normal run of the mill kids and go out as total brain-dead addicts. I didn't buy their excuses, their flimsy reasons for doing dope; they did what they wanted to do. The one thing that most of them had in common was that most of these people, in the end, regretted that they had ever started. They said that it was just too easy to get it. Anything from Hashish to Heroin. Marijuana was laughed at unless it was laced with something more potent. Even the hashish was laced with heroin or morphine.

I had always been anti-drug. I had always felt that dope was something that I wanted nothing to do with. I know, first hand, how drugs can totally ruin people. I've seen it happen, and seen it happen to friends of mine. I never believed that I could stop the flow of drugs, but I sure as hell could try.

When I came to work for Customs, I felt that I had finally made it to a place where I could join the "War on Drugs". I had now made it to a special team dedicated to Narcotics interdiction. The TROLL Team was a locally established team designed by and for the local environment. The next step would be the Customs wide Contraband Enforcement Team (CET). I thought that if I could prove myself on TROLL, I would have a chance for CET.

TROLL, as previously mentioned, had been created some three months earlier. By design, every three months one Inspector would rotate off TROLL and a new Inspector would take his place. TROLL, at the time, was controversial. There were arguments that it was a waste of manpower. Not only did the controversy come from upper management, but from some of the line supervisors.

During its first three months TROLL had managed to nab only one load, and that had come from a south bound Border Patrol (BP) chase. A Border Patrol Agent had observed a vehicle parked along the border fence being loaded with packages which were passed through a hole in the fence from Mexico. When the vehicle left the fence, the BP Agent attempted to stop the vehicle, which fled. A pursuit ensued and headed southbound toward the Port. The vehicle, rather than return to Mexico as usual, pulled off in a parking lot just north of the Port. A

TROLL Inspector, working southbound traffic, saw the vehicle pull in and park. Shortly after the vehicle parked, the pursuit vehicles arrived at the border and, assuming the vehicle had entered Mexico, departed. The sharp-eyed TROLL Inspector, rather than advising BP of their quarry's whereabouts, walked over, nabbed the offender and the load of Marijuana.

The seizure created one heck of a stir. There was quite a bit of criticism directed at TROLL, and rightly so in my opinion. TROLL was initiated to interdict narcotics entering the United States. Why was this TROLL Inspector working Outbound? That is a direct contradiction to TROLL's reported mission. Also, the Inspector had an opportunity to advise the Border Patrol of their violator's location in the parking lot. Instead he waited for them to depart and then nabbed their load.

The first three months of TROLL's existence was in reality, a failure. That first "Team" was doomed from the day that they were appointed. The reason is simple. The first appointments were **Political**. You would think that the Chief of Passenger Processing would have known better. After all, the whole concept and creation of the TROLL Team was because "CET is not doing their job". Why was CET not doing their job? Because CET appointments were political!!! They had NOT earned their positions. The most productive Inspector in the Port, the only one getting any loads, had been passed over on the last CET selections and on the first TROLL selections. The only reason I was finally selected for TROLL was because of the controversy over the BP load and the lack of Port loads. The District Director would have abolished TROLL if it did not start producing *northbound* narcotics loads.

So, there I was, free to do my thing, go after Dope. Concentrate on Narcotics interdiction. Devote total mental and physical attention to DOPE. Well almost. There was only one slight ripple on the pond; I was NOT a *"political"* selection. This ripple cost me any kind of fair rotation between the Ports. We were supposed to avoid setting patterns. One means was to rotate Inspectors between Ports daily.

Now, at the time, the Mariposa Port of Entry (POE) was fairly new with very little traffic. It was assumed by management, and by most Inspectors, that there was little or no dope entering through Mariposa. 'The vacation spot' for line Inspectors, but the pits for a special team Inspector whose job is interdicting Dope. I soon realized that Mariposa would be my home as long as I worked for Senior Inspector (SI) Jonathan Thorny. The only times that I was assigned to Grand Avenue were when the Supervisor, Goose, made the roster rather than SI Thorny.

I was totally taken by surprise at the animosity directed towards me from SI Thorny. I honestly thought that he would welcome me to the team. At the time I had no idea how "Political" the U.S. Customs Service was, so I did not realize that I had upset the cart. I have since learned that what was going on in Nogales on a small scale ran rampant in Customs on the large scale. The biggest problem in Customs, in my opinion, was POLITICS. The people who ran Customs, from Washington to the Port Directors got to where they were through politics, not knowledge.

As an example, we had an Acting Regional Commissioner (Southwest Region) who climbed his ladder at the Los Angeles International Airport (LAX). This guy didn't have a clue as to the working environment, problems, concealment methods, anything about the Mexican Land Border. Yet, this political appointee dictated policy for us.

At any rate, politics or no, I was determined to do the best that I could despite the handicaps. This separation actually ended up working to my advantage. I got the freedom that I wanted (even though it was mainly at Mariposa) but best of all, SI Thorny hung out with his pals and left me alone.

I nabbed my first load very soon after my appointment to TROLL and I led the team with seizures until my departure to CET.

The TROLL tally sheet below was created from the official Search, Arrest and Seizure reports by one of the Port secretaries. The search parameters were by seizing officer using my employee number in the seizing officer field and the beginning and ending dates of my TROLL assignment. There is one seizure that was not included due to circumstances that excluded me as the seizing officer. The seizure resulted from a request from the Chief Enforcement Officer for me to examine an abandoned vehicle. The vehicle was abandoned in secondary by a subject who fled Secondary and returned to Mexico. The entire story is included in one of the upcoming chapters. If you have guessed that SI Thorny was at the root of this exclusion: congratulations! Read on my friends, read on and maybe you will get a chuckle out of it.

```
                    OPERATION TROLL
                      USCI DAVIS

          DATE          SEIZ        SUBS           AMT

        90/02/23        0204      MARIJUANA       25.00
        90/03/01        0216      MARIJUANA       24.00
        90/03/08        0225      MARIJUANA       12.80
        90/03/27        0247      MARIJUANA       32.00
        90/03/31        0255      MARIJUANA       51.50
        90/05/10        0301      COCAINE        607.00
        90/05/25        0316      MARIJUANA       18.00
        90/05/29        0318      MARIJUANA       51.25

   Count:        8
   Total:                                        821.55
```

BILLION $ DOLLAR $ HIGHWAY

Oh Boy, An Alpha Charlie
February 24, 1990
25 Pounds Marijuana

Almost the end of February. More than a month had passed since my last significant seizure and I haven't made my first TROLL seizure yet. The TROLL Senior Inspector (SI) Jonathan Thorny and I, for whatever reason seem to have a personality conflict (to this day I don't know for sure but as stated earlier politics would be my guess). I had been assigned to the Mariposa Port of Entry since my appointment to TROLL. So much for not setting a pattern via the daily Port rotation. Mariposa had really dried up, both narcotics wise and traffic wise. I had a burning desire to get to the Grand Avenue Port of Entry where I was sure that the dope was still moving through.

I had discussed the rotation, or lack thereof, between Mariposa and Grand Avenue with TROLL Supervisory Customs Inspector (SCI) Goose. SCI Goose agreed that there seemed to be some favoritism with the rotation but insisted that the Chief Inspector had given SI Thorny the authority to run the roster his way. Goose, however, also agreed that there seemed to be a definite lack of narcotics being put on the table and it was obvious that the lack of productivity was very concerning. February is still within the high peak of the produce season in Mexico and much of that produce is shipped to the United States. Nogales is the point of entry for most of that produce. With the thousands of trucks on the road that haul the US bound produce quite a few of them are used to move thousands of pounds of narcotics as well. The Mexican drug enforcement for what it was worth, also focused on big loads in big trucks so that left many mom and pop drug smuggling ventures wide open as well. It is a win-win for the dopers. The bottom line for us was that produce season is drug season.

Goose came up with an idea, or so I thought, to test my theory that the dopers had moved their operations to Grand Avenue. His assignment would allow me to work Grand Avenue without changing Thorny's precious rotation.

I give Goose a ton of credit for having the guts to stick his neck out, not only with the Chief Inspector, but with the Union. Goose instructed me to go ahead and work Johnny's rotation, but to come over to Grand Avenue on overtime at the end of my shift. This was an overtime assignment which bypassed the overtime schedule (Union), was designed purely to let me work Grand Avenue (Thorny) and test my theory that dope was moving through Grand Avenue (Other TROLL members were missing it).

Goose advised me that we would run this clandestine operation until we got caught. He said that he guessed we would probably have three or four days before someone complained. He asked me only one thing, "Please get a load so that when the ax falls it won't hurt quite as bad!"

Goose's estimation of a time-frame was slightly wrong. With exactly one overtime shift under my belt we (Goose and I) were called to the carpet of the Chief Inspector Gerry Utlee.

I knew that trouble was brewing on day one when Mr. Utlee "welcomed" me to his handpicked TROLL team. The indoctrination went something like: 'You are here because of your seizure record. My hand-picked team will set new standards and CET will be mandated to follow those standards should that team survive. I am the Chief and Thorny runs the team for me. Goose is the Training Supervisor and TROLL is a collateral duty for him. You work for Thorny who reports to me. Do not disrupt my team.' When he said "my hand picked" team it sounded like a threat. In fact, the whole welcome sounded like a threat or an ass chewing at best. He made one thing obvious; the only reason that I had been placed on TROLL was because TROLL was hurting for dope. I got the feeling that Mr. Utlee was in danger of having his special team abolished due to lack of production. I was leading the Port in seizures thus, necessity placed me on TROLL.

The post operation meeting was ugly of course. Mr. Utlee ranted, raved and threatened. We, Goose and I, would never again run any operations without his approval. I would get no more *special* treatment. I need complain no more about the favoritism as this was Mr. Utlee's special team and he and his Senior Inspector would assign me anywhere they desired. If I didn't like the conditions, I was welcome to resign from the team. I was an unwelcome trouble maker who had been placed on TROLL at the District Directors request.

Mr. Utlee ended the meeting with: "Would you like to resign from TROLL? I can have the secretary type up the letter for you right now."

"No, no." I replied, "If the District Director wants me on this team maybe I should stay."

As I left the Chief Inspectors office, I actually felt pretty good. The reprimand issued by the Chief actually turned out to be an at-a-boy from the District Director. That was good; I had no idea that the DD had selected me to TROLL.

Remembering the previous night's unauthorized "Operation" I felt even better. I knew that Mr. Utlee's blood had to boil when he read about it.

I had left the Mariposa POE at about four PM and arrived at the Grand Avenue POE at about four fifteen. I was the only TROLL member present, apparently the other three members all worked eight to four at Grand Avenue. 'That's good' I mistakenly thought, 'Maybe I'll make it through the first night unnoticed.'

As I walked out to the lanes that I had manned many times I was thinking that I had finally made it. My first day of pre-primary roving at the very busy Grand Avenue. I was not standing in a booth waiting for vehicles to come to me; I was going after them. I took up a position out in front of the primary booths and looked out over four lanes of traffic that stretched as far as the eye could see. Here I stood solo. Just me and, not hundreds, but literally thousands of vehicles entering the Unites States from Mexico.

Who knows what percentage of those vehicles have narcotics secreted within? One per thousand, one per five thousand, who knows? I do remember, however, just how overwhelmed, alone and isolated I felt. I remember thinking, 'I must be crazy to think that I can pick out that one loaded conveyance out of this vast array of vehicles.' There I stood; just me and a moving sea of potential smugglers.

I began roving the primary lanes checking for any signs or abnormalities that might indicate that the conveyance might contain something other than legitimate border crossers. I was looking at the people as well as the vehicle. I was determined to pick up on some anomaly that would lead me to my first TROLL load. This load was for Goose regardless of what was said in my indoctrination. Collateral duty my ass. I have known Goose long enough to know that he is a drug interdicting Inspector just like most of us.

I walked down the fourth or fifth vehicle that I had looked at. It was a Ford LTD driven by a female with one child in the front seat and one in the back seat. When we got to secondary, I took a secondary declaration and everything seemed just fine with her, the car and the kids. I checked every inch of that car and ended up watching her and the kids heading north out of secondary. They were going home after visiting her aunt in Mexico.

About ten minutes later I walked down a pick-up truck because the driver didn't fit the truck. After another inspection that would not have missed a marijuana seed, off he went heading home.

This went on until about eight PM when I realized that I was just trying way too hard. I felt that I had to get a load. I had been killing myself all night on vehicles that I would not have sent to secondary if I were working the line. I thought 'What in the heck are you doing? You can't will a load to be there.' The bottom line is that willing or just wanting is pretty much what I was doing.

I took a step back and said to myself 'just do your job, there is dope out there and if it comes your way you will be ready if you are here roving. You can't get that load if you are in secondary looking at a want-a-be'.

Never again did I try to manufacture a load; not even when the Commissioner came to visit. I clearly wanted to get a load but if it is not there, it is not there. For the rest of my career I made quality exams, not quantity exams. I suppose it worked or I would not be writing this book.

I did have several good prospects during the evening, but none had drugs. One of those prospects was a husband and wife team in an RV. They were Canadians with thirty bottles of alcohol in a stairwell compartment built under the steps leading into the RV. I knew the guy was nervous, but his poor wife was way at the far end of the nervous spectrum. I almost felt sorry for her when I found the booze. Not drugs so I didn't want it. I called an inspector who was working secondary and asked her "Does that step look funny?"

She looked at the steps and said "No, which one?"

I said, "The middle one, it looks like it might lift up."
She looked at it then reached down and lifted the compartment door. "Wow this is loaded with booze. Look there must be twenty or so bottles of booze. This will make the morning report!"

A couple of hours later I strolled into the office for a drink of water and the Inspector (to this day I can't remember her name) looked up from the report she was writing, and she stated more than asked "You knew that booze was there didn't you?"

I looked at her and said "You found it during your inspection. It is your seizure and you also discovered the load. What more needs to be said?"

She laughed a bit and said "Thirty bottles of booze. I think that is very good for my first seizure. Not only that but like you said, I am the seizing officer as well as the discovering officer. I will take that any day!"

Hey, she got a very good seizure out of it that made the morning report. She was seizing as well as discovering officer to the Customs world. Her seizure report made it to Washington, DC and who knows how high it was briefed there at headquarters. She was very happy, and I was happy for her. If I was not on a "drug team" I would have been all over that one myself. That was her first and last seizure in Nogales however because she twisted her ankle stepping off the curb on her way to primary a few days after the seizure. She was assigned to the Tucson International Airport (TIA) for light duty and she never came back to the Noggie. TIA was and still is a very desirable location to be stationed. I was very happy for her. She did very well at TIA for a couple of years then moved on to the Office of Enforcement as a Special Agent. Not bad for thirty bottles of booze.

I looked at my watch and it was 11:00 PM just one hour from the end of my overtime shift. I don't think that Goose will be too happy at the morning briefing with only the alcohol to talk about. I thought that maybe I should have written it, but that would sure put the word out about our special operation. Let Passenger Processing have the glory, better I stay surreptitious. While I was thinking that with any luck we still had a couple more days before the ax fell, a Ford LTD pulled up next to me. Just over a month ago I had discovered a natural void area where the LTD could be loaded so I opened the passenger door, shined my flashlight in the same area and there was no void. There was a very non-factory cover over the void. As Yogi Berra would say "It's like déjà vu all over again."

I told the primary inspector that I would walk the vehicle to secondary and asked for the two occupant's immigration documents. I instructed the driver to park in lane one in secondary. In secondary I took a secondary declaration and then escorted the two male occupants in for pat downs. The pat downs were negative and the subjects were secured in our holding cells.

I returned to the vehicle and removed the plastic cover on the kick panel giving me access to the trapdoor. There was an identical cover in place over the fresh air vent just exactly the same as the previous vent load. The previous load came with the tool to remove the cover stashed under the seat. I looked under the seat and there was no socket this time.

I went to my car and retrieved my socket set and headed back to the car. When I got back to the vehicle there was a dog team just starting to run the vehicle. I have no idea where that team came from but news travels fast in the Customs world. I watched as the dog ran the vehicle starting at the rear bumper. When the dog, Moozer, got to the front fender area he stopped, sniffed a few more times and attempted to remove the fender for me scratching like there was no tomorrow. Moozer kept looking back at his handler like he was saying 'Well here it is, where is my reward?' I was going to remove the cover no matter what the dog said, but I have to admit that it is always nice to have the alert. The drawback it that the dog alert draws an audience. All the inspectors in secondary were now watching.

I removed the trap door and sure enough sausage shaped packages were clearly visible. Squatting there looking at those packages I thought 'This is going to be a long night.'

I got the load Goose had asked for, but one thing was now certain. Before I finish the seizure reports Utlee and Thorny will know I was working a TROLL operation. I had been on duty since 8:00 A.M. and it was now 11:00P.M. I was certain about one more thing; the reports would have to be perfect because Utlee would be looking for anything to bash us on.

One difference between this load and the previous one was the weight. This one weighed in at twenty-five pounds and the previous one had fourteen and a half pounds. These guys went all the way into the firewall area whereas the previous load only loaded the lower vent area.

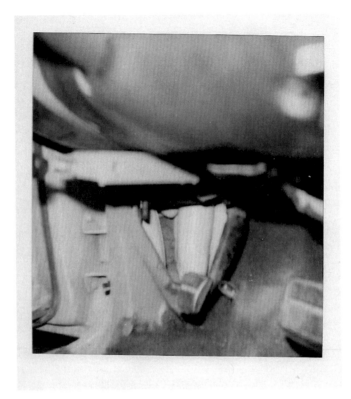

Illustration 20: Packages visible in driver side air vent.

Illustration 21: Sausage shaped packages after final weight.

As Goose and I left Mr. Utlee's office after our post seizure meeting, as stated above, I was feeling pretty good and I said to Goose "Was that an at-a-boy or an Alpha Charlie (ass chewing).

Goose answered "Yes!" and began laughing.

We walked to Goose's office and he said, "Close the door."

I did as instructed and sat down.

Goose asked me what time I had arrived home "this morning."

I told him it I pulled into the driveway at three and hit the bed by about four. It took me an hour to shower and to wind down. He then asked how many hours of sleep I had managed to get in and I told him two, I was up at six and on the road by six thirty.

Goose shook his head and said "Utlee is an idiot. He is listening to Thorny and Thorny is going to be his undoing if he doesn't wise up."

50

"Well I just hope that the DD is happy." I said, "If he is half as pissed as Utlee we may well end up in Alcan" (Alcan Alaska).

Goose looked at the door, I assume to ensure it was closed, and said "I called Mr. Fredericks yesterday and advised him of our plan. He agreed wholeheartedly, his exact wording, with your overtime assignment. I know that Mr. Utlee is in the DD's office as we speak or is on his way at a minimum to be briefed on Mr. Fredericks operation. I had just hung up the phone with Mr. Fredericks when I got the call to proceed to Utlee's office. I know that the ax will fall this morning but not on us."

Goose walked over to the door, opened it to look up and down the hall and then closed it to return to his desk. He continued "A couple of days ago Mr. Fredericks told me to get you to Grand sooner than later, so when you and I talked everything just fell in place and here we are. Mr. Fredericks was right and you proved that. Are you sure you didn't talk to Mr. Fredericks?"

"No Goose, if I had maybe I would have managed three hours of sleep by not worrying about today. Winding down was laying bed tired as hell with my eyes wide open." I told him. "I think I will be able to sleep tonight. This is a load off my mind."

Goose then chuckled "When Utlee offered to accept your resignation I was disappointed when you declined. I would have loved to be a fly in the corner of the DD's office when Utlee tried to explain that you were offered a resignation and took it."

Mr. Utlee never mentioned the meeting with the DD nor did he ever mention that first load. He gave me a few at-a-boys during my tour on TROLL but nothing more and those few at-a-boy's came only when others were present and he had to put on a show. From that point on both he and Thorny avoided me like the plague until I left TROLL. I did get my share of work at Grand Avenue and I led the TROLL team in seizures by a good margin. Six months after my departure from the TROLL team it was abolished by the DD for lack of production.

BILLION $ DOLLAR $ HIGHWAY

The Commish Wants To See It
March 1, 1990
24 Pounds Marijuana

It is a warm day for March and there is quite a stir today at the Port. I am working the Mariposa POE (Map) as usual and the Commissioner will be visiting the Commercial Facility just east of Map. That is about all I know, and I had asked around the port for more information on the visit but nobody knew anything more than I did. I had been working for about an hour watching the Office of Enforcement (OE) clowns running around with their radio earpieces in and looking very much like the USSS (United States Secret Service) but none of them are even talking to us. Oh well, I am so low on the totem pole that the visit is neither here nor there as far as I am concerned. As I am roving the lanes the inspector on lane one received a phone call and called me over.

"Soldier Buffalino just called and he said that Supervisor Goose wants you to call him at his office ASAP." she relayed.

The TROLL supervisor very seldom called me and 'ASAP', yep everyone and I mean everyone are jumping through their ass for the Commissioner's visit. ASAP has never been in his vocabulary.

I headed to the office and made the call "Rick here Lacky, what's up?"

"Hey Rick, I was just talking to Mr. Fredericks (the District Director) and he asked me to relay to you that today would be a good day to get a load." he said just as lackadaisical as ever. Well so I was wrong, Goose does not seem to be jumping through his ass for the Commish. He continued "You got one last week and the boss said you jumped the gun. Oh, and one more tidbit, but this stays between us understood?"

He paused waiting for a confirmation "10-4 understood sir." Now I was just a bit uneasy, WTF, I haven't heard that concern in his voice ever.

"Thorny told the rest of the TROLL team here at Grand Ave that they need to get a load over here before you get one over there." he whispered in the phone. "Don't let them know that I called you, keep it just between us."

"10-4 sir, I am always looking but now there is even more incentive to knock one down." I now whispered, why I whispered I don't know "The one last week was only 25 pounds in the air vents. But the one prior to last week was 88 pounds and it would be awesome to top that. A double bed or something would be nice."

"Well, Mr. Fredericks was impressed with the 25-pound sausage looking packages tucked so neatly in their compartment. He said the air vent concealment was top notch, but I think he will just be happy with whatever you get." he added. After one more "10-4" from me we hung-up.

I headed back out to the lanes to see what I could come up with in the way of a somewhat larger load and ran into OE Special Agent Juan Remous carrying some folding chairs. I never cared for Juan and never felt really comfortable with him and his arrogance but thought I would ask him about the Commissioner's itinerary. Maybe I could get some kind of a timeline not that it really mattered; I sure as heck can't schedule a smuggling attempt. But still...

"How is it going Juan?" I asked.

"Watch it man I am in a hurry, we have a VIP coming into town and I am the duty agent today, so I am very involved in the security aspects of the visit." he said swishing me away with his arm; folding chairs and all.

'Holy crap, is this idiot full of himself or what.' I thought.

"Yea I know, I was just wondering when she is due to arrive." I asked.

"*That* Inspector Davis is need to know only!!!" his arrogance now gushing from his every pore like a river of crap that he was full of.

"Well, I am sure I will know when she gets here." I said. "Don't let me hold you up. I saw you guys and the CET team over there setting up the VIP chairs so my apologies for the delay. Sure, don't want to keep someone standing and I am sure that for security purposes you will have to check them all. One missed whoopee cushion would be a disaster."

I guess I can be a jack ass myself, but he deserved it. I had to get back to roving so if fate is on my side I can comply with the DD's request. As I stated earlier, I can't schedule a load. You just have to cross your fingers and hope one happens along.

I did hurry however as I returned to the lanes. I was now almost running from vehicle to vehicle and nada. Also, no Commissioner in sight. I thought she would have a motorcade or something but in reality no Commissioner had visited Nogales since my arrival. For all I knew she had come and gone. As it neared noon my trusted ally and very good friend Velo Raptor was on lane two and his relief was due at noon. The traffic had petered out and Velo walked over and said "Well, has the Commish come and gone?"

"I have no idea." I said, "But I haven't seen any activity over at the dock for a while. I would have thought we would see something."

Raptor then informed me that when I was in the office about twenty cars entered the truck dock through the exit gate and he asked "Have you seen a convoy leave there? You have been out here roving ever since they went in."

I thought about it and laughed. Then replied "No I haven't but they may have exited the north gate and we wouldn't see them leave. I hope so because I saw Remous carrying some folding chairs as I was on my way out. It sure would make my day if he missed the Commissioner while he was over here gathering chairs. Yes Velo, *that* would make my day, maybe my week. I asked him when she was supposed to arrive and was told it was need to know only. I think he was offended that I even knew she was coming. Need to know, you know."

Velo came back with "Yea I hate that idiot and I trust him even less. Here comes my relief and I am starving. I am going to run down to the KFC for some chicken, do you want anything?"

I never, or at least very seldom ate anything when I was working. But I had doubled the previous day and I got home after 1:00 AM, took a shower and crashed. I was up at five and the wife, who waited up for me to get home, slept right through my departure today. My poor wife put up with crazy hours, crazy work, death threats (including me being shot at on my way home only to have bullet holes in the car) and other challenges; so when I could sneak out without waking her I did so. She usually made sure I had something when I got home and if I was too worn out to eat, she would make sure I had something before I left the next day or more accurately the same day just a few hours later. Today she was just too worn out to wake up. My hard hours took a toll on her with never a complaint. God Bless her I don't know how she did it. Anyhow I gave Velo some cash and said "Yes, I am starved also, can you get me one of those personal meals, white meat?"

"You got it." he said and off he went.

As I watch him leave, I am thinking that I can't remember the last time I had KFC and I am now hungrier than ever just thinking about it. As I turned around there are about ten cars coming from Mexico. I thought 'What did a light change.' There are no traffic lights anywhere near the border on either side in reality but it sure seemed like it, that or they somehow knew that I was now on the verge of starvation. I strolled over and began checking the vehicles that had split between the two lanes. I checked the one on lane two and nothing but as I am checking it, I hear the Immigration Inspector in lane one ask "Donde viene?" (Where are you coming from) and the driver answered "Magdelina". I turned and there sat a Ford Maverick. I hurried over and checked the rocker panel where I can see into the void and there is no void. I can see a package.

I walked over to the II and told her "I will take this one." and she handed me the passports and instructed the driver to park in secondary. I escorted the vehicle to secondary and took a secondary declaration. The usual, going to the stores in Nogales. No store in particular just the stores. I escorted the occupants into the holding area and secured the driver in the holding cell then advised the Senior on duty that he had some occupants in the holding area. I returned to the car and probed the rocker panel and extracted Marijuana. I had a load.

Just as I started walking back into the office to call OE, Raptor came walking over with the KFC. "Are you ready to eat?" he said.

"No, I got a load. You go ahead and have at it." I said.

54

"Damn I leave for ten minutes and you get a load." he said, "That is just not right."

I walked into the supervisors' office and there sat Buffalino. "Well is it loaded?" he asked.

"Yep, rocker panels." I said as I displayed the probe.

"I will call OE and get that ball rolling." he said. "Is it from Magdelina like the last few loads we got here?" he asked.

"Yep, déjà vu." I said, "I am going to get a sample and test it to confirm it is MJ."

I retrieved a test kit and headed back to the vehicle. Raptor was standing there waiting for me. "Show me how you probed this without drilling."

"You get the sample Raptor here is the probe." I proceeded to walk him through extracting some 'green leafy substance' without drilling and we tested it. The conclusive result was positive for the properties of Marijuana.

"So that is it. Hell, I didn't know that access point was even there." he said "That was easy. Quick and easy as a matter of fact."

By the time we completed the confirmation the OE duty agent was just exiting his car. He had only a short drive from the Commercial Facility where everyone was waiting for the Commissioner.

Agent Remous was obviously furious. He ranted and raved that I did this just to steal the thunder from the Office of Enforcement. I had no desire to confront this idiot, so I let him rant and rave away. Then Buffalino really ruined his day. "Rick, Mr. Fredricks wants you to take the car over to the truck dock ASAP. The Commissioner is on her way and the DD wants your load over there."

"You can't move that car." Remous said "It is evidence."

I wheeled around and there he stood with his lips smugly closed in a manner that put them somewhere between a pout and sneer. His head was cockeyed and nodding so he looked like a bobble head. I was done with Remous and I started toward him. I am not sure what I was going to do, talk or sock but I had had enough of his high and mighty crap.

Buffalino probably saved my ass as he cut me off and got in Remous's face where he said with decisiveness "Take it up with the DD Remous, it is going over *now*!"

"Is it OK if Raptor goes with me?" I asked somewhat calmed down for now as I watched Remous retreat to the door leading to the holding cell.

"Sure, this old thing may not make it so you guys may have to push the damn thing there." he was actually laughing but he was right, the damned old car had seen its better days.

I jumped in the driver's seat and started the car as Raptor came around an entered the passenger's door. "Thanks man." Raptor said a bit excited "I guess we will get to meet the Commissioner!"

Raptor was never one to get to excited. In fact, he was very laid back. Nonchalant was pretty much his middle name. So laid back that he blew me away one night when we were working Map. Mariposa closed at 10 PM and on this night at about 9 PM a hail of gun fire came in from Ephraim Canyon.

Illustration 22: Looking southeast from Mariposa POE into Ephraim Canyon with Mexico to the right.

The supervisor Christchurch Colon closed the Port and sent all but the three Vietnam Era veterans' home. Christchurch, Raptor and I remained at the Port for "Port Security". Christchurch asked "Do you guys have a long gun with you? I am breaking out the AK."

I said "Yep, got my SKS." and Raptor shrugged his shoulders and shook his head 'no'.

Colon said, "Let's go down there and show them that Nam experience wasn't a waste."

Being I had no more common sense then than now I said "Hell I am game. Let's GTA." GTA was a term coined by my old CET partner Gordo and was an acronym for Get Them A-holes. So off Christchurch and I go down into the canyon in performance of our mission to protect the USA. It is a bit ironic but during the Battle of Nogales in 1915 only one death was recorded.

Troops from Camp Nogales located in Ephraim Canyon were fired upon by Pancho Villas supporters who had occupied Nogales Sonora. The soldier killed war rumored to have been related to Gordo. I wonder if during that skirmish he said "Hell I am game. Let's GTA." Anyhow we did not encounter enemy forces on that night and when we returned to Map there stood Raptor in exactly the same position as when we left; puffing nonchalantly on a cigarette. He tossed his cigarette and said, "I suppose we are on our way home now?" and we packed up and left.

I guess meeting the new Commissioner took the 'non' out of 'nonchalant' (I know, chalant is not a word but you get the point). Word or not a word Raptor became more and more excited as we entered the truck compound through the exit gate. Past all the nice neat rows of chairs and over to the dock where the Chief Enforcement Officer (CEO) was awaiting our arrival. The only enforcement activity I saw was the National Guard checking the few trucks that were making their way through the maze of Commish preparation. I noticed that all Guard personnel were equipped with hand drills.

Upon my arrival the CEO was elated. "Thank God you managed to nab a load. Mr. Fredericks was counting on you and you sure came through."

"Just good luck Mr. Crow but I will take it. It is a Maverick with rockers loaded so it won't break any records but like I said, I will take it." Now I am starting to get excited, maybe this is just what the doctor ordered.

I continued with the CEO "What is with the National Guard? Is that a show of force? I didn't see any Customs there with them for a photo op."

"No, they are drilling the floor on every trailer that comes through. A guy walking southbound through Mariposa stopped in and told Buffalino that a cartel was going to use the Commissioner's visit as a distraction and run a floor load through the facility when she arrives." he said.

"He told Buffalino?" I said almost offended "I have been over there all day and this is the first I have heard of this informant. Where is he?"

"In Mexico. Buffalino didn't even get his name, just took the information, including a trailer number, and let the guy walk on out the door" he almost growled obviously not to happy.

"Everyone thinks it is BS so Mr. Battle assigned drilling to the Guard so the Inspectors could be present for the Commissioner. We have to fill all those chairs somehow." he snarled waving at the sixty or so chairs. "Oh, there is Mr. Fredericks, she must be on her way."

As he walked off towards the District Director I said to Raptor "Well Juan and his 'need to know' just went to crap. I guess Mexico knows she is coming. Or maybe the informant had a need to know. Hell, I bet everyone in Mexico knew long before we did. I would be willing to bet that they have her itinerary."

As we stand there laughing about the arrogance and raw stupidity of Special Agent Remous I hear a helicopter approaching. "Well that sounds like a Black Hawk, what do you think?" I asked.

"Yep, I guess now we know when she is coming and how she is getting here." he said, "And just think, we are the main attraction!"

"Well Velo, I don't know about the main attraction, but it sure looks like we will certainly have our moment in the limelight at the least." now I am almost as excited as Raptor.

We watch as the Black Hawk grows from a dot to a helicopter and lands on the north side of the compound. Before the props even start to slow a mass of our VIP's, the Special Agents and the CET team all converge on the door of the bird. We can just barely see the entourage disembarking when a National Guardsman comes running over. "Do you know where Klug Lancelot is? We got this on the drill bit when we drilled. The truck number also matches the lookout!"

This guy is holding up a drill with a six-inch bit and fresh marijuana filling four inches of the groves. "You got this from the floor?" I asked.

"Yes, in three places." he just ruined my day. The limelight has all but burned out.

I looked over at the mass of humanity gathering around the Black Hawk and see Klug. "He is over there." I point to where Klug is standing behind the crowd.

"Oh, I see him, thanks." the Guardsman says as he breaks into a trot. I stand there and watch him as he talks to Lancelot and off they both go running towards the suspect trailer.

A few moments later as the now moving mass of humanity is heading our way Lancelot runs screaming through the crowd "We got a load, we got a load." he is announcing. For some crazy reason it reminded me of a guy named Paul Revere, I don't know why and he was not carrying a lantern just a damn drill with marijuana on it. Waving it over his head like, well like a dad gum lantern.

Velo and I stood there watching our once sure audience move like a flock of starlings, head east and engulf the offending truck. We began walking that way, but not in any real hurry and I saw CEO Crow heading our way. "Well guys I think you can head back to Map and finish your seizure. Your show has been trumped. Sorry guys, but that floor is definitely loaded."

As Raptor and I slowly dragged our backsides on now very heavy legs back to the ugly Maverick, Raptor came up with the phrase of day "Well at least we can eat our chicken. I forgot how hungry I was with all this excitement."

Ah there is life after all and now that he mentioned it that dad gum chicken was looking better than ever. "Yea Velo, now that you mention it, I think I will just eat that before I even start unloading this flipping dope."

58

When we got back to Map Velo said "You watch your load and I will get the chicken."

I waited in secondary by myself until he returned with the two little personal meals and the drinks now somewhat watered down. We stood there leaning on the ugly beast munching in silence, tossing the bones and other trash from the now tasteless meal into the back seat of the rolling hemorrhoid. When I finished my first meal in two days, I felt no relief as my stomach was in somewhat of a knot. I removed the rear tire on the passenger side to get to the trap door covering the rocker panel and, as with the previous loads, there was the roped to pull out the dope. I began pulling and nothing. I pulled harder and still nothing, the dope had swelled up in the rocker panels to the point that the packages were not moving. It was one of those days. After replacing the tire, I broke out the air chisel and began cutting the rocker panels open. When cutting with an air chisel the chisel leaves the cut metal razor sharp. I have on plastic gloves, but they are no match for the sharp metal. I finally finished retrieving the dope on the passenger side with just a few cuts and minor bleeding and started on the back-driver side rocker panel. When the rocker panel was sufficiently open enough to remove the now visible marijuana, I opened the front door to start there. Just as I am ready to engage the air chisel Buffalino came running up.

"Rick, take that car back to the truck dock. The Commissioner wants to see it." he said. Now he was excited.

"What, are you kidding; this thing is cut to pieces. Why does she want to see this when they nailed a thousand pounds over there?" I said incredulously.

"They told me she said that load was not a cold hit, they were drilling every truck, so it did not impress her. She wanted to see the concealment and how it was detected on a cold hit. They are waiting at the slot where you had parked earlier." Wow, I think Soldier Buffalino was actually impressed. I am not sure if it was the load or the Commissioner he was impressed with, but he was impressed. "Raptor is on the line, so you are solo, get going, the Commissioner is waiting."

I jumped in the old Maverick and hauled buns back to the truck dock and right where I had previously parked there was a large crowd. As I pulled up to park I was waved in by Mr. Fredericks and the Regional Commissioner. I knew I was in the right place so I got out of the car and the Commissioner walked over. She introduced herself and put her hand out obviously to shake hands. I started to shake her hand but as I looked down at our hands I noticed that my hand still had the somewhat shredded plastic glove on it and thanks to the razor sharp metal everywhere I had been cut several times, therefore I was looking at what was left of the glove and a hand that was covered with blood.

I stopped and apologized "Ma'am I was in the process of cutting the rocker panels to get the marijuana out and the process produces some razor-sharp metal. It is a messy process and my hands are a mess."

She said, "It is part of the job and I want to shake your hand, mess or no mess." I removed what was left of the glove and shook her hand. She had just earned my upmost respect and to this day I respect her as much as I did that day. Gutsy lady is all I have to say about that.

She wanted to see the compartments, so I showed her the passenger side first with empty compartments and then the driver side back seat which was cut open, but the dope was still present.

Illustration 23: Commissioner Hallett viewing the Maverick load.
Back seat driver side where packages are visible in the open compartment.

We then moved to the driver door where the rocker panel was intact and untouched. As it turned out the little break for lunch was a God send since she was able to see the entire process, step by step. A God send and, well I wouldn't quite say curse but nearing a curse.

The Commissioner was quite impressed and had a few questions that I fielded with no problem. How did you find it? What were you looking for? Was the driver the owner of the car? With the usual answer on the Mexican border "No ma'am, he claimed it was borrowed."

Easy to answer questions and then she hit me with a comment that solicited an answer. "I see someone was eating KFC and just tossed the bones and cups in the back seat. I have noticed that most load vehicles seem to have nonexistent owners." Ms. Hallett was definitely observant and we are surrounded by the District Director, the Assistant District Director, the Regional Commissioner, and a slew of other HQ VIP's.

I thought this is embarrassing, 'yes ma'am Raptor and I had lunch and used the load vehicle as a trash can because I am going to cut it up and trash it anyhow so why not just toss our waste in the back seat – burp'. So I said "Yes ma'am, eating is a tactic used by many smugglers to cover up signs of anxiety or nervousness. When the occupants are eating KFC we know that someone met them in Mexico with the food because there are no Kentucky Fried Chicken places in Mexico or at least not in Nogales, Sonora."

I certainly did not lie to the Commissioner, she said "I see someone was eating KFC and just tossed the bones and cups in the back seat." True statement Raptor and I are guilty. Then she said, "I have noticed that most load vehicles seem to have nonexistent owners." I then tossed in that "Eating is a tactic used by many smugglers to cover up sighs of anxiety or nervousness. When the occupants are eating KFC we know that someone met them in Mexico with the food because there are no Kentucky Fried Chicken places in Mexico or at least not in Nogales, Sonora." True statement, I did not say this was the case in this seizure, just stated a fact about tactics and observation techniques.

Illustration 24: Commissioner at driver door.

OK now that I have that as clear as mud lets continue. When the show finally ended and the entourage moved on Mr. Fredericks and the Assistant District Director Rudolph Macho stayed behind. Rudolph said "Well, this was a good catch and really good observation knowing they were hiding their nervousness with KFC. I think she was impressed."

Mr. Fredericks laughed and said "Yes that was great observation. How was the chicken?" He laughed again and said, "Quick thinking and well done." then walked away before I could answer.

I drove the old clunker back to the Mariposa and cut the last panel. The marijuana weighed in at a whopping 24 pounds. Certainly not my biggest load but an unforgettable one. A load that made the newspapers and Customs Today magazine.

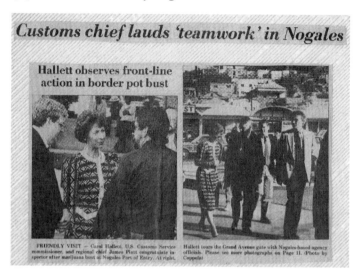

Customs chief lauds 'teamwork' in Nogales

Hallett observes front-line action in border pot bust

FRIENDLY VISIT — Carol Hallett, U.S. Customs Service commissioner, and regional chief James Platt congratulate inspector after marijuana bust at Nogales Port of Entry. At right, Hallett tours the Grand Avenue gate with Nogales-based agency officials. Please see more photographs on Page 11. (Photo by Coppola)

It was also enough to start a skirmish with the Office of Enforcement. When I started to take some pictures of the load the Assistant Special Agent in Charge (ASAC) who had come over from the truck dock disallowed me. "You can't take pictures and if you do, we will seize them as evidence. The AUSA informed us that any pictures taken are clearly evidence so no more pictures of loads." Fortunately, the US Customs Service sent me the two press release photos that are included in this chapter and the newspaper clip is from the local Nogales newspaper.

One more caveat to the I&C/OE battle. The following week I attended a pretrial meeting with the AUSA for a previous load coming up for trial. Of course, OE was present. Special Agent Negame Wasish one of the most beautiful people I have ever met, who had both the appearance of a model and an outstanding personality, joined us. We were very good friends and to this day she is one of my favorite people. Oh, and she is still knock down gorgeous! I have only seen pictures of her, but she still makes my heart skip a beat or two when I see them.

At the close of the pretrial I asked the AUSA about the photo ban placed on loads and she said "I told them any pictures taken are evidence so have them make two copies. One for evidence and one for training or whatever. As long as a copy is in the case file."

I was very fortunate that Negame was there and heard the AUSA. She was instrumental in ensuring that OE upper echelon was made aware of the "two copies" instruction. From then on until my retirement if I took pictures, I had two copies made, one for me and one for "evidence".

When the battle subsided, I guess you could say I, at a minimum, came out even. I look at it like this, it is a win for you the readers who can enjoy the pictures, READ ON AND ENJOY!

BILLION $ DOLLAR $ HIGHWAY

A Traitor to God, Country and Us
May 9, 1990
607 Pounds Cocaine

Yesterday was my wedding anniversary and I didn't even get the day off. Today I have already worked my eight hours at Mariposa and am now on an overtime assignment at Grand Avenue. I was very happy to see that SI Thorny had departed before my arrival since our relationship or rivalry if you prefer had taken a nosedive the previous month.

The nosedive started with a note from SCI Goose (the TROLL supervisor). The note directed me to report to him at 8:00 AM the following day at Grand Avenue regarding a discovery request on one of my cases heading to trial. I reported as directed and learned that Goose had not yet arrived, so I had headed to Secondary to hang out there and await his arrival. I was in the Secondary office hanging low and in walked flipping Thorny.

"What the hell are you doing here?" he asked, "You are supposed to be at Map (Mariposa POE)."

"SCI Goose left a message at Map last night for me to meet him here for some paperwork housekeeping." I replied knowing that Thorny was going to go ballistic.

"Yea well Goose isn't in yet" he snarled "and I don't even know if he is coming in today."

"I know he is not in and I assume he will be in since he ordered me to report here." I replied, "That is why I am helping out in Secondary just until he gets here."

"You can help these guys out in Secondary but stay the hell off the lanes." Yep ballistic on cue "You do your roving at Map, not here."

'No duh!' was my thought but I just replied "10-4 understood."

As I watched Thorny walking across secondary heading to his office at District, I emerged from the Secondary office and headed to the Secondary Inspection Area, no need to lay low now. Maybe I can make his day and pick-up a load in Secondary then he could really blow up. As I am standing in Secondary watching Thorny top the District stairs and enter the District building, I hear someone calling me. I looked over and it was the Chief Enforcement Officer (CEO) Vance Crow who was walking towards me at a fast pace and waving almost frantically.

"Rick I am glad you are here today, I need you to take a look at a vehicle for me." he said.

"Sure, which one." I asked waving at the three or four vehicles in Secondary.

"Oh no, not one of these. Last night we had a runner from Secondary (the driver had abandoned his vehicle and ran back to Mexico). Everyone including CET has checked the truck and found nothing." he said and added "We have also had three K-9's run it with none alerting. SI Corona who was on overtime seized the truck on an abandonment since she is the seizure clerk, but I would really like for you to take a look at it."

"Sure thing, not a problem." I said looking in our small fenced-in seized vehicle lot. "Is that the truck?" I said pointing to a truck in the lot.

"Yes, and Corona is in the Supervisors office with the keys and the paperwork." he replied.

I headed to the Supervisors office and there stood Dee Corona. "I see Vance recruited you to check the truck." she said with a twinge of nervous chuckle. "We were talking about the incident and unless the guy had immigration issues, we found no reason for him to run. That is unless everyone in the Port missed something. Vance said he was going to call you at Map and there you were standing in secondary. He took off so fast his vortex almost sucked me out the door with him." she added, laughing at her last comment.

"Well let's go, do you have the keys to the lot and the truck?" I asked.

"Yes, and if you find something I am going to pound you! Everyone in the Port has looked at that damn truck." she said and she could probably do it, pound me that is, Corona was one tough Inspector.

Corona and I headed to the mini seizure lot and on the way there ran into Thorny of all the bad luck.

"Where are you guys going?" he asked.

Corona answered "Rick is going to check the seized truck from last night. Everyone's already checked it but Mr. Crow asked Rick to look at it. I already threatened him with a pounding if he finds anything."

"Crow? Well I will come with you then. Mr. Crow should have let me know he was going to talk to one of my guys." Thorny whined.

Corona stopped dead in her tracks and said "I don't think Mr. Crow needs *your* permission. You are a Senior 11 and he is a Chief. Last I heard that is a 13. Besides you already looked at it."

"Well I will look again." Thorny said now a bit on the defensive. Since the seizure lot is a controlled access area, Corona could deny his entry to the seizure lot due to the fact that she is the seizing officer of the vehicle as well as the Seized Property Custodian and a GS-11 herself. Basically, she owns the lot and determines who has a need to gain access to it. Thorny had already looked at the seizure (that explains his presence in the secondary office) and a GS-13 Chief requested me, not Thorny. That made him spare baggage, just along for the ride. Back then a GS-13 was way the heck up there in the Port hierarchy. My goal was to make GS-11. I knew many Inspectors who retired as 9's. An insult was to refer to someone as an NFL – Nine For Life. They were never going to get above Journeyman.

"OK but it is double for you Jonathan, you better not find anything either under the circumstances." Corona said. Knowing Thorny was on the defensive she immediately went offensive. "You will be right there with the rest of us 'missed a damn load' inspectors."

I must admit I enjoyed that exchange immensely. My thought was 'ouch, I bet that hurt' Thorny's pride and his ego. Yep, I was eating that up like a bucket of popcorn at the movie.

As we got to the truck, I tapped the tail gate and said, "Here it is, I found it."

Corona yelped "What? You found it already?"

I laughed and said, "No just kidding Dee, there is nothing here." I walked up to the rear tire and checked it and repeated the 'discovery'. Dee's reaction was the same and we repeated at the driver's door. Jonathan opened the hood and 'discovered' the non-existent load as the old grump actually joined the game. I walked over to the passenger door, opened it and checked the dash area with nothing there and then looked at the fresh air vent. It had a non-factory trap door. I looked in the glove box and there sat a socket wrench that fit the bolts on the trap door. Two minutes later with the trap door removed I saw a package in a Kmart bag. A quick probe and as the probe was extracted from the suspect object a white powder gleamed on the probe. I stood up and said, "I found it, it is here." Dee laughed and said "Are you finished? Let's go."

I said "No Dee. I am serious this time, it is here in a Kmart bag and it's cocaine."

Poor Dee went ashen, came over and said, "Where is it?"

I pointed it out and as she looked at the powder on the probe then at the kilo package contained in the Kmart bag and she said "Well, I just can't believe it. Everyone including CET and a passel of K-9's has checked this damn truck and there it is, it took you to find it. I just can't believe it. Let's go tell Mr. Crow. He was right when he said if there was anything there you would find it."

Jonathan finally came over and asked where the package was, and I pointed it out to him. He reached in and pulled the package out with his bare hands. Dee pointed out the fact that he should have donned gloves, but he was way beyond that.

He removed the package of cocaine from the bag and looked at the white powder just visible where I had probed the package. He then set the package on the floor of the vehicle and said "Yes, you guys go get Mr. Crow, I will guard the scene." His voice sounded so dejected that it was more of a mumble, almost unintelligible.

Well, he was my supervisor, so the scene was his. We went about 10 yards and we saw Mr. Crow already headed our way. He yelled "Anything?" and Dee yelled back one word "Coke."

Mr. Crow broke into a run and covered the 30 yards like a wide receiver. I may be mistaken but I just might have seen Dee's vortex on that run. We headed back to the truck and there sat the kilo of cocaine with Thorny still looking at it like it was a snake.

"I knew, I just knew this wasn't an immigration thing. Is it just the one package?" Mr. Crow bellowed.

"Yes sir, the driver side hasn't been tampered with and this is the only one on this side." I replied. My years of experience now tells me this was probably a sample or a payment.

"Drive the truck down to lane one and I will let OE (Office of Enforcement) know that we have a cocaine load. I can't remember the last time we saw coke here." Mr. Crow said beaming.

I would have to guess that in the morning staff meeting he had probably told them that he was sure there was more to this than immigration issues. Well he was right.

I drove the truck to secondary lane one and by the time I got there the District Director (DD) and the Assistant District Director (ADD) were on their way over from the District building. Not ten minutes later OE arrived and took pictures. I felt real pleasure when OE asked who removed the cocaine and the Kmart bag from the concealment area. I enjoyed watching Jonathan squirm when he had to admit that it was him and no, he had not donned gloves. Touché, chock another one up for me. First Dee verbally smacking him and now OE, yea baby I was just loving this. Immediately after receiving a lengthy and stern lecture from the Special Agent in Charge (in front of the DD and the ADD) Jonathan headed to the supervisor's office, I had assumed to hide and lick his wounded pride. I would find out differently.

OE finished taking their pictures from every conceivable angle as well as a book full of notes and asked who the seizing officer was. I told them it was Dee and she immediately told them that she was going to cancel her Search, Arrest and Seizure (SAS) report. She said her SAS was for an abandoned vehicle and she would not amend it to add cocaine as a line item. She said I would be executing a new SAS for the cocaine seizure and the vehicle would then be a line item rather than the main concern of the SAS. We argued a bit on it and Thorny came strolling up. He listened to the debate for a bit and said that our argument was moot because he had already executed a new SAS and he put himself as the seizing Officer. He handed a copy of the newly created SAS to the OE case agent who asked how he could possibly be the seizing officer instead of me and he stated, "I am his supervisor and he was working under my direct supervision when he found the load."

Dee came unglued, I had never seen her that pissed off and OE made it clear that they were none too happy either, but at the end of the day Jonathan Thorny was the seizing officer with me as the discovering officer. Thorny did not even mention Dee who, in reality, made the initial seizure. She should have been at the very minimum a witness. Cocaine was extremely rare on the Mexican border back then and it was a big deal to get even a kilo. This would probably be Dee's only opportunity for an honorable mention on a cocaine load other than TOT (turned over to) seizure custodian Corona.

Illustration 25: The lonesome kilo of Cocaine.

Illustration 26: What an improvement, Thorny has never looked so good.

Anyhow, here I am a week later roving at Grand Avenue and I was still practicing my self-imposed 'pick a vehicle every day and check every one of them that I encounter'. The vehicle of the day was Chevrolet pick-up trucks. Chevy trucks were very popular in Mexico, so I had my work cut out for me. There were times when three of the four lanes had a Chevy pick-up in them and I would practically have to run from lane to lane. Many of the Inspectors, especially on the Immigration side, would cut their primary inspection short just to try to keep me from checking a vehicle on their lane. On many occasions I would be reaching under a vehicle to tap a tank or the drive shaft and off the vehicle would go. Roving was very dangerous in those days from our own side as well as from the criminal element. One had to move fast, very fast.

I was on lane four and looked over at lane one to see a Chevy pick-up just pulling in. I started that way and recognized the truck as that of an Immigration Inspector Rudy. We used to call Rudy the preacher as he was very religious. I had heard that he would fill in for the reverend at his church upon occasion. Religious to the point that when he was in the immigration secondary office where one could break out a radio and listen to music, he would break out his tape recorder and listen to church sermons he had taped. As soon as I recognized the vehicle I slowed down and almost ignored it thinking 'that is only Rudy coming from his Wednesday church service' (in Nogales, Sonora, Mexico). Just as I thought this, I corrected myself and told myself 'Chevy pick-ups are the pick of the night. You have to check them all'. I walked over to the truck and could hear the Immigration Inspector on primary and the driver chatting more than actually taking a declaration. Oh well it gave me time to get there and check the vehicle. I looked at the gas tanks and reached under the truck and tapped them – nothing. I then tapped the bed floor and received a clunk instead of a clang. WTF I thought, I tapped it again and again a clunk. That sounds and feels like a double floor, I thought. I walked to the back of the

69

truck that was equipped with a camper shell and I opened the window on the camper shell. There sat two very young girls the oldest about seven, sitting on a carpet kit. A carpet kit is plywood with cushion and carpet that is installed in the bed of the truck to form a passenger area on top and a storage compartment underneath.

Illustration 27: Carpet kit, the carpet covered plywood pieces lying on the floor were installed using the ledge where the red arrows point. The installation made a floor with a compartment beneath.

As the girls looked at me, I said "Excuse me mija[1], I need to lift this." referring to the carpet kit. The girls moved to the front of the truck bed and I lifted the carpet kit to see into the compartment. What I saw was numerous white plastic trash bags all exactly the same tied off on top containing what appeared to be bricks stacked in them. My first thought was 'This is not Rudy; it must just be a similar truck.' Fearing that the truck would be released I hurried to the driver's door. As I rounded the back of the truck, I saw Mary Fidel the Immigration Inspector assigned to that lane chatting with the driver. When I reached the door, I ripped it open and physically removed the driver. It *was* Rudy. At this point I thought 'Maybe those are Bibles.' I was sure he was coming from church. Before I had a chance to say anything Rudy said, "I don't know what is back there, I loaned my truck to someone at church."

---

[1]Mija-literal interpretation daughter but used also as sweetheart for any very young girl

Illustration 28: Primary booths are just visible on the left; Mexico is to the right where the concrete ends. The rear tires of the blue car are in Mexico and the front tires are in in the US.

Now I did one of the most idiotic things I could do, I walked Rudy to the back of the truck about three feet from Mexico (before the rebuild Primary was even closer to Mexico than it is today) and I opened the camper shell. The opening on top is a window that stretches the length of the shell and comes from the top of the shell to the top of the tailgate. To fully open the cargo area the window is secured up and the tailgate is dropped. I had just the top open and Rudy reached up and held it in place. I then raised the carpet kit and as I was doing this he again said "I don't know what is back there, I loaned my truck to someone at church."

I said, "You are telling me you don't know what is in these bags?"

"I have no idea, I loaned my truck to a guy from church. I don't know him very well." he answered. Again, I thought 'Bibles, maybe these bags contain Bibles.'

I reached down and pulled out my probe which was an old screwdriver. I stuck it in the closest bag and I knew it was not marijuana or bibles. I pulled the probe out and it was covered with cocaine.

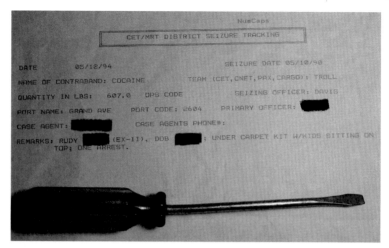

Illustration 29: Probe with seizure tracking report as background

When I saw the cocaine on the probe, I realized what I actually had there in the truck and it hit me in the face like a Muhammad Ali punch that brought reality to the magnitude of this bust. I grabbed Rudy and put an arm lock on him. Ali's second punch was realizing that we were just feet from Mexico and that thought sure as hell made this an 'Oh shit' moment. I walked him back to the door of the truck and I reached in, shut off the engine and took the keys. From here everything went into slow motion. I looked up to our destination which was the supervisors' office about 75 feet away. The Supervisor, Mustang Corners, had just emerged from the office and I watched him light a cigarette. We took about five steps and he saw us, me escorting Rudy in an arm lock. He watched for just a moment and yelled "Is he loaded?"

I yelled back "Yes" and tossed him the keys, then added "and it is coke."

I remember seeing his newly lit cigarette go straight up in the air, Mustang catching the keys and I still have no idea where the cigarette landed if it landed at all. Mustang headed our way and we crossed at the midway point and he relayed that he was going to move the vehicle to secondary. He asked how much cocaine and I said, "Mustang it is a big load, the bed is full."

Mustang's jaw dropped and his eyes almost left the socket, then he said, "Never mind secondary, I am moving it just outside the office door."

I walked Rudy to the supervisors' office and to the detention cell. I asked him "Rudy do you have any weapons on you?"

"No." he replied.

"Not even your service weapon?" I asked. Again, he replied that he had no weapons. I then performed a frisk for weapons which was negative. I secured the door and went to where the truck was parked just outside the door to the supervisors' office. Mustang was standing there with a couple of other Inspectors.

"Where is it loaded?" Mustang asked.

"In the bed under the carpet kit." I replied, "Are his kids still back there?"

"I guess; we haven't touched the truck." he said.

"I am going to get his wife out and have her get the kids." I said pointing to his wife in the passenger seat.

"Hell yea, good idea." he said "Then we will begin on the vehicle. Are you sure it is coke?"

"I haven't tested it and I have only seen coke once and that was last month but, yes I am relatively sure that it is coke." I said shaking my head yes. "Also, it felt like coke when I probed it. Coke feels somewhat different than, well anything I have probed before."

I walked over to the passenger door and opened it. Rudy's wife was sitting there with both hands on the dash holding on as best she could. She didn't look at me or even move a muscle when I opened the door. "Ma'am I need you to step out of the vehicle." I said. Not a move, not a twitch: nothing to register that she heard me.

"Ma'am step out of the vehicle please." I repeated but got the same non-compliant reaction as the first try. I directed her several more times each time a bit more forcefully. She never made as much as a twitch.

"Ma'am I will remove you with force if necessary, now get down from the vehicle NOW." I was now to the point that I would remove her by force and as I just started to drag her out, I changed my mind.

Mustang was standing off to the side of the vehicle watching and I began walking toward him. As I took a couple of steps he came over and we met midway just out of earshot of the vehicle. He said "Go ahead, pull her out. You gave her enough rope."

I said "Well I damn near did but I don't want those kids to see some man in uniform wrestle their mother out of the vehicle. I think we should get Elantra Malta to do it. She is strong as an ox for being a little over five feet tall in heels."

"Damn I am glad one of us is still thinking." Mustang said "She has pissed me off so much I almost came over there and tossed her to the ground, jumped dead into her back and slapped the handcuffs on her myself. You are absolutely right, let me get Malta."

About two minutes later Malta came over and walked to the door. She stared at Rudy's wife for a couple of minutes and in a very stern voice ordered her out of the vehicle. There was still no response from the occupant. Malta then called her by name and said "I am asking you (Rudy's wife) to get out, don't make me pull you out of there in front of those babies. I love them you know."

Rudy's wife looked at Malta and put out her hands to Malta. Malta helped her get out and helped her walk to the back of the truck where the two helped the kids out. As the group walked into the supervisors' office, I noticed tears streaming down Malta's face. I did not know that Malta's family and Rudy's families were very close. Mustang came over and said, "OK where is the coke?" then he added "Poor Malta, that was tough on her but sure as hell it was the best thing for those kids. Pobresitos[2]."

I had always liked Rudy and even when I brought him in, patted him down and secured him in the holding cell I felt no aggression toward him. His wife also obviously knew exactly what cargo their daughters were sitting on. I knew one thing after that scene; I would not go near either one of them for a while because I now felt they both deserved a good ass whipping. Not only for the kids but for poor Malta and I was the one responsible for bringing her into a terrible situation. Those two parents used their children and put them through this. They obviously love money more than they loved their own children. I still get mad as hell when I remember that scene. In 2016 I saw the now retired Malta and of course this load came up in our very short meeting. It brought that night back for both of us. "It still hurts me because of the babies." she said with tears in her eyes. Malta was not the only one with tears in their eyes that day, but mine were for Malta.

I looked at Mustang and said, "It is under the carpet kit Mustang and you won't believe how much is there."

We walked to the back of the truck, opened the window and I raised the floor of the carpet kit revealing the bags of cocaine.

"Holy shit! Are they all loaded with cocaine?" he asked.

"I am not sure. First, why don't we test this to confirm that it is coke. I am going to go get a test kit." I said.

"No, you stay here and watch this. I will have one sent out and before we start unloading this, I am going to get some firepower. Hell, there is a crowd watching from across the line." he said pointing to Mexico. I looked south and he was right, we certainly had drawn a crowd.

Shortly thereafter an Inspector came over with a shotgun in one hand and a cocaine test kit in the other. He handed me the test kit and I retrieved my probe. I once again probed the package using the previous spot and ran the test. I looked at the shotgun wielding Inspector and told him

---

[2] Poor kids

"Tell Mustang it turned blue. It is cocaine."

Illustration 30: Shotgun wielding Inspector who transported the cocaine test kit.

Mustang called every Law Enforcement Organization in the area and before we started to remove the load, we had back-up from the Nogales (Arizona) Police Department, US Border Patrol, Santa Cruz County Sheriff and the US Customs investigators (Customs Office of Enforcement).

We began removing the cocaine two bags at a time with each trash bag weighing about twenty-five pounds. When all was done and the cocaine was weighed on our calibrated scale, the total came out to 607 pounds of uncut cocaine with a wholesale value of over twelve million dollars at the time of the seizure.

Dee Corona had been called in to perform her duties as the seizure clerk. She observed the weighing of the bags, verified and recorded weights as well as kept us going with her constant mock complaining. About half way through the weighing process she said, "My God, this is going to take all night." and Mustang replied, "No problem Dee, we've got plenty of coffee."

Just as we finished weighing the packages Dee said to me "Hey Davis, go ahead and say it. Eat your heart out Jonathan Thorny."

Being at the bottom of that Totem Pole I just held my hand up and laughed "I will pass."

This was, if not *the* largest, one of the largest cocaine seizures on the southwest border at the time. Among those that responded to the port along with OE were Internal Affairs and of course the TROLL supervisor who was also involved with the training office. When Goose arrived, he brought this new piece of equipment called a Video Camcorder and he recorded the event. A couple of days later he gave me a VHS tape of the seizure that I still have today. It is hard to get still pictures off it, but I did manage to get some.

Illustration 31: Inspector Malta in the truck and an unnamed Inspector holding the window up. Bags of cocaine are visible in front of Malta, to her left and on the tailgate.

* * *

Illustration 32: The author carrying two bags of cocaine Nogales PD in the background providing security.

* * *

Illustration 33: Cocaine packages in two lines ready to be weighed.

The following day I went directly to Grand Avenue (a couple of hours late because the seizure did not conclude until the wee hours of the morning, and after a double). As I arrived at work, I noticed that I was receiving some very cold shoulders from many of the Immigration Inspectors. Many of them seemed to have taken the seizure as a shot at their agency. One however came over a couple of hours after my arrival and she said "Great seizure. I am so glad that you got Rudy. He was using me, and when you opened the tailgate on the truck to unload it, I went over and looked in that truck. I could see all the packages. It was then that everything hit me: the enormous amount of cocaine, my lane, our agency and the reality that he was using me and all of us because of our friendship. I walked back to primary but literally got sick and had to go throw up." The inspector was Mary Fidel, the inspector on primary when Rudy was making his entry from Mexico. She then told me that she could not work primary anymore because she had lost all faith in everyone. She could not release a vehicle from primary, so she sent every vehicle that entered her lane for a secondary inspection. The repercussions for "flooding secondary" were numerous complaints from her fellow inspectors, Immigration and Customs. She said that she asked and was granted a reassignment to adjudications. She never worked the lanes again.

Illustration 34: The author sitting on the pile.

* * *

Illustration 35: Dee and I laughing just after her "Hey Davis, go ahead and say it. Eat your heart out Jonathan Thorny" statement.

* * *

Illustration 36: Packages on display for press conference.

Illustration 37: Each package with seizure tag.

This could be the end of the chapter but with the amount and value of cocaine there were two investigations that I am aware of. Of course the Office of Enforcement had their investigation on Rudy and his organization which was somewhat routine. The other investigation that I am aware of was that of Internal Affairs. That would include an investigation of both Customs and Immigration employees. I won't get into the investigations and actually know very little about them anyhow, but I will say that I was asked for my opinion on practically everyone that was working that night. My answers were pretty much the same. I really didn't know anything. IA finally gave up and as they were leaving told me to "think about it" and they advised me that they would be back in a few days if I came up with anything.

I lived in Tucson 65 miles from the Port. I had the most beautiful wife and three great kids at home so there was no "choir practice" or hanging out with anyone. I got in my car and went home. Socially there was nothing with any of my co-workers, Customs or Immigration, so I couldn't tell you where anyone lived much less anything about their life style.

At work I was always very keen on situational awareness. I watched the cars and people crossing north bound and south bound. I paid extreme attention to what was going on in Mexico and who seemed to be your basic border crosser verses those who appeared to be "spotters" watching us. I watched the people, the traffic and all other goings on in Mexico. This was especially true when roving. When you have one foot in Mexico you want to keep keenly aware of any possible threat or threatening event *before* it gets to you. All this and still inspecting four lanes of constant moving vehicles.

That being the case I, at this point in my career, had not really watched or thought much about co-workers. Rudy changed that and I never forgot the lesson we were given that night. I never looked at co-workers the same. I don't think anyone did.

The IA questioning did get me to thinking however. I found myself that night on my 65-mile journey home re-creating in my mind every moment of the night of the seizure. I kept thinking about the lanes. There were four lanes open, two manned by Customs and two manned by Immigration. It only made sense that Rudy would go through an Immigration lane since he was one of them. Why Fidel, what made him choose her? Was it by coincidence or was it part of the smuggling operation.

Now my head was really spinning with just me and the road. I now felt that I must be a suspect also because I had no answers for IA when they questioned me. I was now mentally pre-seizure roving the lanes in my mind. Probably not good when you are driving but – just me and the road. There was no traffic that night.

Only two things jumped out at me, both had to do with Inspector Fidel. First, she was one of the very few Immigration folks to talk to me since the seizure to say she was glad that I got Rudy and that she was so upset that she threw up. Well I sure can't confirm her state of mind regarding Rudy nor did I see her heave. I was not watching her even though now I think maybe I should have been doing exactly that. I spun the two points around in my head and decided I will never know her state of mind so stick with barf.

Suddenly at about km 40 (I-19 is marked in kilometers) one more thing slapped me upside the noggin and it was her demeanor. As I said earlier, when I was inspecting the vehicle, I could hear Rudy and Fidel chatting more than taking a declaration. That just makes absolutely no sense if the primary inspector is a conspirator passing the largest load on record. In my mind I would want that load there and gone! I sure as heck would not be keeping it on my lane while we discussed the weather or whatever. By km 60 or so I was convinced that Fidel was just being used. In my opinion she was not part of the smuggling attempt. In fact, she aided the interdiction greatly by "chatting" rather than waving the load through. I thought maybe I should tell IA about my great deduction – **NOT**!!! Hell, if they find out that she *was* a co-conspirator I may end up in jail. If they come to me again and ask, I will tell them but I am not hunting them down. I don't think I was ready to reveal that not guilty judgment just yet without them asking me for it.

I have about 40 more clicks to figure out the barfing. Why would she come over and congratulate me then tell me how happy she was that I got Rudy and tell me she threw up? Was that a story to cover-up her contribution to the smuggling attempt?

As I pulled into the driveway I was still in a fog. The 40 kilometers was not enough to solve this mystery, but I still felt strongly about her demeanor. I still can't confirm her state of mind, but I think I can give an educated assessment of my deduction regarding it.

Her throwing up remained a mystery for a day or so. I even went and looked for barf to see if I could confirm Fidel's story. The reality of finding where she may have evacuated her stomach was unrealistic because the rest rooms are right there. Oh well at least IA had not come back with more questions.

Then one day Goose handed me the video tape. I could not wait to get home and show my wife and kids. Heck you never know I might get a little kiss or something a bit more exciting for letting my much better half see the craziness. I called her to tell her that Goose had given me the tape and asked if she wanted to see it. Well her demeanor on the phone was just maybe the 'bit more exciting'. She had already seen the news on TV, but this was the actual seizure not just a picture of cocaine and the truck with me talking to the news reporter showing only my back.

Illustration 38: News interview

When I got home my wife was standing there with her hand out. "Where is the tape, let's get it going." she said.

I handed her the tape and she cranked it up. There it was me unloading dope, lots of dope. There was video of the guys with long guns, a bit of the Port and as I was watching Goose happened to have the camera on the bathroom door behind what he was shooting. Right there on the tape you can see Fidel heading in probably to throw up. I will never know for sure, but to this day I believe she was just the poor Inspector who happened to be on the line when her co-worker decided to abuse their friendship by using her lane and it ruined her life. When IA finally returned for their encore, they asked me if I had anything else now that I had time to think about it and I relayed my thoughts blow by blow.

We went to the training room and viewed the tape together and they saw the same thing I saw. We agreed that getting sick and throwing up could have been her reaction to getting caught. When one's life gets turned upside down, the stomach and bowels sometimes react. Weather that reaction is fear of getting caught, devastated at being used or realization that you screwed up and missed something is anyone's guess. But when you put it together with her demeanor that resulted in a delay that was critical to this interception, we all agreed that the preponderance of the evidence indicated that she was not involved.

Fidel and I talked several times after that including the pretrial and the trial with each encounter fortifying her innocence in my mind. She ended up moving out of state in an attempt to put the fateful night behind her. I never saw her again after she left so I pray that she was able to put it behind her and get on with a normal life.

Illustration 39: Fidel entering the bathroom. Part of the crowd gathering in Mexico is also visible and was the object of this portion of the video. Capturing Fidel as she entered the bathroom was just God's hand at work.

The trial was another point of interest. Rudy agreed to a plea bargain that, on the day of his trial, became almost hilarious. I do not know all the details of the bargain, us grunts never do, but I can tell you what I knew, what was rumored and what I saw.

The rumor was that he was looking at ninety-nine years if convicted with a reduced sentence landing him about twenty years with the plea bargain. I do know that this was a huge case for the US Government, so big that the Department of Justice sent some big dogs down from their headquarters in Washington, D.C. to "assist" the local AUSA.

In the courthouse the day of the trial Fidel and I were sitting in the hallway just outside the court room waiting to be ushered in. Sitting opposite from us just a bit down the hallway I saw Rudy's wife and children for the first time since the seizure. She was with a couple of older adults that to this day I do not know the relationship. I do not know if they were friends, relatives or whatever. The girls were playing and laughing where the adults sat there whispering and occasionally giving Fidel and me sly, sideward glances. During the 15 minutes we sat there in silence Rudy's wife came over to me twice with an unlit cigarette in hand and asked for a light. Each time I pulled out my Zippo and obliged. Both times she polity thanked me, but her expression was a far cry from polite.

I must admit it was most uncomfortable and looking at poor Fidel she obviously felt the same. I was quite relieved when one of the HQ AUSA attorneys stepped out in the hall with the OE case agent and engaged in a whispered conversation not far from Rudy's wife. I motioned them over as I stood up and they looked at their audience and walked over.

"Isn't that the wife?" Hecburt Bobries the OE special agent asked.

"Yes Burt it is and the kids. I have no idea who the others are." I answered and then added "Is there an open witness room? I think Fidel and I would be more comfortable in one if possible."

At that point the attorney chimed in and said, "There better be, you two are witnesses."

Sixty seconds later we were ushered to a witness room where we were sitting with Burt and the attorney. "How is it going?" I asked.

"There is a delay but once we are all in the court room I will send for you." the attorney said. "Since this is a plea with no testimony you two can come in and watch the proceedings."

When they departed and Fidel and I were finally alone she looked at me and she had the most beautiful smile on her face. Fidel was very attractive, great personality and would have been a great catch. Just an all-around beautiful girl and this was the first time I saw her smile since that night. She said "Oh my God, this is like a dream. It is just unreal."

I answered "Yes I agree, surreal. I just don't know if it is a nightmare or a really good dream."

"I think it is kind of both." she said "One minute I am excited and the next I am terrified. I have to pinch myself to see if it is real."

"Well Mary, I am relieved to see that it isn't just me." I said. "That is Rudy in there, a person I once considered a friend."

Mary stood up, came over and gave me a hug. I stood up and gave her a hug back and she held on and said "It isn't just you Rick; I haven't known which side is up and which side is down for a long time. Thank you for letting me know that I am not alone. Ever since that night I have felt isolated, totally alone." now she had tears in her eyes. "I hate going to work where no-one talks to me and I feel like I have a demon on my shoulder. They hate me and I didn't do anything."

We held each other in silence for a while and as we broke our hug and sat back down, I said "Yea, I know that feeling too. I think you are the only person from INS that has spoken to me. By the way, if you look in a mirror that is not a demon on your shoulder, it is an Angel. The demons are those who you work with. Oh, and if you see that glow over your head don't worry, it is a halo."

Just then the door opened, good timing or bad timing? I don't know, none the less we were on our way to the court room.

Very shortly after sitting down in came Mrs. Rudy and the kids, all of them wailing and crying. What a difference ten minutes makes. Just moments later they brought Rudy in and it was kick off time.

The judge started and Rudy was read his rights, the judge read the charges and took care of other preliminary business. He then got to the plea. He asked Rudy if he was going to plea and Rudy answered in the affirmative. He asked him if he was of sound mind and again affirmative was the answer. There were a few more questions and then the judge asked if there was anything that might have an effect on his thoughts or judgment. The answer to this surprised everyone in the front of the courtroom judging by their reaction. This answer was also in the affirmative and when the judge asked Rudy to explain. His answer was that he was on pain medication that might have that consequence.

The judge turned to Rudy's attorney and asked him if he had an explanation. After the lawyer picked his jaw up off the ground, he said "One moment your honor."

He then leaned over to Rudy and went into a deep but whispered conversation. After a few minutes he told the judge that his client now understood the question. The judge thanked the flabbergasted attorney and went through the latter portion of his sound mind. When he got to the part where he asked about anything that might have an effect on his thoughts or judgment Rudy's answer was the same, he was on pain medication that might have that effect on his thoughts or judgment.

His attorney looked at Rudy, then the judge, then back to the Rudy and back to the judge. The poor defense attorney had the most helpless look on his face and just shook his head no. Wrong move! The judge grabbed his gavel and slammed it down on the bench, then looked at the bailiff and said "Clear the court room of witnesses and bring in the jury. This court is going to trial by jury!"

The defense attorney, now in a panic, jumped up and asked the judge for a fifteen-minute recess. The bailiff had already started clearing the court room and Mary and I were directed back to our witness room.

As we exited the court room, I heard the judge grant the recess and then go directly into a lecture session with the defense. The lecture was ongoing as the door closed behind us.

Back in the waiting room Mary looked like she was in shock. "What just happened?" she asked.

I said, "I am not sure, but it sure looks like we are going to end up on the stand after all. I think Rudy changed the rules in mid court and the judge was far from happy."

Mary shook her head and said "I really don't want to testify Rick. It terrifies me to think about getting on the stand and having to defend myself. I was told by some of my friends who have been to court that the defense will try to save Rudy by crucifying me."

I hate to say this but after testifying in court numerous times, probably somewhere around one hundred, those friends probably hit the nail right on the head. I have had them try to discredit me on several occasions. In one instance there were about seven or eight Hispanics on the jury and when I walked in the defense attorney said in Spanish, "Here comes another lying government witness." This comment was completely out of line for an Officer of the Court from what I have been told, mainly because it was directed to certain members of the jury. The non-Spanish speakers on the jury would have no idea what was said. It is also improper to influence the jury in that manner.

At any rate about half an hour later we were directed back to the court room and the plea took place with a guilty plea entered by Rudy. I believe he saved himself seventy-nine years by going that route because there was a great amount of evidence confirming his guilt and two of his co-conspirators (both Mexican Customs Officers) were also listed as witnesses for the prosecution.

One last item I promise. In the early days of my career I did not carry a camera. The pictures were taken by other people and given to me. Many of them came from OE Agents who would get double sets and graciously give me a few. Pictures were never a sure thing but as time went on I began to carry my own camera even though at times I was not allowed to use it. Several pictures in this section with the exception of the screwdriver/probe and a couple of others came from two old VHS video tapes. Most were from the tape made real time during the seizure. The video was made by SCI Goose and it was the first time he used the video camera outside the training room. The screwdriver/probe picture I used my smart phone just a few days ago. Yes, I still have the screwdriver/probe and the 18-year-old document (District Seizure Tracking Report).

The other pictures from video came from a VHS tape that my wife made using a VCR hooked to the TV and were from news reports. My deepest apologies for the poor quality of the pictures but during this seizure security was the main priority and as far as I know only one still picture camera was on scene and the OE case agent had it.

COCAINE BUST
Customs officer finds 607-pound load
in truck driven by former INS inspector

By MANUEL COPPOLA
Nogales International

A former inspector of the U.S. Immigration and Naturalization Service in Nogales was arrested last Wednesday after authorities made the largest cocaine seizure ever in Santa Cruz County.

The "high-quality" cocaine has an estimated wholesale value of about $12 million but could bring dealers up to $27 million when diluted and sold on the streets, said U.S. Customs Service officials.

Rodolpho Lopez, 35, of Nogales, was attempting to cross into the United States from Mexico at the Grand Avenue Port of Entry, when a "roving inspector" discovered 607 pounds of cocaine hidden in the bed of the

(Continued on Page 13)

HEFTY HAUL — More than 260 individually-wrapped kilo packets of cocaine take up all of the counter space in office of U.S. Customs Service at Mariposa Road. At right, Cleve Ainsworth, contraband enforcement supervisor, checks inside bed of Ford pickup truck where load was discovered as ex-INS inspector Rodolfo Lopez attempted to cross border at Grand Avenue port of entry. (Photos by Coppola)

* * *

The pictures below were taken by OE on the night of the interdiction. When I arrived home that night or early morning if you prefer, I noticed that I had cocaine on the probe and on my gun belt where I kept the probe tucked in behind my speed loaders. Twenty-eight years after the seizure, while adding the pictures to this chapter I noticed that the probe and cocaine residue from the probe are visible in the pictures. Amazing!

Illustration 40: Mustang and the author. Note screwdriver/probe on gun belt below the elbow.

* * *

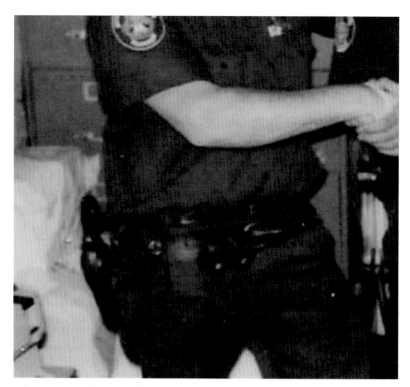

Illustration 41: Screwdriver/Probe with cocaine visible on gun belt.

BILLION $ DOLLAR $ HIGHWAY

El Gigante
May 25, 1990
18 Pounds Marijuana

For the rest of the world it is Friday. Most everyone is in a good mood and full of Happy Fridays. For me it is my Monday. Monday on the 6 AM to 2 PM shift. I absolutely detest the six to two. I would rather work a midnight to eight than get up at four flipping AM to go to work. Four AM going to work sucks, four AM going fishing or for other family activities is puraimu, primo or in English prime time.

I had just come off my only day off this week and to my family the one day meant going to bed at midnight at the earliest. I instigated the late night more than my family because with all the overtime and six-day weeks, that one day had to cover a lot of missed time. I lived for that family time and to this day regret the hours I worked that cut family time to almost nothing.

I arrived at the Grand Avenue Port of Entry at about five thirty. The drive in seemed like it took forever and the road kept moving on me. I was so tired that I just sat there in secondary where I had parked the car listening to music on my car radio for about fifteen minutes. Secondary was not used until the eight to four shift arrived so there was no one else there to bother me. All secondary exams were done in front of the office since the midnight shift was manned very lightly, a skeleton crew you might say.

I finally managed to exit the comfort of my car and push myself to the office. I stopped in at the office and let the Supervisor Selok Montana know that I would be roving. Selok was a very laid-back supervisor and his response was "OK" and then he looked at me with a puzzled or maybe disgusted look and said "You know it has been over three months since the Bowling Alley massacre in Las Cruces and they still haven't caught the pieces of crap who did it. Apparently they don't have a clue as to their identity."

Selok and I are both from New Mexico and I spent my last two high school years in Cruces. Selok was from northern New Mexico but we were still homies I suppose. The murders involved the execution and the attempted execution of seven people. One male and six females with four of the female's children ages 2, 6, 12 and 13. Four died and three survived. One of the survivors was twelve years old at the time and she managed to call the 911 emergency number even though she had been shot in the head. Her miraculous and heroic phone call is what saved the survivors from certain death in my opinion. Selok and I had talked about this many times after the senseless and gutless act. The description and sketches of the suspects were two Hispanic males with dark completion and of course there was a lookout for them possibly heading to Mexico. You better bet your last dollar that we were on the lookout. This happened in the town where I graduated high school. The take for these lives: five thousand dollars.

We talked about the murders and the survivors. When I finally headed out of the office it was after 6:30 and I walked past a vehicle parked where the midnight crew performed secondary exams. The vehicle had been there when I walked in but on my way out my mind was on looking for some dark-skinned Hispanics who did not look Mexican. South American, Cuban, Dominican Republic maybe but probably not Mexican. We did have quite a few Cubans cross so there was a Cuban community somewhere near Nogales. Yep this is what was going through my mind, not why the car seemed to be a permanent resident in the inspection area.

As I started roving my mind cleared somewhat and I mentally returned to the here and now. That is when the light went off regarding the car. I turned and looked at the car. No inspectors were near it and none were inside running names. I headed back to the office and asked Selok about the car.

Selok replied "Oh they told the driver to open the trunk and he did not have the trunk key. He called his brother and told him to bring the key."

"Oh well I just saw it and it looked pretty lonely with no one checking it." I replied. I am on the TROLL Team and I didn't want Selok to think I was butting in on his operation.

"Yea they did what they could, but the last thing is to open the trunk. The driver is still sitting in the passenger seat, isn't he?" he said looking out the window.

"No, there is no one anywhere near it." I replied. We headed to the door together and when we opened the door there sat a very empty car.

Selok called out to one of the Inspectors and asked, "Where is the driver?" as he pointed to the car.

The inspector walked over, looked in the very empty car and said, "He was right here a few minutes ago?"

The other midnight inspector Salvador Cidillo exited a booth where he had been hanging out on one of the closed lanes and walked over. "Yea he was waiting in the car. We told him to sit on the passenger side and I took the car keys or key, there is only the one ignition key." Cidillo said holding out a single key.

My thoughts were 'Are you kidding me?' How many people have only the one key? Not even on a key ring just a lone ignition key.

I looked at Selok and said, "If it is OK with you, I am going to pull out the rear seat back rest so we can see into the trunk."

"Yea, I think we will see a load in there. It sure has all the signs of a trunk load." he said.

I went over to the car and unceremoniously removed the seat. Using my flashlight, I lit up the

92

trunk and there was no load to be seen. The trunk was almost empty except for a small pile of clothes and as I shined the light around I came back to the pile of clothing. WTF! A pile of clothes? As I looked closer at the clothing what I saw was pants, shirt and boots.

I shouted at the pile of clothes "Hombre, hey hombre."

There was no response. I reached in with my three cell Maglite and prodded the subject calling out to him again as I did so. There was no response and there was no reaction or resistance from the body.

I backed out and said "Selok I think we have a dead body. I am going to pop the lock and open the trunk."

Selok said "Hold on Squirrelly Cat from Nogales PD was hanging out with Janna in the Immigration Office earlier. Salvador, see if he is still there and if so ask him to join us. If it is a dead body, it is theirs anyhow."

The Immigration Office on the midnight shift was only about fifteen yards from where we were standing and in about thirty seconds Squirrelly Cat joined us.

As I went to my car for a large screwdriver and sledge hammer Cat was prodding the body from the back seat area with his PR24 nightstick.

When I got back about two minutes later Cat was now convinced that we had a 10-7 subject as he put it over the radio.

It took me about thirty seconds to pop the trunk and there certainly was a body lying there. As we stood looking at the dead body Cat reported over his radio that the body was confirmed. And then out of the blue the dead body looked up at us and said, "I guess you found me."

Holy crap; literally. Hell, every one of us jumped about ten feet in the air. Cat drew his weapon which made the not so dead body cover his face with his hands and scream the most awful scream you never want to hear.

When we all got our wits about us Cat called off the NPD response but requested an ambulance to check the guy out. All was medically OK with him and he admitted he was being smuggled into the US, his presence in the trunk was an alien smuggling attempt. The driver was never seen again and the not so dead body was VR'd (voluntary return) back to Mexico by Immigration. We did ask him why he didn't answer us when we were prodding him from the back seat and he said "Oh that was you? I was wondering what was poking me because there was only the seat there." It never dawned on us that the guy had no idea that we had gained access to him from the back seat. I would make some remarks about stupidity and if you keep your eyes closed no one can see you, but I have to admit that it never dawned on my fellow Inspectors to remove the back seat either. Best to keep the snide remarks to myself.

The most astonishing thing about this whole fiasco was that during the remainder of my career not one time did I hear anything about it. Normally within an hour the entire Customs world knows and everyone would be poking fun of us for weeks. Had one of us drawn our weapon it would have been a different story but since CAT was Nogales PD their policy was followed and no report was necessary.

I looked at Selok and said "I am going to put my tools up and go rove. I am really looking forward to roving all of the sudden."

Selok's response was "It is seven o'clock and I am out of here in one hour. That hour can't pass fast enough. I think I may have soiled myself. I was not ready for that!"

I walked over to my car in secondary and as I was putting the tools away a dog handler Cratchit Singer came over. "Hey Rick, Rob just alerted on a car as we were walking to Primary. I had the guy pull into the lane next to the Secondary Office. Will you check it out?"

"Sure, where did he hit." I asked.

"The front fender. It looks empty to me, but I don't know." he said and then added "I had a three-day break and I think Rob is just looking for attention."

"Rob is really coming around and I consider him one of the top dogs in the Port." I said, "Have faith in your dog."

"Thanks, that makes me feel good." he said now standing a bit taller "Manor just called me up to the office, so I am headed that way. I should be back in five or ten minutes. I am going to tell him what you said if that is OK."

"Sure, I am just telling it like I see it." I answered truthfully.

I headed to the far north end of Secondary where a white Dodge sedan was parked next to the Secondary office. It was just a little past 7 AM and I am the only Customs person in Secondary. The only other person is the driver of the Dodge who is still sitting in the car.

I walked up to the driver's door and the driver looked up at me. I was looking at a male in his early to mid-twenties who made the car look like a kid's toy. The guy was HUGE. I thought Cratchit had to have seen this Goliath so I was sure he will hurry the meeting along.

I took the secondary declaration and the driver said he was not bringing anything from Mexico and was headed to the local stores. He gave his occupation as a farmer and lived in Magdalena Mexico. I had him exit the car and escorted the colossal farmer to the secondary office where I frisked him for weapons and secured him in the holding area while I checked his vehicle. I will say one thing, everything about this enormous individual told me that he was exactly what he said he was; a farmer. A farmer from his boots, to his overworked hands, up to his young but sun hardened face and all the way to his well-used hat with a tractor on it. Yes, this guy's physical features confirmed to me that he was a farmer.

When I arrived back at the car, I checked the fender and nothing but dried mud. The dried mud has some partial hand prints and some very pronounced brush marks. I knew exactly what story the mud was telling me. It said, 'Check the rocker panel'. I chipped the mud away from the area where a trap door would be located if there was one and just as I suspected there it was. A trap door with screws that had signs of recent tampering.

I had just a few loads under my belt but classically this type of concealment warranted a check for the tools to open the trap door. I had detected that the most common places were the glove box, under the seat or in the trunk. I opened door number one, the glove box. If I were playing the game show I would have lost. The glove box had only one item in it and that was the Mexican vehicle registration. I looked at the paperwork and noticed three things. First the registration had been issued only a week prior to out encounter. Second was the owner's name, not the same as the farmer in the lockup. The third and last piece of information with evidentiary value was the owner's city of record. It was not Magdalena but Hermosillo, Sonora, Mexico. Just those three pieces of information alone told me there was dope present, I was sure of that.

Door number two was under the seat. Since I was digging in the near empty glove box my first shot at door number two was the passenger seat. As I looked under the seat door number three became moot. There sat a socket wrench with a bit on it. I donned some gloves, retrieved the tool then walked to the trapdoor and removed the bolts holding it in place. As the trap door fell to the ground, I was looking at bright white packages. Didn't even need a flashlight to see them.

I probed the first package and it looked (green leafy substance) and felt like marijuana, therefore I ran a field expediency narcotics test. I wiped the probe then took a sniff of it and it smelled like marijuana. I will add one caveat, if there is white powder or it does not feel like I am pushing through plant like material I do not under any circumstances get it near my nose or mouth. Only in Hollywood does any narcotics officer do a taste test. If it looks and feels like marijuana once I wipe the probe the green leafy substance is gone but the marijuana odor is still there.

With the now confirmed load of narcotics present I headed back into the secondary holding area to transport Old MacDonald or Young MacDonald who had a farm to the supervisor's office where I could secure him in a holding cell. In the secondary holding area I had the driver stand up, turn around, spread his legs to an almost unbalanced position and put his hands behind his back interlocking his fingers. In this position it is very difficult for a suspect to put up a fight.

He complied and I approached him with my handcuffs ready. Using my right hand, I grabbed the first two interlocked fingers of both hands holding them tightly together. This was a chore as even his fingers were like tree trunks.

Using my left hand with the handcuffs I properly placed a cuff on his left wrist and just like I had done many times I before put pressure on the cuff so the single bar or locking bar will pop through its position and the locking bar will come around and catch the locking mechanism. One little teeny-weeny problem, the locking bar did not catch; it dropped back to a now open position. I tried to remedy the situation with my left hand holding the cuff, but I could not get the bar to come up and even get close to the locking mechanism.

I tried numerous times, but the cuff was just not having anything to do with it. I finally released his fingers with my right hand and now using both hands began struggling to get the bar to catch. I finally got one click on the mechanism and it was secure. Now I look at the guy who is stand there with his right hand reached out to the wall and I realized he was pushing his left arm up struggling as hard as I was to get the darn cuff on. I told him to give me his right hand and he brought it back behind him. I took his right hand and began trying to get the handcuffs on it. His arms were so big that he could just barely interlock his fingers and the cuffs could not reach his wrist. Finally, Young MacDonald said "Please, one moment." With that he took two steps closer to the wall and put his head on the wall. He reached his right hand back again and began struggling to close the gap between his wrists as I stood there holding the cuffs still with only the left cuff secured.

I looked at this giant of a human being and said "Sir, stand up straight and relax."

I pulled out my handcuff keys and opened the cuff that was one click in place on his left wrist. I said "Please sir sit and rest. Do you want some water or anything?"

He said, "Yes please, I would be very grateful for some water."

I said, "Follow me." and we walked around to the officer's side of the Secondary Office where there was a water cooler. There was a chair next to the cooler and I told him "Help yourself and sit down."

We sat there for a few minutes and he said, "Thank you I am ready to try again." as he turned and put his hands behind his back.

I told him "Senor, no es necesario." (Sir, that is not necessary)

Sometimes realization is like a new dawn. My new dawn here was that this mammoth could probably have turned me inside out without building a sweat as I was struggling with the handcuffs. Instead he is building a sweat trying to help me put him in jail. The handcuffs were not necessary. I was by myself completely out of sight to anyone in the office or on primary and that was quite obvious. Just the two of us and this guy was nothing but a gentleman to me.

"Let's go to the office." I said and off we strolled. I did not even put him in an arm lock we just strolled like old friends.

We walked into the office and Selok was sitting there at his desk.

"In here please." I directed the gentle giant.

He walked on in to the holding cell, sat down and said, "Thank you."

I looked at Selok who was now motionless with a quite confused look on his face and said "What?"

He shook his head as if to snap out of a dream world and asked, "Who is that and why are you locking him up?"

"Oh, he has a load of weed in his rocker panels so I am calling OE (Office of Enforcement)." I said somewhat nonchalantly.

"That guy is huge. Why didn't you have him hooked up?" he asked sounding somewhat incredulous.

"Oh we tried. The damn cuffs just aren't big enough, so we gave it up and came on over." I said now beginning to enjoy the many different looks Selok was exhibiting. He somewhat reminded me of a shape-shifter or something. It would have been cool if I had brought a camera with me into that office just to get those weird looks memorialized. "That poor guy looked like a contortionist trying to get his wrists together enough for me to get the cuffs on him."

"Well, you could have cuffed him in front." as the shape-shiftier now became a wise man.

"Yea, if I had leg irons. His wrists are bigger than most people's thighs." I said. Then I added "You know Selok, sometimes you just get a revelation when you look at the whole picture that it is time to put faith in your instincts and go with them. My instinct with this guy is that he is good people. I am very interested to see what comes out in his interview."

"I am going to go put someone on the car." Selok said. "Call the agents and let's get this going."

I called OE and the duty agent called back in about fifteen minutes. It was not yet 8:00 AM and the agent was still at his home forty miles away. He would be there in an hour.

I waited for Selok to return and when he did I advised him that I was going to bring the load vehicle to the office where a tow truck was just hauling off the not so dead body's mode of transport. Selok agreed and said he would rather me start the reports in his office than isolated in the secondary office. We still had about a half hour before the day shift arrived and thirty minutes on the border can be a long time. He then added "How did you end up isolated with that inspection all the way down there?"

I told him about the dog alert and that I had expected Singer to return in just a few minutes. I added "He didn't return and I haven't seen him since. Must be one heck of a meeting to keep him away knowing that he was my back-up and the suspect makes King Kong look like a tamarin."

I moved the vehicle up which gave me the freedom to start the search, arrest and seizure report. By the time the agent arrived I was more than ready for a break from writing the report. The day shift started and the office was now buzzing. Selok and the rest of the midnight folks were gone and it was a new day.

After the agent looked at the load vehicle and took some pictures we went in for the interview. The suspect was read his Miranda and we went through the preliminary questions. We finally got to the questions I wanted to hear.

"Do you know why you are here?" he was asked.

"No but I think it must be the car. It is stolen isn't it?" he answered.

"Why do you think the car is stolen?" was our reply.

"Because my wife told me the man, Metro, who asked me to come to Nogales and pick-up some things for him looked like a car thief." he said hanging his head "She told me not to trust him. Last year was a bad year and my corn does not look so good again. He said he does not have a passport and needs these things."

He handed the agent a list and the agent looked at me and said "The interview is over for you. I need you to leave."

That was it. I can only guess the agent flipped him or recruited him as an informant if you prefer but that is all I know.

I went out to the car and removed eighteen one-pound packages of marijuana. I never saw El Gigante again.

Illustration 42: Driver side rocker panel with package.

Illustration 43: Packages from passenger side rocker panel.

BILLION $ DOLLAR $ HIGHWAY

Who Would Have Thought
May 29, 1990
51.25 Pounds Marijuana

For the rest of the world it is Tuesday. Most everyone is in a bad mood after putting in their normally busy Monday playing catch-up for the weekend days off. For me it is my Friday. Friday on the 6 AM to 2 PM shift is the only day that I look forward to this shift. The only reason of course is getting off at two PM. The two hours seem to make the weekend longer. I may even get up at four AM tomorrow since my body is now on that cycle anyhow. Who knows I may pack up the family and go fishing or something. It will probably be the *or something* since I live in Tucson Arizona and haven't yet found a place to fish. I had some folks tell me about a "lake" near Rio Rico Arizona a few months back, so the wife went out and bought each one of our children one of those very nice youth rod and reel fishing combos. On one of my days off we were up bright and early (not 4 flipping AM) and off we went. Rio Rico is just north of Nogales but several miles west of Interstate 19. I had driven by the cut off every day but never seen the "lake". When we got to the lake it was just a bit disappointing. Maybe we went to the wrong place on the lake but there was a facility there with what looked very much like raw sewage running into the lake. My wife, being Japanese, had us back in the car and gone so quick that today I don't know what the facility was. It may have been a bait shop or maybe a small cafe, but I will never know. From what I understand the lake was recently drained, cleaned-up and massively improved so good for the Forest Service. I would like to go there again just to see and maybe even drop a line in the water.

Anyhow I had requested an overtime exemption for the day which was very unusual for me. We were determined to do something on my day off even if it was just to head to the mall. My family time was precious to me and back then in the Customs Service a couple of days off in a row was a rarity. Heck an eight-hour day was even more rare. Generally, the only semi-guarantee that an *overtime exemption* request was honored was if the request was for your BDO day. BDO was *before day off* and if memory serves me the union contract addressed the BDO requests. The bottom line was that I was not on the O/T list, so I was off at two. This was one area that being on TROLL paid off. Everyone else at Grand Avenue was on eight to four shifts so the sick leave and emergency leave calls wouldn't start until after two. By then I would be on my way home that was some 65 miles north of Nogales. TROLL didn't carry radio's and cell phones were for the rich and famous, so I was incommunicado for an hour or so.

I was almost half way through my shift and it had been a busy day. It seemed like the entire day shift was staffed by the sick, lame and lazy. I was bouncing from lane to lane trying to keep up with the traffic flowing into the abundance of weak links in the border protection chain. One of the staff made the same comment every time I got near enough for him to talk to me. He would just say "They are beating us. I can feel it, they are beating us."

One of the other characters working that day (and I use the term "working" in protest) was a retired Air Force Colonel Vance Warren. He was one of the nicest people you will ever meet but extremely far from a good Inspector. He had been a US Customs Sky Marshall who was reassigned as an Inspector when the Sky Marshall program underwent a re-organization. The Colonel as we called him was very bitter and apathetic toward his job as a Customs Inspector. To me he was an integrity problem because of his attitude. I don't believe he would ever get involved with a drug smuggling organization running or passing loads of dope intentionally, but his integrity issue was that he just flat didn't care if a load got through him.

You want to talk about two ends of the spectrum; I have one who is obsessed with being beat by the drug smugglers and one who couldn't care less. Which one is worse, I really don't know? What I will say is that the Colonel was sure more entertaining and obviously well-traveled. I couldn't count the number of times that I heard him take a declaration and ask the traveler where they were going or where were they born. Both legitimate questions during a declaration to determine citizenship, alienage and legitimate travel. Impostors and false claims to US Citizenship were daily occurrences on the Mexican Border and it is the duty of the inspector on primary to release legitimate travelers at primary or to refer questionable travelers to secondary for further exam. Most of the border crossers were local to include Tucson and Phoenix in the definition of local. To verify their claim the inspector could ask specific questions to determine if they were telling the truth or lying about their legal grounds for entry. The alien smuggling organization's (ASO) would have the false claims and impostors practice answering the usual questions so they were prepared when they arrived at the primary inspection station. If an inspector set a pattern of their interview technique and questions, the ASO's had him/her and would direct their customers to the slack inspector. Vance avoided this quite by accident. I would hear him ask where a crosser was born and the applicant for admission would come back with a place I had never heard of but the Colonel would say "Oh, I know where that is at; I lived there for a while. Did you ever eat at Whosits Burger Barn (or whatever)" and they would often answer "Why yes I loved the Flamingo Burger." Then the Colonel would come back with a verification that he had been there such as "Oh yea, they would put that little pink flamingo that served as a toothpick dead square in the middle of the burger." He even got me the first time we met. When I told him where I grew-up he said "Nice town, I used to live on North Mesa Street a few blocks north of the mid high school." I knew exactly where he lived. I lived on North Lake Street but south of Mid High. Yep it didn't matter if the party was from Butte, Montana or Leesville, Louisiana he would know their town.

Since I considered him a weak link, I was working his lane a bit more than the other lanes that day. I had knocked down a load on my first day back, last Friday and had been at Grand Avenue every day but Wednesday when it was my day to pull a Mariposa tour. I had hoped to get a load over at Mariposa just because; but Map was still very light on traffic. Oh well I was still well ahead of the rest of the TROLL team and I hadn't seen Thorny all week. That made this a bonus week; a load and no Thorny.

As I am standing on the lane where the Colonel is chit chatting with every car that pulls up, I see a 1974 AMC Gremlin. I hadn't seen a Gremlin in forever and never at the border. I stood there looking at the relic as it moved on up to primary where the Colonel started in on his extensive chat. If nothing else, he liked to talk so his "declaration" was a long-lasting affair.

I was thankful for the long chat since it gave me plenty of time to scrutinize the vehicles on his lane. I walked around the car that seemed like it was all windows and peered in. I could see from the windows that the screws on the side and rear panels had been recently worked. I walked over to the Colonel and told him that I was going to walk the vehicle to secondary.

Vance said, "This thing?" as if he could not believe that I was interested.

I replied "Yes I haven't seen one of these on the border yet. This will be educational."

As he handed me their passports he laughed "Better watch out you might find some gremlins in there."

As I walked the vehicle to secondary the K-9 didn't even have any interest in the darn car. I took the secondary declaration and secured the two male occupants in the holding cells.

I walked back out to the Gremlin and no dogs, no inspectors, no nothing but a lonesome Gremlin. A lone Gremlin that when the panels were removed revealed sixteen packages with a total of 51.25 pounds of marijuana.

Illustration 44: Packages: on scale and floor.

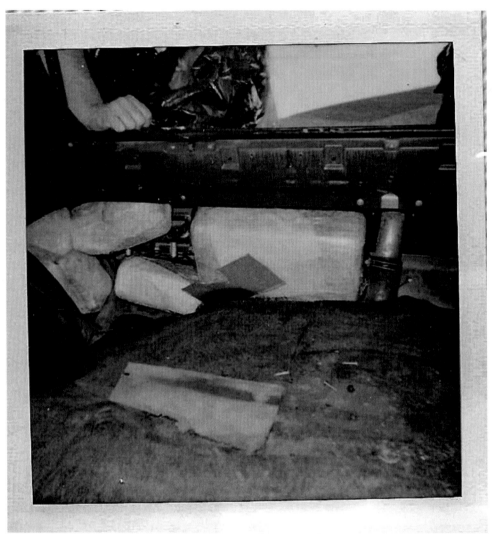

Illustration 45: Panel removed revealing packages under rear window.

Sometime later after the marijuana was bagged, tagged and secured and I was writing the Search, Arrest and Seizure (SAS) report the Colonel came into the office and said "You are still here? I haven't seen you so I thought you left." He then added with sarcasm "You guys on the special teams seem to work variable hours."

I looked at the Colonel and said, "No Colonel Warren, I have to write the SAS on the seizure."

"Oh, you got a load?" he said genuinely surprised.

I looked at him just as surprised "Yes the Gremlin I walked off your lane was loaded with a little over fifty-one pounds of marijuana." I followed with "I thought you knew, my apologies."

"Oh, you mean that the Gremlin you walked down off my lane was loaded?" he asked.

The shift supervisor Cosmos Linex was sitting at his desk and chimed in very angrily "You haven't started your witness statement Vance?"

"A, well no I am getting off soon so I will write one tomorrow. I didn't know." Vance replied.

Cosmos jumped out of his chair and as mad as I have seen or heard him speaking very slowly in an undertone voice said, "I told you hours ago to write a witness statement regarding this seizure that came off your lane."

Vance looked terrified, Cosmos could do that, and Vance almost whispered "I guess I didn't hear you."

Wrong answer, the undertone voice now became a roar "Vance, have you been in the rotation?"

The Colonel had been demoted to Airman One and he dropped his eyes and said "No."

Cosmos asked, "And why were you not in the rotation for the last four hours?"

Poor Vance was trying to squirm out of this one, but the trap was set and it was not going away "You took me out of the rotation to write the witness statement." he whispered "Sorry I thought I could do it tomorrow."

"Wrong! You will be doing it right here *tonight* if it takes that long and I mean in this office not the secondary office where you were supposed to be working on it." Cosmos now very calm.

"But my wife is picking me up and we are going out for dinner tonight." Vance tried.

Cosmos pointed at the phone and said "Well there is the phone. Tell her you will be eating in tonight; in this office. She is more than welcome to bring you dinner right here." and with that Cosmos pulled out a pack of cigarettes and headed out the door.

Vance stood there with an odd look on his face then turned to me and said "Well I told you there might be some Gremlins in it. I didn't know what car he was talking about."

I have no idea what Vance did for the several hours that passed after he was informed of the load but this will go down in the anuses that ran TROLL, oops that is annals of the anuses that ran TROLL as another example of me being a troublemaker as Mr. Utlee had unceremoniously pointed out. My thought: *touché* Mr. Utlee, *touché*!

Illustration 46: Packages crammed in rear under window and on drive side quarter panel.

BILLION $ DOLLAR $ HIGHWAY

Contraband Enforcement Team
District CET Team
June 1990 – CET Disbanded 1995

Illustration 47: CET Badge number 017

June 1990 closed the book on my assignment with the TROLL team and opened a new door for me with Customs. I was finally assigned to the Contraband Enforcement Team as a direct appointment by the District Director. The CET mission on the southwest border was to stop illegal activity at the border with the focus on illicit drugs. CET fell under the Anti-Smuggling Division and that basically meant drug enforcement.

When I first arrived in Nogales CET was commonly referred to as a bunch of prima donnas and it was frequently noted that the CET acronym stood for 'Customs Eating Team'. The word around the Port was that the only time anyone saw them was sitting in a restaurant during lunch. I never went to restaurants or even ate lunch, so I cannot confirm the 'Eating Team' accusation but I can only remember two of them getting a load of dope on their own and a third who's one and only load was nabbed after she asked me to check a vehicle for her. Pictures of her load are added at the end of this chapter.

In the latter 1980's and early 1990's there was a cut back in U. S. Government spending that had a major effect on new employment. As a result of the cutback we were extremely shorthanded. The real money hogs were airports (the biggest money pit) and seaports. The culprit and target for the inflated spending was overtime. Those folks referred to southwest border overtime as 'blood money'. It was very hard to keep Inspectors on the southwest border and virtually impossible to get any Inspectors to voluntarily transfer from airports or seaports to the southwest border. Under the pay system at the time both these entities made triple and sometimes quadruple overtime quite often and even more so on Sundays.

All Inspectors worked split days off and all had Sunday off with one other day of the week. This ensured no one received Sunday premium I suppose but it also meant that every Inspector that worked Sunday was on overtime. With the Service being so shorthanded we worked doubles almost every night on the Mexican border whereas at airports they would go home after eight hours and be called back to work when an arriving flight was due. Each time they went home and were called back they received a call-back and a commute and if my memory serves me correctly that came out to a minimum of four hours of overtime except on Sunday where it was eight hours overtime each time they returned even if they only worked thirty minutes. If they had three or four flights come in sporadically, they had three or four call-backs and commutes. The only time we saw that on the Mexican border was if we nabbed a load on Saturday evening that bled over into Sunday, we then would get eight hours overtime for the few hours we worked on Sunday after midnight and another eight for our scheduled Sunday tour. There were no call-backs or commute because we never left the work site, just the guaranteed eight hours. We called it hitting the jackpot.

Eventually in Nogales we were so shorthanded that not only did we not schedule anyone for Sunday, but they gave up assignments to the Swing shift (4 PM to midnight) which of course meant that everyone on Swings was on overtime. I almost never turned down an overtime assignment, so it was quite common for me to have more overtime hours than regular time (40 hours). I would double every day including my day off (Sunday) for fifty-six hours of overtime. Most of the overtime hours were not CET hours but regular Inspector hours. Sometimes in the rotation but most of the time I was assigned as rover for Passenger Processing.

Along with overtime spending but certainly not on the same scale was CET. CET was one of the targets of administrative cuts and was on the bubble for being abolished nationwide. Nogales was even closer to having the team disbanded due to the establishment of the local narcotics enforcement team TROLL.

The District Director, Mr. Fredericks had battled Customs Headquarters to retain a District CET team and had been approved for extended funding for one more year on the grounds that the special team could improve its production to justify its existence. The bottom line for keeping a CET team was answering the question that Customs Headquarters was asking; what is our bang for the CET buck. Simply put CET needed to put dope on the table.

I must admit that I was somewhat responsible for bringing the limelight on Mr. Fredericks's CET team. Unfortunately, that bright light was focused on the negative side of the productivity spectrum. TROLL had blown the CET team out of the water with drug seizures for the previous quarter and I far outdistanced the other Inspectors on TROLL. To compound the whole can of worms, I not only led Nogales in drug seizures for the quarter, but the entire southwest border.

When Mr. Fredericks brought me on the CET team he congratulated me on my outstanding success with the TROLL team saving it from being disbanded and in the same breath relayed to me in a few words that now the stakes had doubled for the CET team as it is funded from Headquarters who have an entire section in the Anti-Smuggling Division that scrutinizes all counter-drug spending. As he continued his face lit up and a look of pride washed over him. He had one more tidbit of HQ inside information to toss my way. He said "Speaking of the Anti-Smuggling Division the Director and I were talking and he mentioned that you are in the running for Inspector of the Year. Keep up the good work and just so you know that is the first time in my career that I have been able to say that to an employee of mine." As it turned out a female Inspector took top honors for a seizure in cargo. Her seizure netted the largest penalty the Customs Service had ever doled out. Back then the Customs Service was the only government entity that was self-supportive and also added to the Treasury. All I have to say about a commercial violation taking Inspector of the Year is: *Touché ma'am, I am honored to play second fiddle to that. Outstanding work!!!*

I would spend the next ten years on CET or counter-drug teams that splintered off of CET. We eventually were ordered to establish a CET presence in the Commercial Facility and I was tasked with establishing the team and ground rules for commercial CET operations. I also established counter-drug new employee training at the Commercial Facility and developed as well as instructed commercial counter-drug training at the US Customs Southwest Border Interdiction Training (SBIT). SBIT was a nationally funded extension of the US Customs Training Academy. I did not return to Passenger Processing until November 1999 and was reassigned to the Customs Management Center in Tucson less than a month later in December after receiving severe injuries to my right hand and shoulder during a freak incident at Grand Avenue Secondary.

Illustration 48: CET rocker over Customs patch.

Illustration 49: Assist seizure mentioned above. Top of gas tank with trap door open.

Illustration 50: Tank open and compartment containing drugs visible.

Illustration 51: Drugs on the scale and CET inspector who requested my assistance.

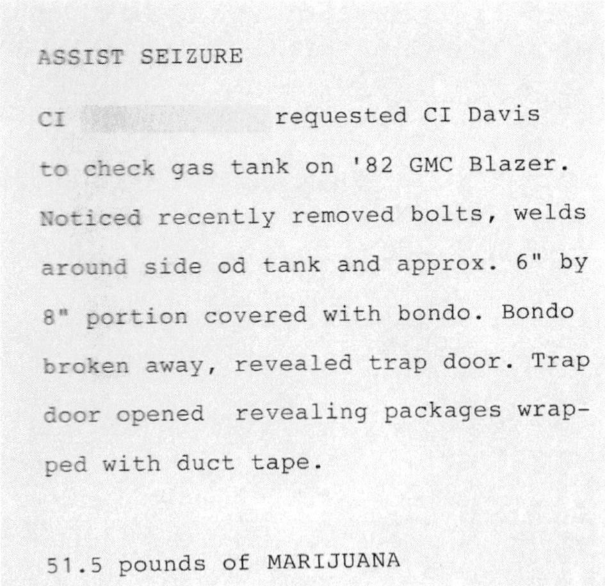

```
ASSIST SEIZURE

CI ▓▓▓▓▓▓▓▓        requested CI Davis

to check gas tank on '82 GMC Blazer.

Noticed recently removed bolts, welds

around side od tank and approx. 6" by

8" portion covered with bondo. Bondo

broken away, revealed trap door. Trap

door opened  revealing packages wrap-

ped with duct tape.


51.5 pounds of MARIJUANA
```

Illustration 52: Note from my photo album, please excuse the 28 year old typo.

BILLION $ DOLLAR $ HIGHWAY

Run Mule Run
June 21, 1990
644.75 Pounds Cocaine

It is15:30 hours or 3:30 PM if you prefer and I am just heading into my overtime shift. I have been roving the lanes since 8:00 AM and really haven't seen anything worth looking at all day. I have been on a rover team for several months and the only difference between this month and the previous few months is that I now wore a CET rocker (patch) over my US Customs shoulder patch. I had been assigned directly to the Contraband Enforcement Team at the end of my TROLL assignment.

When I said only difference, I am referring to the roving technique. Many things changed in the working environment, but the actual performance of the work was the same. The changes include my chain of command. The best part of the change in chain of command is that I now work either port, Mariposa or Grand Avenue. Thorny is no longer impeding my ability to work where I think the highest threat is. This change opened the door to assessing numerous variables in the working environment to work smart.

In my mind one of the top priorities in determining my location changed drastically just over a month earlier on May 9th with the 607 pound cocaine load. That load was an internal conspiracy load. One of our own using his knowledge of our operations and his friendship to circumvent interdiction efforts. As I stated in that chapter, since that seizure I have never looked at my fellow employees the same.

I spent many hours observing my fellow workers and evaluating their performance. The performance measures were all based on an integrity risk matrix I had constructed in my mind. I had even parceled out the matrix into categories such as:

New employee – risk factor inexperience, low to moderate risk with mostly test runs: Apathetic employee – risk factor looking but not seeing, moderate to high risk: et cetra, et cetra.

I never shared any of my thoughts or conclusions, they were just my way of compensating for totally missing any signs that Rudy may have displayed and that ultimately I had missed. Once I came up with probable integrity issues, I secretly worked them. I was not Internal Affairs nor was I gaining legal evidence that should be reported to IA. This was a shot in the dark, like checking every Chevrolet pick-up that entered the port regardless who was behind the wheel.

Such was the case today. I had been observing an Immigration Inspector, Tory Kline who was on top of my extremely high risk list. I had zero evidence of illegal activity; in fact, many of the 'fill in the blanks' on my matrix were gut feelings or instinct if you prefer.

All the same, using my new-found freedom I had been working Mr. Kline for about a week now and was more convinced than ever that he was working for the other side.

114

Mr. Kline and the other Immigration folks that were on my matrix were somewhat more difficult to keep up with and work than the Customs Inspectors that made the list. I had easy access to Customs schedules and therefore I knew when and where my matrix residents were working.

Immigration on the other hand was in a separate area and I did not even know where their schedules were kept much less have easy access to them. Complicating things even more was Immigration's attitude toward me for taking down one of their own with the largest load of cocaine in our district and maybe even the entire southwest border. I was not on their most popular list and would not even dream of strolling through their domain. I was completely in the dark therefore I had to bounce around between ports and shifts to determine when and where they were going to be for that rotation. The rotation was every two weeks if memory serves me so every two weeks the process would start over again. By the way, I did not follow these folks around and watch them like a hawk, my matrix was more of a 'be aware' when we were working together. When we were at the same port, then I watched them like a hawk.

On this particular day all the ducks were in a row, so my plan was to rove as usual but keep a close eye on Tory. Unless his schedule changed, he would be in at 16:00 (4:00 PM).

As I looked at my watch it was 3:30, half an hour before show time. Suddenly I am snapped back to the present as I hear a very familiar voice "I am going to KFC do you want anything?"

Sure enough there stands Velo Raptor, now laughing.

"Absolutely" I replied "but make it a bucket of white meat this time. If a personal meal brought twenty-four pounds of Marijuana imagine what a bucket will do."

I have to admit, Velo and his humor was extremely welcomed and greatly appreciated. It was a humongous relief to talk about twenty-four pounds of marijuana and not six hundred pounds of cocaine along with all the conspiracy theories and such. I had not realized the stress I was under until I felt the relief wash over me at his humor.

That cocaine load pushed me into an area of Law Enforcement that I never wanted to have anything to do with. I was not Internal Affairs, nor did I ever want to be. But Rudy changed my way of thinking. Integrity was not just an IA concern; it was the concern of every sworn LEO (Law Enforcement Officer). Today, until the KFC jab was a prime example. All day I had been consumed with exactly that – integrity.

As we both laughed and talked about observational techniques like detecting discarded KFC personal meals in the back seat of a load vehicle, my fifteen minutes of relaxation came to a screeching stop. I see today's person of concern exit the Immigration section. There he is walking from lane to lane heading to his assigned booth.

I was surprised to see him relieve the Inspector on Lane 4 at 3:45. Immigration was notorious for being late relievers and to see him take the lane fifteen minutes early put up a red flag.

Lane 4 was the last lane and I was on Lane 2 when he opened. As I was watching him relieve the day shift I saw a red Dodge Dart pulled up next to me in Lane 3.

I quickly said to Velo "This one looks good, I have to get a look at it."

Velo stood there for a few seconds and said "Yea, I don't believe that I have ever seen it before." Then he added with a laugh "Hey man, I was just kidding about the damn KFC, don't tell me this one is loaded!"

I began checking the Dart and before I even started I could see the driver was visibly nervous. I opened the back door checked the back seat and nothing there but cushion. I looked at the rocker panel and sure enough there was fresh tampering with the access screws. Unlike the Maverick, this car did not have the easy check location. One has to pull the chrome strip off the rocker panel to gain access for examination.

I told the primary Inspector that I would walk this one to secondary for an exam. The primary Inspector handed me the passport and I told him to have the guy park in secondary lane one.

As I turned around to watch the Dart leave primary, I saw a white Ford Taurus enter lane four from the return to Mexico turnaround. The turnaround is for cars that accidentally get into the lanes and have no desire to enter the United States. It is a one way return lane back to Mexico and the Taurus, traveling the wrong way, slipped to the front of the line in Tory's lane.

I watched as the Taurus pulled up to the primary booth. Normally the Inspector would reprimand the driver and immediately send him to secondary. As I am watching the encounter what I see is far from a reprimand, it is both the driver and Tory staring at me. No declaration being taken, no documents being examined, no primary inspection activities at all.

I looked at Velo who is still standing there watching the Dart pulling into secondary and I quickly handed him the passport for the driver of the Dodge. I told Velo "I think the rockers are loaded, check it for me would you?"

Velo took the passport, gave me an odd look and said "Sure".

I took two steps toward lane four and Tory finally looked at the driver and said something that I could not hear. Tory stepped into the primary booth and the driver door opened, the driver jumped out and three steps later he was in Mexico. The last I saw of the driver was him running the correct direction in the turnaround lane. Once he hit the corner a short distance away, he made a right hand turn around a building and was history.

As soon as the driver door opened, I broke into a run but of course there was zero chance of intercepting the driver before he made the three steps and entered Mexico. I can **not** enter Mexico, so my run ended at the Taurus. Velo and the Inspector from lane three were close behind me. As we reached the Taurus Tory exited the primary booth and said, "What happened, I was going to run him in TECS and the next thing I know he was gone."

I said "Well Tory I am sure there is a reason that he absconded. Was there anything in TECS?"

Tory replied "I never ran him. I saw him get out and run so I didn't get a chance to run him."

I looked for and found alterations to the suspension that I suspected might give a clue as to why he ran. When a vehicle has a heavy load in the trunk the back end will almost drag the ground. To counter the weight the suspension is usually altered. Air shocks are one method that was commonly used. This was not the case for the Taurus, but I will say that an alteration was there, so I strongly suspected a trunk load.

I proceeded to the driver's seat and just my luck, no keys.

There was now a crowd growing in Mexico and fortunately every Inspector from Secondary was now there with us on primary. Sitting in the driver seat I said, "Push me to secondary." and before they began to push, I said to Tory "Give me the driver's documents."

Tory replied "Oh, I don't have them, he kept them."

"Do you remember his name by any chance?" I asked knowing the answer.

"No, I had just started with my processing?" was his response.

I said nothing else, but it sure confirmed my suspicions about Tory. It is quite impossible to run someone in TECS without entering their full name and date of birth at a minimum. 'Driver of Taurus' or 'Absconder' won't work. Either he knew this guy VERY well, well enough to know his date of birth or he was lying. Every answer he gave conflicted a previous answer. You be the judge.

As everyone started pushing the car things went from bad to worse. I had to make one left turn and two right turns to get into secondary. With no keys not only starting the engine is out but making a turn with a locked steering wheel is a near impossible. I was able to get the left and one right somehow. To this day I don't know how we manage that but making the third right into secondary never happened. We ended up parking in the left lane of the two primary departure lanes.

One of the K-9 teams was present and he ran his dog with a positive alert to the trunk. Without keys opening the trunk was another chore. For an immediate remedy we removed the back seat rest and that gave us access to the trunk. Peering into the trunk from the back seat area we could see the entire trunk area was loaded with kilo size packages. Reaching through a small access area I was able to probe a package and retrieve a white powder that tested positive for cocaine.

I notified the Office of Enforcement and they responded in about fifteen or twenty minutes. While we were waiting the Port supervisor decided that the trunk should be opened now that we had verified that it was indeed a load vehicle. Since I was now on CET the Port supervisors were no longer in my Chain of Command, but I still worked with them and respected their position. I agreed with opening the trunk since we were going to have to eventually. Now the Port supervisor and a K-9 supervisor who had just arrived engaged in a debate as to which locksmith to call to bypass the lock. As the debate was in full swing, I went to my car opened the trunk, retrieved a very large flat tip screwdriver and a hammer. I walked over to my seized vehicle and three smacks on the screwdriver later the lock popped out and we opened the trunk.

Illustration 53: Packages visible in trunk

When OE arrived the case agent and Elan Smelly, the SAC (Special Agent in Charge) were both very irritated. The SAC asked me "Who is your informant?"

"Informant, I don't have an informant." I replied to his question.

"You have to have an informant. How did you get these two loads of cocaine?" he accused.

118

"Well Elan, sorry but I don't have an informant and if I did it is in my job description that I can recruit informants, so I certainly would not reveal his or her identity." I replied. I added "If I did have one, I would tell you flat out that I did just so you would know, but I have been on CET for less than a month and I really don't need one it appears. I got these through hard work and observation if you must know."

Well that got a reaction and he had to come up with something, so he asked, "Why is the car parked here and not in Secondary?"

I told him that when the driver absconded, he apparently took the keys. That happens quite often especially if they bail out on primary. Taking the keys out of the ignition when you exit the vehicle becomes so routine that it is a habit that is hard to break. The first load I ever got was a trunk load of Marijuana. I did not write the SAS or get credit for it (my Field Training Officer or FTO for short, wrote it as hers) but when I told the driver to open the trunk he walked to the back of the car and hightailed it to Mexico. I yelled at him "Los llave's" and he stopped about fifteen feet into Mexico and tossed the keys to me. Habits die hard even to stopping and complying when yelled at. People laughed about that one for years. It was a well told story. I once had an Inspector in training tell me the story just as his FTO had told it to him. There was one small discrepancy; the FTO substituted herself in my place. Truth be known she wasn't even there that day, but she had the keys tossed to her in the story. I did not correct it because this lady made the absolute best caldo de queso in Arizona or Sonora. For a bowl of her caldo de queso and a couple of tortillas heck I can still see her catching those darn keys.

Anyhow back to my adversaries or oops our sister agency OE. Smelly had no come back as to how to turn the wheel and get the car into secondary so he decided that Grand Avenue was not the best place to unload the car. He wanted it taken to Mariposa. I told him no problem, give me fifteen minutes. I walked up to the line and waved over a Nogales Transito Police Lieutenant who was over in Nogales Mexico working crowd control. "LT do you or one of your guys know how to hot wire a car?" I asked.

"Sure, our mechanic does, and he is here with us." he replied.

"Can I borrow him?" I asked.

Ten minutes later the car was running, the steering wheel was unlocked, and we were ready to head to MAP. I knew the LT would have his mechanic because their vehicles were very substandard. I also knew that any good mechanic in Mexico or the US should know how to perform that menial task. International relations at its best. We had helped the LT many times and they had helped us many times. On the Mexican border that is called survival.

At this point we still do not know how much cocaine we have but one thing I do know is that it is a big load. Smelly did not even ask how we managed to get the damn car started. These nimrods were so full of themselves that I am sure that it did not enter their mind that we still did not have keys for the car. One would actually have to be aware of something other than the idiot looking back at him when he looks in the mirror. He and his ASAC smoked the biggest cigars I have ever seen and I smoked a cigar upon occasion back then. At any rate we are talking about making the move to Mariposa. I tell them that we should use Mariposa Road rather than Target Range Road for safety. Smelly is totally against that because it would add a few miles to the journey. I told him that Target Range has many places that are perfect for an ambush if anyone knows we headed that way. It is mostly an unimproved road that brings you right down to a canyon known for drug smuggling. The canyon connects to Ephraim Canyon one of the most utilized routes used by smugglers. There have been many armed conflicts in Ephraim Canyon as well as snipers firing at the Maripose POE.

My points were so well taken that one hour later our convoy of one car with two agents in the lead, me in the load vehicle and a trail car with two agents in a pick-up truck is on its way to Target Range Road on route to Mariposa. As we exit Interstate 19 and make a left on Target Range there is a pick-up truck parked in the shade under the overpass. A female with halter top and short shorts wearing heals is standing there with the truck. The lead vehicle in our convoy pulled over immediately and they said over the radio "We will be pulling over to help this girl, she is in dire need of our attention."

I jumped in and said, "I don't like it, I am not stopping."

Smelly, who was in the tail truck said, "You keep going; we will be assisting her also."

As I drove by, I looked in the rear-view mirror and Smelly had also pulled over. I kept on going but my Smith and Wesson .357 was no longer resting in the holster.

When I arrived at MAP a passel of Inspectors were there waiting for me. The MAP Supervisor Lefty met me and said "Man am I glad to see you. I heard OE on the radio and I just cannot believe what I heard. I sure don't see them, so I guess they all stopped."

"Yes sir. No way was I going to stop driving a car with a heck of a lot of cocaine, a hot wire starting system and who knows what else with this car." I said.

Lefty asked "Where exactly was this girl in need?"

"Parked under the I-19 overpass. Perfect place to set-up an ambush." I said.

"Well maybe OE felt that no one knew what route you were taking so it would be safe. We all thought you would take Mariposa." I couldn't believe he was defending them.

"Sure, no one knew the route. It was either Target Range or Mariposa that everyone knows and if I had millions of dollars of my product in this car, I certainly would have a tracking device on it." came my reply. "Even if this got through, I would want to know exactly where my load was from starting point to ending point and everything between. I wouldn't even trust the driver."

"I didn't even think of that, but you are absolutely right. Who's to say that it does not have a device?" Lefty said now looking all around us "Let's get this dope in the vault."

We had about half the load out by the time the Special Agents arrived laughing and joking. That girl was so dumb, all she had to do was put the wire back on the coil. The truck started right up when her knights in shining armor discovered the coil wire had *fallen* off. Yep common problem, those coil wires fall off like – never!

We removed 245 packages of cocaine with a weight of 644.75 pounds. I set a new record by about forty pounds. If there was a tracking device on the vehicle, I never found it, but I really didn't look all that good.

Illustration 54: Not a bad catch.

The CET supervisor was quite happy. My first day on CET he had practically reprimanded me for getting Rudy and the 607 pounds of cocaine for TROLL. That load had put TROLL way ahead of CET in the seizure race. He literally sat there and told me that I should have waited until I was on CET to get the load. Well this load beat the TROLL load, so he is king of the big load. There certainly are times when you just have to sit back and shake your head. Where do these people come from?

Illustration 55: Me and the catch of the day. For those under 30 the blue thing on the lower right is a type writer. It is where I typed the witness statement.

IA didn't show up for a couple of days unlike Rudy's load where they were there during the seizure. This time I did have something to share with them and I gave them just the facts on Tory Kline. Nothing that I had put together on my mental matrix but just the facts of what had transpired. I emphasized his discrepancies and contradictions. If they couldn't put a case together on that well, que sera. The only thing I actually saw come out of this was that all the supervisors seemed to know Tory was being looked at by IA. But in reality, no one was actually doing anything.

I began working Tory very hard. Then less than two weeks later on July 3rd he was supposed to be at Grand Avenue working the day shift. I was there at 8:00 AM and by 10:30 I had not seen him. Immigration had gone through one rotation and he did not show up. I asked one of the Aggies if they would walk through the INS area and check their schedule if she could do so. Ten minutes later she told me that Tory had traded for the 6:00 AM to 2:00 PM shift at MAP. He had now been there for more than four hours.

I jumped into my CET vehicle and took off for MAP. When I arrived, I drove over to the primary lanes and parked on the far side, just off the road and slightly north of the primary booths. As I got out of the vehicle Supervisor Lefty came over and said, "Man am I glad you are here, Kline showed up here today and he is acting very weird."

As Lefty was relaying this, he was motioning with his eyes to Lane one.

I looked at lane one and there was Klien. Lefty and I walked over to Lane two and were standing directly north of the corner of Lane two's primary booth. As we were standing there a pick-up with a camper shell rolled up. As I looked, I really liked that camper shell. I watched the truck come to a stop and then I watched the non-existent declaration. This was *déjà vu*. Klien and the driver were looking at me. No declaration, no document check, nothing that should have been going on was going on. I took one step towards them and thinking camper shell pointed to the hood for Klien to have him open the hood. Klien said something to the driver and the driver floor boarded the gas pedal and headed straight for Lefty and me. We both jumped towards Lane two's primary booth for cover and the truck raced by just missing us.

In ten steps I was in my vehicle and in pursuit. The truck then cut across a very rough median and entered the southbound lanes headed back to Mexico. As I was bouncing along behind him cutting across the median, I saw an object fall off the truck. I just drove by it and kept up the pursuit.

As we approached the Port several inspectors including Klien had positioned themselves near the outbound lanes. As the fleeing truck passed Klien, who had drawn his weapon, he threw his weapon at the truck. As I went by the Port I saw his hand gun hit the pavement to my right and bounce off the roadway and come to a stop on the shoulder of the road. That goes down as one of the strangest things I have ever seen.

As we were approaching the gate at the border fence, I was at seventy-five miles per hour. I slammed on the brakes and slid into Mexico for a bit. I immediately rammed the gears into reverse and quickly backed out of Mexico stopping just north of the gate. I looked up just in time to see the truck go head on into a concrete pillar that supported the roof covering Mexico's primary booths. There were several cars in the primary lanes and the smuggler apparently forgot he had brakes, at least I never saw a brake light nor did the truck slow down. He went between the lanes of cars but that was not an escape route. Just in front of the support was a lawn chair that the Aduana's (Mexican Customs Officers) would sit in when there was no traffic. That poor chair never stood a chance.

123

I pulled out my binoculars to get the number on the Arizona license plate and watch the show down south. I saw the poor Aduana who was manning the booth behind the concrete pillar exit the booth and slowly, on very wobbly legs, walk over to the driver's door. He was joined by three other Aduana's. When the truck hit the pillar, it spun about forty-five degrees so I could see the driver slumped over the steering wheel. The Aduana's stood there looking at him for a minute or so and I believe I saw his left arm move. Just then one of the Aduana's opened the door surprisingly with no trouble, drag the guy out onto the pavement and they backed off looking at him lying there on the ground. In unison all four pulled their night sticks out and commenced corrective disciplinary action on the offender. As I was watching through the binoculars I thought 'Why do they run? Here he would have had a place to stay with TV, three square meals a day and a bed to sleep on. Over there he will be lucky to make it to a hospital.'

Once that started, I knew it was time for me to leave. That is Mexico and it is a sovereign country with their own laws. My place is finding out what fell from the truck during the cross median run. I headed back to the spot where we made the U-turn and found a package of marijuana. I retrieved the evil weed and noticed the package had a very large gash in it. As I looked at it, I realized what had happened. I can't say much about the rest of the vehicle, but I was sure it had contained a hood load. Many hood loads are simple with chicken wire used as flooring in the engine compartment. The dope is then just tossed in on top of the chicken wire. The package must have bounced out of the chicken wire net and fell out between the fan and the radiator. That would explain the gash.

I jumped back in my vehicle and headed back to the gate. Thank goodness the show was over down south but of course the vehicle was still there. Using the binoculars, I now looked at the vehicle damage. The hood and engine were pushed back almost to the windshield with the hood forming a tent like structure over the very visible packages of dope. My thought had been the camper shell, so I pointed to the hood thinking I might throw them off with me looking in the wrong place. Instead I pointed right at my target.

After confirming my suspicions and not even having to wait for Mexico to start unloading the load, I headed back to the Port to write-up my one-pound load. I would find out later that the camper was also loaded. Mexico seized about eight hundred pounds of marijuana, so I wasn't completely wrong. As I pulled into secondary with my package of marijuana Slim Smalls, one of the Vietnam Era Customs Inspectors who came into Customs at the same time I did asked if I saw Tory throw his gun at the fleeing vehicle. I told him that, yes, I saw the gun hit pavement and the last I saw it slide on off the roadway.

Slim walked over to Tory and said, "Hey Kline, did you find your gun?"

Tory answered with somewhat of a nervous chuckle "Yes I did it was over on the shoulder. I have no idea why I threw the gun. I guess it seemed like the only thing I could do."

Slim asked "Would you like for me to look at it for you? I was an armorer in the service."

Tory handed Slim the weapon and Slim unloaded the weapon and began his exam. He checked the action, trigger and the other working parts. He then gave it a visual and said, "Damn good thing you didn't have to use it, there is a piece of pavement in the barrel."

Slim pulled out a knife and gave it a go. That piece of pavement was not moving. Slim handed the weapon and ammo back to Tory and said, "I would get that fixed as soon as possible."

As Slim and I walked away Slim said "Hell I am wondering now if I should have kept my mouth shut. Losing that dimwit would be like losing a hemorrhoid."

When I finished the SAS, I went in to talk to Lefty. I had made up my mind that I was going to call IA to let them know about today's events starting with the shift swap, but my main concern was the *déjà vu*; no declaration, no document check, nothing. Adding the attempted run down of the two of us warranted the call to IA. I thought that since Lefty was also targeted by the truck and IA would probably want to talk to him, I should make him aware of the call.

When I entered his office, he was first to speak, and he told me to close the door.

"Rick there is something you need to know. I know that IA has opened a case on Tory. They met with all the Supervisor's and told us to keep an eye on him and report anything that might help their case. They said immediately report *any* suspicious activities or goings on that occur specifically if he might be involved." he said and then added in a very troubled voice. "That truck coming at us was no accident in my opinion."

"Lefty the reason I came in here was to let you know that I intend to call IA." I said matter-of-factly "I know they have something going and I agree; the truck was definitely aiming at us. I have no doubt about that at all."

Lefty seemed relieved and said, "Let's make the call together then since we were both there."

"That works for me." I replied "But I would prefer to make the call from the Truck Dock. We can walk over there and use one of the processing booths that are fairly sound proof. I am sure that they have one that is not manned since produce season is over. Also, there will be fewer prying eyes and ears but best of all there are no Immigration employees at the facility."

"Yea you are right. I am beginning to think that Rudy may be the tip of the iceberg." was his response.

We walked over and used a booth on the north dock where there was an empty booth and even better the entire north dock was shut down for asphalt repairs taking place in the parking area. We were totally isolated and could have left the door open, but just the same we had it closed and locked.

Less than two months later Tory resigned from the Immigration Service and that was the last I heard of him.

In less than two months I had interdicted one thousand two hundred fifty-one pounds of pure uncut cocaine. That tipped the anti-smuggling scale to our favor in several ways. First it put the small Port of Nogales on the Customs map, or so I was told. It also opened the eyes of our Headquarters in Washington, DC that Mexico had definitely become a transship country for cocaine. No longer was the Miami Seaport the only big dog in the cocaine wars. The Miami Seaport had almost one hundred Inspectors on their CET team. We had five. Headquarters quickly changed that and gave us one more slot. The bright side to me was that we blew Miami out of the water when it came to averages.

We were now so well known that I was looking forward to Hollywood starting a new series – Nogales Vice with detective Jaime "Hijo" Chavarria as the star. I know just the perfect person to play Hijo – coming your way Mustang Corners, white cowboy hat and all!

BILLION $ DOLLAR $ HIGHWAY

Double Play - Out One
October 13, 1990
51 Pounds Marijuana

October the 13th is a bad luck day in my wife's book because she considered 13 unlucky. Many people consider Friday the 13th as an unlucky day or bad luck day as she calls it. Yep, it's a Saturday but to my wife it is not the day, but the number. To me it is just another day of work.

The CET team had only one load in August and two in September. Most of the loads taken down during this time were backpack or drive through loads between the Ports of Entry (POE). By all appearance, the drug smugglers were avoiding the POE's. At least October was looking up with two loads already and the month is not even half over. Word from snitches or informants if you prefer was that the cartels and the mules were very uncomfortable with us rovers. We, as rovers, were unpredictable and that brought the cartel's chances of getting a load through the Ports too low for the guy in charge of the load to guarantee it with their life.

The mules on the other hand did not guarantee anything, they were paid to get the vehicle from point A in Mexico to point B in Arizona. The mules were not willing to use the Ports because if they failed they did not get paid, they were the ones that went to jail and their visa was revoked. The probability of getting caught and ending up in jail is what gave them pause in agreeing to drive a load vehicle through without some assurance that they would not get caught.

It is a bit ironic but just like the SAC accused me of having informants; the bad guys came to the same conclusion. There were many executions in Nogales Sonora, executions of *suspected* informants as well as the operatives that "purchased" the load guaranteeing payment with their life. The Mexican Transito Police lieutenant from whom I had borrowed a mechanic to get the trunk loaded Taurus on the road kept us in the know. In fact, a few days after the six hundred forty-four-pound cocaine load the LT walked over one evening waving to us. My CET partner Gordo and I walked to where he was standing and he said, "train gate".

He wanted to meet us on the east side of the Port at the railroad crossing. The train gate is only a few feet from the Grand Avenue's lane four but there is a twenty-foot-high brick wall that separates the vehicle lanes and the rail crossing. One of the main features of the wall is to significantly reduce the noise at the Port from the train as it crosses. The perfect place to significantly reduce our voices from the ears at the Port. It also hindered the prying eyes that were always watching CET. The port definitely had eyes and ears everywhere.

Any time we heard "train gate" we knew it was probably something good. We never got workable drug information from the LT (he valued his life) but he gave us news and I would say gossip. Almost all law enforcement in Mexico as well as most of the military were on some criminal element's payroll. LT was no different, we did not know for sure, but we just assumed that to be fact. LEO's in Mexico made just a few dollars a day and their real living expenses came from mordida. Mordida was their bite of the illegal pie. Mordida literally means *bite*, but when it comes to government officials the interpretation is *bribe*. In the US we figure in premium pay like overtime, night differential, Sunday's and Holiday's. In Mexico they figure in mordida. Yep that is Mexico; that would never happen in the US. Well unless you are a politician. Remember AbScam and AzScam? I will say no more.

LT's secret meeting was regarding several executions that had taken place in Nogales, Sonora that were believed to be directly related to the coke load. The Mexican authorities had found several known operatives of the CFO (Carrillo-Fuentes Organization) executed by train. In 1990 Amado Carrillo-Fuentes was the King Pin of what is now better known as the Juarez Cartel. One of their most common executions was to tie the condemned subject on the railroad tracks with their eyes facing the oncoming train so they could watch as it rolled up to them. LT told us that there were six executions in total with four on some train tracks leading to one of the maquilladoras. Maquilladoras are commercial assembly plants in Mexico where much of the parts for an end product such as automobiles, chain saws, sterile hospital equipment and many more items than I can list are shipped to Mexico from the US and other countries and then assembled in Mexico. The products are then shipped to the US as *assembled* in Mexico rather than *made* in Mexico. Maquillas were basically a product of NAFTA (North American Free Trade Agreement) and are still surviving today. Seems like every four years there are ripples of rescinding NAFTA but amazingly after November the ripples depart and the NAFTA pond is again calm. Four executions on that set of tracks was probably a distinct message to other cartel members – it is not healthy to work with the Americans. These would be suspected snitches and the other two who were just shot with a single bullet would be the guarantors. I trusted you and you went against me vs just collecting a debt.

I was going to work one morning and headed to my usual exit for the apartment complex that I lived in and as I rolled up there were about a dozen Tucson Police Department (TPD) vehicles blocking the entrance. One of them, an acquaintance of mine, told me the entrance/exit was closed. Then he looked and said "Oh hell I forgot you live here. Someone sent you a message. There is a dead guy in the driveway with his hands tied behind his back."

I don't know if it was a message to me or not but if it was, I never heeded it. I thought about it, but I just don't see it. Why the entrance, why not my porch. Just collecting a debt and that was just where they discarded the trash.

Back bad luck day. So here I am working with Gordo again. Very seldom did we work the same Port together. Gordo was the only hold over from the previous CET team. The rest were all in the rotation. The supervisor said that Gordo and I were first and second on the seizure board, so he was not comfortable with us both working the same Port. It gave the smugglers an open Port to get their wares through. I admit that he had a point because the Mexican radio station gave weather reports, traffic wait times at the Ports and they also reported our location when we were working.

Gordo and I were also trainers for Customs and our training was called *Inspection Techniques* We later renamed the training: *Sign Cutting – Compartment and Concealment Detection*. The training started when I was still on TROLL and continued when I was appointed to CET. My

128

first assignment on CET was to travel to Springfield, Illinois where Gordo and I presented our class to the Illinois State Police (ISP) Drug Interdiction Squad at their Academy.

CONTRABAND ENFORCEMENT TEAM
'INSPECTIONAL TECHNIQUES CLASS'
on
JUNE 13, 1990
at
ILLINOIS STATE POLICE TRAINING ACADEMY

Springfield, Illinois

by
·| and R. DAVIS

Illustration 56: Today as I am writing this is June 13, 2018 exactly 28 years ago to the day we gave this class. No I will not attempt to remove these items from their protective covering, sorry for the distortion.

Gordo was working his regular 6:00 AM to 2:00 PM shift and I was working the 8:00 AM to 4:00 PM shift. Just before I arrived, Gordo had taken a call from our point of contact at the ISP counter-drug guys. He called to let us know that the previous afternoon one of the team had intercepted a double bed pick-up truck following the techniques we had taught during our class. We had instructed the class that by using a particular observational technique they could sit on the side of the road and pick out a double bed as it drove by. That was exactly what the officer did. He detected the discrepancy from the side of the road as the truck went by.

As Gordo and I were talking about how well the class went and that the ISP had nabbed another load, a 1985 Mercury Cougar pulled up a couple of lanes over on lane three. I told Gordo that I wanted to check the Cougar out and he said "It's a local, we never get anything from locals. We are on the radio right now." Gordo never checked a local crosser. I don't know if it was a mental block or self-preservation, but until his retirement he would not check them.

I strolled over to the car and straight to the quarter panel. I tapped it and it felt solid to include the fact that it was definitely missing the usual hollow sound. I opened the door and checked the screws and sure enough there had been recent tampering.

I motioned Gordo over and said, "See what Buster says on that quarter panel."

He stooped down and ran the Buster then said, "Well Buster agrees with you, the readings are high."

I told the primary inspector that I was going to walk the vehicle to secondary for an inspection and he handed me the driver's passport. I told the driver to proceed to secondary and park the vehicle in lane one.

The driver complied and I took a secondary declaration. He was not bringing anything from Mexico and was going to Safeway to buy milk. Truth be known, the guy could park his car in a lot in Mexico and walk across then proceed the short distance to Safeway (so close it would be measured in feet), purchase the milk and return to Mexico in far less time than he just spent waiting in the long vehicle lines. The odd part is that his story was very common. I once asked why they would wait so long in line when they could walk faster and the lady told me; "The car has an air conditioner, my house doesn't. On hot days the car is much cooler."

I walked the driver into the office and secured him in the holding cell. I returned to the vehicle and began removing the inner wall of the quarter panel. These panels are made of some very hard plastic and it is sometimes a bear to remove them. Once off there is another somewhat more flexible plastic liner. Bending the flexible liner revealed the open cavity of the quarter panel. Open but quite stuffed with packages wrapped in silver duct tape. I removed thirty-four packages of marijuana with a total weight of fifty-one pounds.

One caveat that I will toss in: The ISP training was June 13th, twenty-eight years later, I wrote this on June 13th, this seizure was October 13th. All pure coincidence as is the 13th in the next chapter.

Illustration 57: 1985 Mercury Cougar. This one had glass packs and had a big cat roar. Sure beat my Escort.

Illustration 58: Packages visible in the driver side quarter panel.

Illustration 59: A close up view of the packages and no I am not a zombie, close but no. That is powder from the rubber gloves.

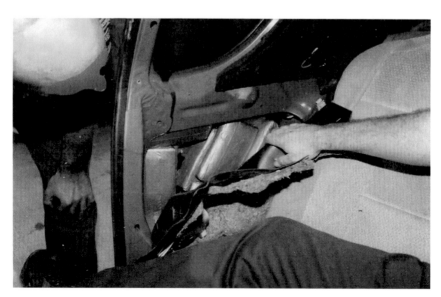

Illustration 60: Packages in passenger side quarter panel with Gordo checking it out.

BILLION $ DOLLAR $ HIGHWAY

Double Play – Out Two
October 13, 1990
137.5 Pounds Marijuana

October the 13th is a bad luck day in my wife's book because she considered 13 unlucky. Many people consider Friday the 13th as an unlucky day or bad luck day as she calls it. Yep, it's a Saturday but to my wife it is not the day, but the number. To me it is just another day of work.

The CET team had only one load in August and two in September. Most of the loads taken down Arizona during this time were back pack or drive through loads between the Ports of Entry (POE). By all appearance, the drug smugglers were avoiding the POE's. At least October was looking up with three loads already and the month is not even half over.

I arrived at the Mariposa POE (MAP) a little after 5 PM for my overtime shift. Since MAP closed at 10:00 PM. I am relatively sure that this will be a fourteen-hour day rather than a sixteen-hour day. I should be home between eleven and twelve this evening rather than between one and two tomorrow morning. I just might be able to eat and get some sleep.

Another little bonus is that I knocked down a load at 10:10 AM over at Grand Ave so I spent most of the day removing the dope, writing the reports (SAS and witness statement) and inventorying the seized vehicle. When I arrived at MAP I felt pretty fresh and welcomed getting back on the line and out of the office chair. Writing reports was not my favorite part of law enforcement; very necessary grant you, but still not exactly my favorite portion of a good seizure.

I will tell you when those pesky reports, chain of custody forms and inventories did become my favorite time spent. That would be when I planted my backside in the chair next to the judge in a court room. Yep, when that defense attorney walks up in front of you and starts his or her bashing one piece of ammunition in their arsenal are the reports, notes, chain of custody, rights statements and several other items most folks never think about. If they are not perfect, they will become your worst enemy on the stand.

I have been to court many, many times and have learned many ploys in the arsenal of the defense. Remember that in this country all suspects are presumed innocent until proven guilty in a court of law. That sure as heck does not interpret to *they are innocent*. They are **presumed** innocent.

I will add my two cents on the presumption of innocence. The law very clearly stipulates that I must presume a guilty person innocent until the verdict is in. When the verdict does come in, he or she is either innocent or guilty *in the eyes of the court*; or by law if you prefer. It does not change the facts. The fact is he or she is either innocent or guilty period. The law adding until **proven** otherwise does not change the facts or the truth. Many guilty defendants walk out of the court room after being declared innocent, but they know that they made out, got lucky or whatever. I guarantee you that when the guilty party hears the "innocent" verdict they know damn well that it was the wrong verdict. They know they are guilty as sin.

There are always at least four other people that know those people are guilty but respect the law and can only grin and bear it. Those other four are the arresting officer, the prosecuting attorney, the defense attorney and the judge.

I learned a long time ago that my job is not to convict. That mission belongs to attorneys and the actual verdict sits squarely on the shoulders of the jury. The judge and the attorneys are there to ensure the jury has enough de facto evidence to deliver a correct verdict.

It may work that way in utopia, but the real world; not so much:

The judges begin to think that they know how the law should be, so they start legislating from the bench. An example of this was during a motions hearing. I interdicted a load in gas tanks. The driver like many others fell asleep in the holding cell. That is part of what I call the adrenaline rush also called the fight or flight response. I am no doctor (I have morals) but I will explain it the best I can as a witness to this reaction many times. As the smugglers approach primary, they get more and more nervous and a physiological reaction is an adrenaline dump or adrenaline rush as some call it. At any rate the body goes into a massive rush preparing to fight to the death or run for your life. Everything is racing. Again, I am no doctor, all I can tell you is what I see. When the cell door locks many of these people fall asleep. I don't know if it is because they know it is over, they know they are caught or what, but when the handcuffs are removed and they sit on the hard bench their shoulders slump and their body melts. Those are the ones you know are going to be asleep in five minutes. The fight is over. Normally these folks sleep for a very short time, ten or fifteen minutes at most. I put it this way, I have seen them asleep but never had to wake one up. By interview time they are wide awake.

When interview time came in this case, we went into the holding cell and read the very wide awake and alert suspect his Miranda rights in Spanish (Fifth Amendment rights warning established after Miranda vs Arizona). We also had him read the warning with English on one side and Spanish on the other, his choice. He then signed the rights statement validating that he understood his rights. Standard procedure for court purposes. The subject was asked if he wanted a lawyer and he declined. He was then asked if he was willing to waive his right to be silent and answer some questions and he agreed. He gave us the entire story of how and why he agreed to transport the load of marijuana. Open and shut.

At motions the defense attorney began with a request for his statement to be excluded as evidence on the grounds that the defendant's rights had been violated. The prosecuting attorney argued that his statement was crucial to her legal proceeding as it was the foundation of her case. She also pointed out that there were no grounds to dismiss his statement bringing out the signed Miranda documents. The judge then asked the defense on what grounds where the defendants' rights violated, and the defense attorney answered that the defendant was too tired to understand his rights. It was a long trip from Guadalajara to Nogales. The judge then became a law maker re-writing the law and said, "Motion granted, the statement is inadmissible."

The prosecuting attorney pointed out that he was verbally read his rights, he visually read his rights himself and validated that he understood his rights. She asked on what grounds does the defense make his case that the defendant was too tired. She emphasized that there is nothing in his entire statement that indicated he was tired.

The judge didn't even bother to ask the defense attorney to provide his response to what the mysterious grounds were for the basis of the motion. The judge answered, "He said he fell asleep in the holding cell." The judge then looked at me and asked, "Did he fall asleep in the holding cell Inspector?"

I know my job at court hearings; it is to tell the truth. "Yes, your Honor he did. I checked him after running him in TECS as is standard procedure and he was asleep just like many other suspects. But when we went in for the interview, he was wide awake."

The judge came back with "I asked if this defendant fell asleep, I didn't ask about other suspects or the interview. Why did you throw that in, are you biased?"

I answered "No your Honor, I was just trying to answer to the best of my ability to draw a complete picture. I should also add; as is typical of many others who appear to have gone through the fight or flight response." I knew this judge and I was sure this case was already beyond the toilet and in the sewer.

Oh boy did the judge let me have it. He asked if I had a Medical Degree, asked if I were a certified Psychologist, asked again if I was biased and then blurted out what the real issue was, he said "This is just a poor mule trying to make an honest living. Why do you want to put him in jail?"

I answered "I don't sir, I just want to do my job to the best of my ability. Here, under oath, it is telling the truth. It is up to the jury do put him in jail or set him free. My job ends when I walk off the stand."

Surprisingly the judge had no response to me. Not even a dirty look. He looked at the AUSA and said "The statement is inadmissible. Do you have anything else?"

Her response was "If the statement is inadmissible, I have no case at this point. I am dropping all charges."

And with that the judge re-wrote the law to his own satisfaction. *He is presumed innocent until proven guilty in a court of law* became *he is innocent if the judge thinks he is just a poor mule trying to make an honest living.* You see in the real world there were several laws that were violated: general smuggling, failure to declare, possession of a controlled substance and others. Unfortunately, this judge lives in his own world that he controls without oversight. In fact, he remained on the bench for many years. He was and still is touted as a great judge and community influence. He even has a few things named after him. His community influence is seen at many gatherings. You can usually smell his influence burning before you see the funny cigarettes.

This being said, I also named something after him. Upon occasion one of the K-9's would have an accident and the handler would have to put him away and get the scooper to clean it up. When this happened, I would say "Watch out, one of the dogs just took a Judge Whosit over there."

I don't know about anyone else but none of my cases ever ended with a conviction in his court. Now on the other hand the attorneys and I admit that upon occasion Law Enforcement Officers (LEO) have a somewhat different approach at ensuring that the jury is properly informed of the *true* facts. They re-write those true facts.

The defense attorney is paid to get their client off no matter what the facts show. That is why there is an attorney/client privilege clause. If their client is innocent, they don't need to hide facts. Yep in my humble opinion that privilege is not for the innocent, but for the guilty who are attempting to circumvent the law. The defense will use whatever means necessary and at times manufactured evidence to get a client off. If you look up a good defense attorney it is not the one who ensured justice, it is the one who wins the most cases. These attorneys are very sought after if they have a list of guilty clients who walked. I could mention the white Bronco case and how those attorney's firms skyrocketed. It seemed like the entire country thought the driver was guilty with the exception of the twelve jurors. An example of manufactured evidence will be annotated in a later chapter during a trial for a heroin smuggler.

The prosecutors and LEO's who go beyond the law think their job is to put the defendant in jail. Perjury is probably the most common violation here but if you believe Hollywood all cops carry a throw down gun to taint the evidence. I have no examples of this because I never saw it, but in order to taint the evidence we come full circle to the paperwork. To taint the evidence, one must also taint the reports leaving a paper trail that can, will and should be ripped apart by the defense. If jury deception or tampering is used by any party it taints the groundwork of our country, The Constitution of the United States. Whoever does it is smearing the Constitution, squatting there like the K-9 mentioned above and dropping a Judge Whosit. Many Americans died for the Constitution, some friends' others unknown but for us prior military all are Brothers and Sisters. When we enter the armed forces, we all swear to **support** and defend the Constitution of the United States and that is never rescinded.

The short story, yes, I was very meticulous with the paperwork and it could take hours getting it as accurate as possible. That is a lot of butt time in a chair for a rover. So, I was happy to get back to roving now that I am at MAP.

The best part of this assignment was the Senior, Kindrick Pauls. Pauls was very sharp, easy to work with and I am very proud to say he was a good friend. When I arrived he was as happy as a pig in well you know. We took a little bit of time catching up on things and he was very enthusiastic about a pellet burning stove he had purchased. I had never heard of a pellet stove but from what I understand they are very popular these days. Pauls was the first person that I know who bought one. To be honest with you he is still the only person that I know that has a pellet stove. I have never seen one in use. I never even saw Kindrick's but heard about it almost every winter after he got it.

I finally got down to business full time without distractions and there was a good flow of traffic. Just enough to stay busy but not enough to beat me up. Even though I had been off the line for most of the day it was still eight plus hours and that wears on the body.

As I was roving a VW bug rolled up to the first in line behind primary and was waiting for the vehicle on primary to depart. I looked at the occupants. There was a young girl about late teens driving, an old male probably in his late sixties or early seventies in the front passenger seat and two late teen females in the back seats.

I waited until the vehicle pulled up to primary and when it stopped, I opened he passenger door to check the interior. I greeted the older male sitting there with "Good evening, what are you bringing from Mexico?" The only reason I asked was so I could check the interior transmission tunnel and floor. When you open the door and start shining a flashlight under the seat and elsewhere in the car it is only common courtesy to say something. These areas have been used often for smuggling, so I am going to check the interior, but I was always mindful that I was invading their personal area. In VW bugs the engine is in the rear and there is a tunnel about six to eight inches high for the transmission linkage. The tunnel can be accessed from a trap door in front of the vehicle (I checked this while they were waiting pre-primary) and the other access is from the interior. The floor is deep an made for an easy double floor compartment.

When he answered I had already looked under the seat and saw nothing but a bag of cone shaped brown sugar candy. I then moved to the tunnel but quickly lost interest for two reasons. The first, it had not been tampered with. The second and most shocking was his answer to me. I expected the guy to declare dulces (Spanish for candy) instead he said "Panochas nada mas." All three young girls giggled and partially hid their faces in their hands.

I understood why, panocha in my not so great Spanish refers to a females, shall we say private parts. Not the breasts but somewhat lower. I looked at the female inspector Janna Adaporo who was on primary and was a native-born Spanish speaker. I saw that she was also giggling. Jan and I got along very well and she was tough. I would take her as my right-hand Officer in any situation and know that my right side was covered. She was a faster draw and a better shot than me any day. Obviously, she had heard our exchange. I expected a referral to Secondary for immigration status on the lot because prostitution is one of the crimes of moral turpitude that will result in inadmissibility (as written: offenses relating to owning, controlling, managing, or supervising a prostitution business).

I looked at the driver and noticed that her blue jean cut-offs were unbuttoned and the zipper was down. I also noted that she did not appear to be wearing anything under those shorts and she was not a natural blond. I looked again at the girls in the back seat and they were still giggling and continued to cover their face with their hand.

I was somewhat in shock and backed up putting a little distance between me and the rolling house of ill repute. That is definitely an Immigration thing, not a drug thing. Those girls were almost babies. Jan then told the driver to park in Secondary lane number one. I watched them head north and make the turn into Secondary lane one. I looked back at Jan and her relief was standing there. I asked, "Where is Adaporo?"

"She headed to Secondary last I saw." was his reply. I guess that I was so absorbed in watching to make sure the car did not bypass Secondary and head north that I completely missed the Inspectors rotation.

I headed to Secondary still watching the VW as it came to a stop and saw the driver exit the car, button and zip her shorts then head toward the MAP office facility where Jan met her. Jan said something and pointed to the west entrance to the facility. Immigration was actually around the building, not through the west entrance. In that area there are offices, holding cells and employee bathrooms. Now I am at a total loss as to what is going on.

The driver practically broke into a run as she rushed in the west doors. I walked over to Jan and asked her "Are they going to Immigration?"

"No" she said "She just needs to use the bathroom. I don't think she could have made it to the public bathrooms in the Immigration office."

I was shocked and asked "Did you hear what that old man said? He said he was bringing panochas! He called the girls panochas!"

Jan began laughing and said "Panocha is not what you think. That panocha is slang. His panochas are a type of candy. Only old people still call that candy panocha. My grandfather used to do the same when I was in the car crossing the border as a young girl and I would get the same looks I saw on your face. I would be so embarrassed. I know what those girls were feeling."

I said "Oh, is it the brown sugar cone looking candy? I saw some under the seat."

Now laughing harder she said, "Rick you are quite observant. Yes, you were looking at panochas under the seat, not sitting in them."

I said "Well I saw panocha in the driver seat. Well not quite but close enough to know she is not a natural blond. Her shorts were unbuttoned and unzipped and there is nothing under those shorts but her."

With that revelation I had to wait for a couple of minutes for Jan to catch her breath due to her now gut-wrenching hysterical laughter. She was finally able to say "She told me she had to pee so bad that she had to undo her shorts. That is why I let them park in secondary for her emergency run to the bathroom. I came over here to make sure no one ran them off without a referral slip on the windshield. Poor thing was about to burst at the seams."

So, one more lesson in the Spanish language verses the Spanish slang language. Why does it seem like when learning a new language, immersion into society style, we always learn the curse words and slang before the proper language and pronunciation? The first word I learned in Japanese is *Oppai* and the first word I learned in German was *Scheißkopf.*

So now I have to go back to the line and somehow concentrate on drug interdiction. Just as I was thinking that I need to get my head out of the driver seat of that VW I look up and see a 1988 Dodge pick-up truck with a double bed. The panochas are now ancient history, both translations. I walked over to the primary officer and told him to have the driver open the hood. As the driver stepped out to open the hood, I took him into custody and walked him into the office where we would now head to the west side and the holding cells I had mentioned earlier. As we passed the supervisors office, I advised SI Pauls that the vehicle on lane one had a double bed and asked if he would bring it around to secondary. As I reached the hallway where the holding cells were located the driver of the VW was just exiting through the door that led to secondary. I had managed to go back to roving and snatch a load before the poor gal finished peeing. I guess she must have REALLY had to go.

I patted the driver down and secured him in the holding cell. I headed to secondary and Pauls had already started to remove the tail gate for access to the compartment. We removed the gate revealing the trap door access to the compartment. A few screws later and the compartment was open and it was not empty. We could see numerous packages wrapped in wood grain contact paper. I still haven't figured out if the wood grain was supposed to fool us or if it was just what the smugglers had on the shelf but either way we retrieved 42 packages with a total weight of 137.5 pounds of marijuana.

This was one of the easiest and quickest loads of dope I ever interdicted. The smugglers even made it very easy to extract the packages by using a rope on the first packages they inserted. The rope ran the length of the bed and every package inserted after the first one went in over the rope. All we had to do was pull all the ropes at an even pace and voilà, the compartment is completely unloaded. No cutting, no tools just doper innovation. Sometimes you have to appreciate your adversary's innovation.

I called the Office of Enforcement and when the duty Agent arrived, I was somewhat disappointed. He was one of the arrogant but very lazy crew. As we walked into the interview room I felt that the paperwork on this one would play no role in court. This guy almost never brought a case to court. I was right. The driver denied knowledge and the five-minute interview ended with a call to the AUSA who declined prosecution. I was not surprised.

As far as I know this was the first and only time that an Inspector knocked down two loads in one day. Not only two loads but at two different Ports. I guess that put something in the books somewhere but what it did for me was put my butt back in a chair writing more reports. Just can't get away from them! Oh, and if you are curious, I was still just as meticulous with the paperwork as I was with an arrest. Why? That is just me.

Illustration 61: Load vehicle

Illustration 62: A very well constructed double bed truck.

Illustration 63: Packages with ropes for easy removal.

Illustration 64: Deuces were wild - double seizure day with one being a double bed and two Ports.

Two caveat's that I will toss in: The first is tied to the first seizure of the day. Neither the driver or the vehicle was local. Both were from California. This pick-up and the driver were from Nogales, Sonora – both local.

Second: when I got home, I couldn't wait to point out to my wife that thirteen was not as unlucky as she thought. I told her it was a lucky day for me! She, being brilliant, trumped me of course. She came back with her usual wit and made it very clear that if it wasn't for bad luck, I would have no luck at all. On the subject of getting two loads in one day she said that luck did not come into play for me, just long hours and hard work. She looked me in the eye and as serious as I have ever seen her said "You proved that I am right, the 13th was bad luck for those idiots that tried to run a load through you. Bad luck day all the way. For them that is." Yep, time to stand-up, look her in the eye and say, "Yes Dear, I stand corrected."

Illustration 65: My wife patiently waiting for me to shut up so she could correct me on bad luck for them vs hard work for me. I was stupid enough to bring a camera for her reaction.

ベイビー、愛してるよ

BILLION $ DOLLAR $ HIGHWAY

Gone Fishing
November 17, 1990
5 Pounds Heroin

The middle of November and the day has been absolutely boring. I started the day at the Mariposa Port of Entry on the 6 AM to 2 PM shift. When the Port folks opened the gate there was nothing there. There were no cars or trucks waiting in line as is usually the case. I suppose a probable reason for the lack of traffic was the season. Produce season was gearing up and Nogales was on the very edge of an oncoming Tsunami. The Tsunami or tidal wave if you prefer was thousands of commercial vehicles hauling produce for grocery stores in the United States. Much of the produce imported during the winter months comes from Mexico. Their produce is world class and we in America are lucky enough to enjoy fresh tomatoes, cucumbers and most every other type of produce all winter long with that salad fresh off the vines in Mexico.

Both Nogales, Arizona and Nogales, Sonora were days or maybe just hours away from five or six months of this deluge. My thought is that everyone was sleeping in and just spending time with family.

That is a good thing for the populace as well as the Port Inspectors, but it makes for a long day as a rover. With the lack of customers there was only one lane open and the Secondary Inspectors were off somewhere enjoying whatever they were enjoying.

The only excitement came at about 8:30 when the Aduana's or Mexican Customs Officers fired a few bottle rockets our way. Fireworks were prohibited from crossing the border, so they were seized and destroyed by Customs.

They caught us off guard and they were somewhat amused; if laughing their heads off is *somewhat* amused. I suppose we did look a bit funny at first, at least until we realized what was happening. Well we had our seized fireworks container also so some of the Port Inspectors fired a few back. As it turned out the fifteen-minute exchange of bottle rockets broke up the morning but fifteen minutes after the last rocket impacted the laughing was over and we were back to humdrum.

I will say one thing; international relations back then were much better than they are today. Both sides were bored to death and after the skirmish was over both sides were laughing and waving at each other like old friends. No one took offense and no one ran around crying foul. I was right there with the Port. I watched, laughed and enjoyed the show. In fact, the Senior Inspector and I walked the half mile to the border to meet with the Aduanas and shake hands, laugh our butts off and pat each other on the back. This would never happen at Grand Avenue; only at Mariposa would you ever see that.

The rest of the morning was spent working on good looking prospects, but nothing panned out. The most irritating was a pick-up truck with a very suspicious gas tank that seemed to say, 'seize me'. My CET partner Gordo was working at the Grand Avenue Port of Entry and called for assistance removing a stubborn gas tank on a Ford pick-up. I jumped in my vehicle and left the bottle rocket war zone in the rear-view mirror.

Vern Werth the CET Supervisor had gone fishing and Gordo was the acting CET supervisor so having us both at the same Port was authorized. That authorization came from Gordo of course, but as acting supervisor it was his call. Vern was an avid fisherman if going to the same "lake" on every fishing trip qualifies as avid. He apparently had his share of fish out of that lake because he was always trying to give some of them away. I never knew of anyone taking him up on his offer due to the questionable purity of the water. There were a few folks who claimed to have reeled in three eyed fish but that was never confirmed. Vern had many pictures of him holding stringers of fish, but I never counted the eyes. In fact, there were some folks that claimed several of the stringers loaded with fish were loaded with Safeway trout, but they looked good hanging from a stringer. Either way he was off with his line in the water and that was almost like a day off for us.

When I arrived at Grand Avenue Gordo was sitting there in secondary on the pavement next to an older truck that he was using as a back rest. The look on his face was oozing frustration and downright anger. As he smoked his cigarette, he looked like a dragon just about ready to release a gusher of fire. I almost made a U-turn and headed back to Mariposa where the bottle rockets were all used up ensuring no smoke or fire was brewing there.

I parked in secondary and headed over to Gordo who was now using the remainder of the cigarette he had been smoking to light a new one. 'Oh boy' I thought 'I should have made that U-turn.'

"Hey Gordo, watcha got?" I tentatively asked him.

"These expletive expletive dopers. They have this damn tank so jacked up that I can't get the damn thing off. It has to be loaded, why else would they screw this damn thing up so bad." he replied at almost a shout.

Now I was a bit confused and asked "Why? What did they do, weld it to the frame?"

He just stood there looking at me mimicking a dragon shaking his head. Yes; no, I wasn't sure because it was somewhat in the middle between the two.

Trying to calm him I said, "We can always take the bed off to get to it."

"Yea, yea we may have to." he answered, "But it is not welded, the a-holes stripped the bolts so bad you can't get a wrench on them."

Gordo had my attention now. This was actually semi good news. When I first started with

Customs my first shift was the graveyard shift, midnight to eight in the morning. On my second or third night I encountered a gas tank on a car and tapping the tank returned a very solid sound rather than a reverberating ring. I don't even recall what make or model the car was just that it had two occupants, and both were very nervous.

There were three Customs Inspectors and a Customs supervisor working that night along with three Immigration Inspectors. The car arrived when I was on primary and I referred it to Customs Secondary to have the tank checked. The other two Customs Inspectors were well seasoned or well-done crispy critters if you prefer and Immigration Inspectors work people not merchandise and that included dope. Merchandise was our job. I couldn't count the times I heard the term *search for merchandise* used in the old Customs days. In fact, a patdown was a search for merchandise whereas a frisk was a search for weapons. The technique was exactly the same, but the legal justification was totally different.

The two well-seasoned Customs Inspectors immediately punted the referral back to me. "You want it checked we will take your lane." was their response and both did exactly that. I walked the vehicle to Secondary, patted both occupants down and secured them in the holding cell as was the procedure on the midnight shift.

As I headed back to check the gas tank Johnny Climbs the midnight supervisor stopped me and asked, "Why did you secure those guys in there?"

"Their gas tank sounds solid." I responded.

"How many loaded gas tanks have you seen?" he asked.

My not quite good enough response was "Well none, but I have been tapping almost every gas tank that I encounter on the line. I started tapping them to get a base line for the sound normal tanks should emit."

"OK, that is what I thought. Check it but make it quick. I am not a baby sitter for your guests." he snarled.

I had met this man a couple of nights ago. I would learn over the years that he was a *big load-big problem; small load-small problems; no load-no problems* guy.

I headed to the car and crawled under the back to check the tank. The bolts had been stripped just like Gordo's tank. Sockets were useless and the other tools from my personal tool box just made matters worse. I went inside and asked Mr. Climbs where the tool box was located. He laughed and said "You have to bring your own tools. This is Nogales and we don't supply tools." He followed with "Is the tank loaded?"

I replied "I haven't dropped it yet. The bolts are stripped and all I have is a small socket set and some wire pliers."

Climbs turned his back to me to lean on his desk and said "Well get with it. I am already tired of babysitting."

I headed out to the other Inspectors and asked them for tools and the response was nothing but laughter.

I returned empty handed to the car and continued my ill-fated attempt to break the bolts loose with the pliers and a few minutes later Climbs came out and asked, "Is it loaded?"

I shimmied out from under the car and replied, "I am still working on it."

Climbs replied with "Can you tell me that the tank is loaded; yes or no."

"No sir I can't tell you that it is loaded." I replied.

"Get them out of here, your inspection is over." was the reply that forced me to miss my first load. With all the tanks under my belt today I can state unequivocally that the tank was loaded.

The next night I had a tool box with a brand-new pipe wrench as part of the inventory. Granted it was the smallest one I could find, but it was high quality.

Jumping back to the present I blurted out "Hell's bells Gordo, I think I just might have the answer in my tool box." As I hurried to my vehicle I thought 'finally a test subject has arrived to test my little friend'.

Well the small pipe wrench was perfect. Twenty minutes later we were looking into an empty tank. No dope, not even fuel. It looked like the tank had not been used for years.

Gordo went ballistic, cussing everybody and everything. He then put the tank in the bed of the truck and said, "I will give them a form for a tort claim but we are not putting that expletive expletive gas tank back on." and that was that.

I said to Gordo "Well I have had that pipe wrench for exactly this purpose and finally was able to try it. It sure was a good investment the way it worked out. I am on my way back to Mariposa . . ." and Gordo quite rudely interrupted me.

"Like hell you are. You stay right here. Werth is off fishing and the District Director is in DC with the Assistant District Director, so I am answering the phones for them. If Werth can go fishing knowing those two are in DC I can go home at two." he said and added "As of right now you are answering the phone calls for the District Director."

About 1:45pm I took a phone call for District from Headquarters and when I hung-up Gordo was standing there. I started to relay the gist of the call and he said, "I am out of here, it is yours."

He headed to his car, a VW Thing, and the last thing he said was "I want to forget this day. Call me if you get a load so maybe I can forget how bad this damn day was."

I was now roving solo but much less distracted with Gordo gone. Once again able to concentrate on roving I spotted a decent looking Ford LTD in lane two with a fairly short driver that looked like he was lost. I thought I would check him and his vehicle out, so I headed over to give it a look. The primary Inspector who was one of my "keep an eye on" candidates and who was notoriously slow began his methodical questions for the declaration. I knew I would have plenty of time to check the tank, fenders, doors, floor and everything else as well as listen to his declaration. I opened the passenger side rear door to check the floor and back seat while eavesdropping on his answers.

As soon as I opened the rear passenger door the rocker panel screws jumped out at me. The screws had recently been tampered with. I took a step to my left and checked the fender well. Just as I suspected, the fender well area had also been tampered with very recently. Things are looking better for a load so at this point there was no need to eavesdrop, I would be taking my own declaration from this guy in secondary.

I walked over to the driver side of the car and waited at the back door until the primary Inspector completed his declaration. Jay Operacia took a very good binding declaration. Slow methodical and very predictable. He never changed his routine and that is also very good for a load. Spotters don't miss routine either and it is one of the integrity flags I used to target what I considered weak primary officers.

When the declaration was finally completed, I asked Jay for the driver's documents and told Jay to send him to secondary. Jay handed me the resident alien card and said "Coming from Jalisco and lives in California. I got nothing else from him."

Jay was very honest but as I said a bit weak. The guy was as nervous as a child on his second trip to the dentist. I was going to use an old military cliché regarding church attendees, but some things are just better left with the troops.

I walked the vehicle to secondary where I attempted to take a secondary declaration. By now the guy was so nervous that he had trouble understanding the questions in Spanish or English and he had more trouble trying to answer or for that matter speak. The guy was literally falling apart.

I solicited what I could from the guy from Jalisco which was about as much as I could get out of him and then walked him to the secondary holding area where I performed a patdown and secured him in the holding area.

I headed back to the vehicle and took a closer look at the suspect areas. I had already checked the rear passenger side rocker panel, so I checked the front passenger rocker panel cover and it had also been tampered with.

I walked to the driver side and checked both front and rear rocker panel covers and neither had been touched.

I removed the rocker panel cover from the front passenger side and attempted to insert a probe, but its progress was blocked. I attempted to push the probe through the blockage but that was not happening. Whatever was blocking the way was first, not natural or factory and second extremely hard.

Not a problem that is why CET carried drills. I broke out my trusty drill and went to town. This move drew several Inspectors over to watch. When the drill broke through there was very little resistance. I was fairly sure I had not hit either marijuana or cocaine but when I pulled the drill bit out what I saw was totally unexpected.

The bit had a weird light brown crystalline or maybe melted glass like substance on it that had a tail and swirl resembling soft serve ice cream. I knew that whatever I had drilled through was very hard and that also told me that the drill bit was extremely hot when it completed its task. Hot but hot enough to melt glass? I didn't think so.

One of the Inspectors said, "What the heck is that?"

I answered "I don't know but I know what it is not. It is not marijuana or coke so that leads me to think it must be heroin."

So now we all went brain dead and started doing what I tell folks never to do; we started sniffing the substance. We all agreed on one thing, whatever it was it had no odor.

One of the bystanders asked, "Why do you think it is heroin?"

I answered "Just a matter of elimination. I am very familiar with marijuana and somewhat familiar with cocaine. I am not at all familiar with heroin so through reasonable deduction, my guess is heroin.

One of the guys said "Get Velo over here, he had a *flower power* helmet when he was in Vietnam, so he should know what cooked heroin looks like."

I said, "I might have had a peace symbol on my helmet when I was in the mean green, but it sure doesn't mean I know what cooked heroin looks like." Just for clarity, I did not have flowers, paisleys, love with the o being a heart, none of that just a little peace symbol.

My comments went unheard because not five minutes later here came Velo. He looked at the substance, sniffed it then looked at me and said, "What is it?"

I looked at the other Inspectors and then at Velo and I said, "My guess is heroin, but I won't know until we test it."

We all headed to the supervisor's office where I ran a field test for heroin. The test confirmed that it was indeed heroin.

This brings me back to the dumb move of the day. If a small piece of that Mexican Brown heroin broke off at just the wrong time whoever was attempting to play drug dog would have snorted pure uncut heroin. Not good. God made test kits for a very good reason.

I returned to the offending vehicle and began removing the rear rocker panel cover to see if there might be a trap door under it but it no such luck. The rear panel looked exactly like the front panel and when probed the probe met resistance at the same depth as the front panel. There was definitely something non-factory in there as well.

Since there were no trap doors my next move was to check the rear fender well area where access to the rocker panel would be gained. Under the mud, dirt and tar in the fender well there was a trap door right were the rocker panel ends. I removed a couple of screws and pried the trap door open.

Looking into the now open rocker panel what I saw was nylon ropes crammed in the void. By pulling the ropes out the answers to many questions were revealed. Attached to the ropes were metal canisters. The canisters were numbered apparently to ensure that for whatever reason the right box was in its designated location.

Further inspection either gave me some insight into their engineering or threw me off into left field as my deduction was nothing more than a guess. We will never know I suppose but I could see where the rocker panel screws had been altered by cutting a portion of the bottom of the screw off. Looking at the metal boxes I could see where the screws had made contact with the boxes. My deduction is that each box had to be in the exact location for the screws to clamp down on the boxes to keep them from sliding in the compartment while at the same time fitting flush on the rocker panel cover. If the screws were not flush the screws would have been a dead giveaway that something was amiss. Even Jay might have noticed the altered screws if he opened the doors on the passenger side. Not likely but when you have that much heroin at stake who would take a risk that the primary guy might just wander over there for whatever reason and open the doors. Nope, they wanted everything to be perfect and it was to the untrained eye.

I brought the canisters to the supervisor's office and secured them in a dope locker. The Passenger Processing supervisor volunteered to call the Office of Enforcement, so I told him that while he was making the call, I was going to move the driver from the secondary holding area to the more secure lock-up or cells if you prefer in the supervisor's office. I walked to the secondary holding area, placed handcuffs on the driver and began the walk from secondary to the office. The car was sitting two lanes from the secondary facility with the passenger side away from the secondary holding area. As we approached the vehicle and began to walk past the car the driver was looking very intently at his vehicle. As the passenger side of the car became visible first, we could see the wheel lying on the pavement. Next was the fender well cover and then the fender well area with the open but empty rocker panel.

Illustration 66: Illustration 1: View seen by the driver as he was being transported to the supervisor's office.

As soon as the rocker panel was visible the driver collapsed in a dead faint. I had him in an escort hold so he did not hit the ground as I was able to hold him up. I carefully laid him down and several other Inspectors who were watching came over to assist. Moments later he was back and was able to walk to the supervisor's office.

We had an ambulance respond and the medics determined that he had fainted with no further medical attention necessary.

Talking about an involuntary admission of guilt! The subject was arrested and his guilty plea solidified his involvement and his knowledge in this smuggling attempt.

When the OE case agent arrived, I opened the metal canisters and removed the packages. I used a probe in an attempt extract some of the product from each package, but nothing came out on the probe. I then made a small incision that revealed a brown crystalline like substance that when tapped with a screwdriver broke into chunks. A minute piece of crystal from each package was tested with all testing positive for the properties of heroin. The packages were weighed on the calibrated scale with a total weight of five pounds.

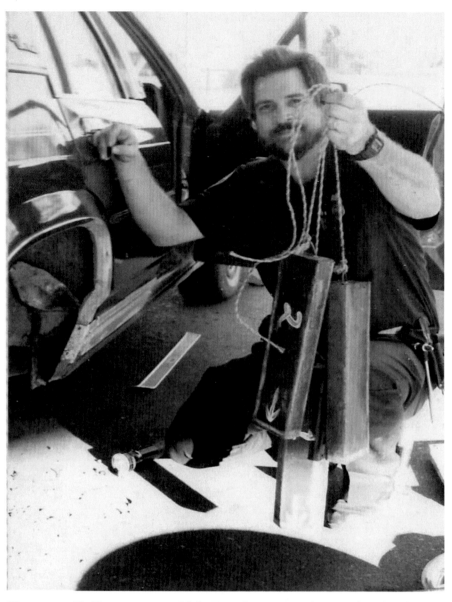

Illustration 67: Not a stringer of fish. Trap door into rocker panel is clearly visible as are the loading sequence for the canisters.

Illustration 68: Another shot of the catch of the day.

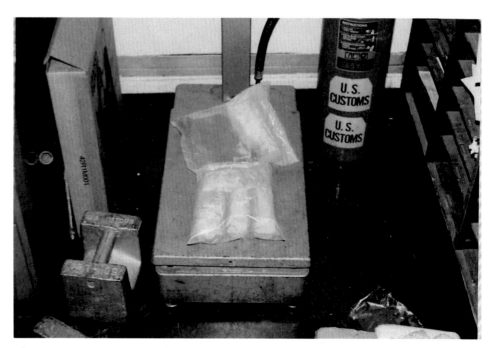

Illustration 69: Packages of heroin on the scale.

Illustration 70: As I have stated previously, money is their god.

BILLION $ DOLLAR $ HIGHWAY

Operation Shadow Wolf
1991

The Grand Avenue Port of Entry was preparing for a face lift, a face lift that would also bring the Port a new name, the DeConcini Port of Entry (POE) in honor of Senator Dennis DeConcini. The renovation was very extensive with a total rebuild still in the planning stages at the time of this chapter. Bids had already gone out, been awarded and one of the construction companies had just began the per-construction ground work gearing up for the surveyors and other preparation folks. One contractor (on the management side) had arrived with a small Airstream tow-along trailer for temporary quarters and had been granted permission to park his camping trailer in a remote corner of our extended parking lot (soon to be the temporary port). The guy was staying there at his own risk and that is not to be taken lightly. There are a few things to consider with this arrangement including the fact that back in the 1990's in Nogales the smugglers ran drugs and illegal aliens anywhere they thought they would be successful and pay the lowest Gatekeeper (or Plaza owner) fee.[3] This included our parking lot, the very one with a new Airstream resident.

Illustration 71: Imagery courtesy of the U.S. Geological Survey. Visit the USGS at https://usgs.gov.

My position on the CET team ensured my knowledge of our guest and the fact that he drove a white full-sized Bronco. I also knew that he could not be given the access code for the employee entrance to the parking lot, so he was given special access to enter the area from the

---

[3]Gatekeepers are covered in another chapter.

east *EXIT* gate.

Totally independent of the reconstruction plans at the Port, the District Director (DD) instructed the CET team to develop an operation that would include Customs Patrol Officers (CPO) also known as the Shadow Wolves. He emphasized that this operation would be to bring the CPO's to Nogales on a detail and the area of the operation was restricted to urban Nogales.

The Shadow Wolves worked the west desert almost exclusively on the Tohono O'odham Indian Reservation (TO). The Shadow Wolfs were non-uniformed Customs Officers who were expert trackers and knew how to blend into the landscape wherever they worked. One requirement was that they must be all or part Native American. The DD wanted to get new eyes and new thoughts on working the narcotics smuggling outside the port in the metro area. The operation was planned and I was the lead point of contact for the operation. We had several known smuggling areas lined up as target areas for the week-long operation. On day one the CPOs were going to drive over from the TO and I would brief them on the operation and the areas where we would be running the operations. Each night we would work designated locations known to be used by drug smugglers. After the briefing we would all head out to do a physical drive-by of each area. Our initial meet and greet was in the secondary exam area at the Grand Avenue Port of Entry.

As the Shadow Wolves arrived at the POE, they pulled into secondary at about 5 PM where I met them. Some of the Wolves were familiar faces and some I had never seen. We proceeded to the CET office where the briefing took place. Then off on a tour of the areas where the operation was to take place. With all the pleasantries complete I told the detail that the briefing and tour was close of business for the day and told them to enjoy the evening and that we would meet the next day and kick off the operation. The team leader promptly advised me that they still had three hours of their shift remaining, so they would like to get started with the operation to complete their shift. I told them that it was not part of the operations plan, but we could wing it with a verbal plan.

For time, ease and safety I decided that we would run an operation west of the Port that included the Customs employee parking lot. We kicked the operation off shortly thereafter and I had the Wolves set-up close enough to the area of the parking lot for a quick and easy response time. Everything was set for our impromptu parking lot operation with a simple operation order (verbal only, nothing written). My mission was to find a place to *lay in* where I could see any incursions and direct the Wolves response to interdict the smugglers. I knew of a good location just inside the parking lot near the exit gate. There were some hedge type bushes that I could lay up in and should be fairly undetectable. I cautiously moved in and took up my observation of the known smuggling route hoping for a smuggling attempt. I remained in my concealed position for a couple of hours and the only activity came when a large group of illegal aliens breached the fence near the Blind center (a center operated by the Santa Cruz County Association for The Blind). The group ran to I-19 and headed east in a direct line to where one of the Wolves was set-up. Now back then we were Customs not immigration, so the group was a Border Patrol problem, not ours. I was sure they did not have dope, so I made the broadcast that they were not our target. As they ran past the Wolf his comments threatened to expose me and my observation point as I had to use every cell in my body to prevent me from erupting in laughter and remembering those comments still make me chuckle today. He called out over the radio to his fellow Wolves in his usual monotonous tone and uttered the now infamous words that ended with, "you guys should see this, looks like the damn Boston Marathon".

My thoughts and hopes were that this large group was either testing the waters or was bait to lure any law enforcement out if there were any present. If the group got through the dope would follow. Well – no. No dope, nada. Therefore, we waited and watched. A bit later I saw our guest, the construction supervisor come in the exit gate and proceed to his home sweet home. Just as he arrived at the Airstream, I hear running footsteps approaching the pedestrian entrance to the parking lot. The pedestrian entrance is very near the exit gate and only Port personnel had access to the parking lot through this gate. This being the case when the gate opened, I was sure it was someone from the Port. Sure enough two probationary Inspectors, Herman Duggan and Kim Blair, opened the pedestrian gate and ran past my location not three feet from where I was laid in. They continued to run for about ten yards and then stopped.

As they stood there looking Herman said, "Where did it go?"

Kim shrugged his shoulders and answered, "I don't know, I am sure it came in here."

To which Herman replied, "Yea me too."

Then the pedestrian gate opened again! "What the hell are you guys doing?" It was Supervisory Customs Inspector (SCI) Cosmos Linex from the Port. Cosmos was one of the best supervisors ever to wear the uniform, hard as nails but fair, and he was far from happy.

"We saw a vehicle come in here, so we were chasing it." replied Herman.

"You are chasing a vehicle by yourselves and didn't tell me where you were going or what you were doing?" Cosmos asked as if what he had heard was unbelievable or maybe just unbelievably stupid.

Yep, Cosmos was on the warpath and rightfully so. The POE and for that matter all areas adjacent to the border with Mexico are dangerous areas. When you add a suspicious vehicle entering a controlled parking lot through the exit gate the danger and need for caution is escalated exponentially.

Poor Herman tried to save it with "Well we didn't have time."

"You didn't have time? You didn't have time to go through the office rather than go around the office?" Cosmos actually seemed dumbfounded.

Before reconstruction the office Cosmos was referring to was located between the outbound lanes and the inbound lanes. What Cosmos was saying was that one could come in the east door to the office walk through the office and exit the west door, in essence a short cut to get to the parking lot. The hole that Herman was digging was filling with quicksand now. I remained motionless and concealed through the meeting that was going from bad to worse by the minute. It finally ended with "Where is the vehicle" from Cosmos and Herman saying, "We lost it."

That ended that with Cosmos telling the two Sonny Crockett's to get back to the Port. I watched the two heading back to secondary with their tails between their legs following Cosmos.

I remained where I was at for another hour or so until 2200 hrs or 10:00 PM and then got on the radio and ended the operation affectionately known as 'Operation Boston Marathon'. The name was never officially or unofficially for that matter put into writing because explaining the name was, well – better omitted.

I radioed the Shadow Wolves that Operation Boston Marathon was terminated and directed them back to Grand Avenue Secondary for a quick debriefing. As the Wolves departed secondary after the short debriefing, I saw Herman and Kim sitting on one of the examination tables watching us. As I headed to the now famous employee parking lot, I had to walk by the car chasing duo. As I approached, I heard them talking about "that fucking SCI Cosmos". I respected Cosmos as a supervisor and also knew what these guys were talking about. I also knew that the fucking SCI was absolutely in the right.

Now I was pissed off and thought it was time to educate these two rookies and adjust their attitude. I walked over and asked, "Are you guys ready to see Mr. Fredericks (the District Director) tomorrow?"

"See Mr. Fredericks, why would we be seeing the District Director?" as expected it was Herman, the apparent self-appointed spokesman.

"Well after you two screwed up our operation tonight I had to let him know that it went bust. He had brought in the Shadow Wolves from the Tohono O'odham Indian Reservation to run a special operation in the parking lot and everything went as planned until you two showed up" I may have stretched the truth a bit, but it worked, and Herman played right into it.

With eyes as big as saucers Herman mumbled "Shadow Wolves, what are Shadow Wolves?"

"What? You didn't see me with them here in secondary today and tonight?" the truth, the whole truth and nothing but the truth. "They are Native American Customs Patrol Officers that work almost strictly on the TO. They are the best trackers you will ever see and for this operation they are totally unknown to the MFJP (Mexican Federal Judicial Police) here in Nogales."

Herman perked up a bit and said "Oh yea, I saw all those guys. We were wondering who they were and what they were doing here." Yep he stepped right into it again.

I continued "What they were doing here was working Operation BM. One of my informants put us on to an MFJP Coke load that was to be run through our parking lot tonight. They had a rig to get it over the fence and load it into a white Bronco. Once in the Bronco they would head out of our parking lot to I-19. To any Law Enforcement who happened to be in the area and on the Border Patrol cameras it would look like one of us departing. No one would stop it under the assumption that if was a Customs employee."

I certainly had their interest, so I continued "A janitor had arranged for the Bronco to come in the exit gate and if things hadn't gotten fouled up, he would be in jail tonight. Since it was coke and MFJP there were spotters everywhere and to the spotters the Wolves looked like anything but law enforcement."

Hmmm, dead silence. I rambled on to my now captive audience of two "Everything was going like clockwork until you two guys came bouncing right into the area of operation. The damn Bronco never even came to a stop. He blew out the west exit gate and was gone. This was humongous to the DD so he was waiting for me to call him on the outcome. I made the call and there was dead silence for about 30 seconds then he said he wanted to see you guys tomorrow before you go to the line, then he just hung up. I am going to let your SCI know to have you report as soon as you go on duty."

My wishful thinking is that these guys will learn a lesson that they will not forget. It could save their life someday. Unfortunately, there is always a 'but' and in this case the 'but' really pissed me off. Herman jumped up from the table where he was sitting and said, "SCI Cosmos sent us."

I was shocked and said "Really? I saw and heard differently. I saw you guys come in the pedestrian gate on a dead run and you asked Kim where the vehicle had gone. Kim answered he didn't know. Then Cosmos came in and chewed your asses for not informing him where you were going and what you were doing. He sure as hell didn't send you from the conversation I heard."

Kim finally broke his silence and asked "Where were you? I didn't see you."

I answered "I was laid in not ten yards from you when your conversation with Cosmos took place. And no, you didn't see me; neither did the driver of the load vehicle or the spotters. But I was right there with you."

Kim was now doing the talking and he said, "We are on probation for another month, are we going to get fired?"

Poor Kim was almost in tears, so I let him have it, I said "If I were telling the truth you probably would be job hunting tomorrow, but the truth is the Bronco you were chasing is a contractor for the construction company surveying the port. I was laying in on Operation BM and the CPO's were my interceptors *if* I spotted a load. I heard you cussing Cosmos who could have really jacked you up, but he didn't. This scenario I just played through could very well have been true. If so, Cosmos would have been briefed and when you checked with him, he would have stopped you from screwing it up. If this scenario was indeed reality but take me and the CPO's out of the picture where would you guys be now? You would have walked into a full-blown drug cartel cocaine smuggling attempt alone. You would be lucky to walk out alive. Let this be a lesson, when you ran past me, I was less than three feet from the path you took. When you stopped you were no more than ten yards from me. Remember, I am a good guy but if I were a smuggler where would you be right now?" I did not expect or receive an answer, but I could see the point was made. Training session over.

God must have been watching as He always is. On day three of Operation Shadow Wolf God put an exclamation mark on the training. We were working the Trade Zone that is west of the Mariposa Port of Entry. The area was very remote at the time and used quite often to run loads normally as vehicle drive throughs. A drive through is where the drug traffickers use vehicles to drive across the border many times cross country and sometimes on unimproved roads. Some of the warehouses in the Trade Zone are literally built on the edge of Ephraim Canyon with maybe ten yards from the south side of the building to a thirty-foot drop into the canyon.

The trade zone is a very dangerous place to run drug operations. So, the ConOps and the OpsPlan specified very clearly that there would be no Customs presence in the Trade Zone. When I gave the CPO's the driving tour of each night's area of operations the Trade Zone was the first one I hit. I referred to the OpsPlan and clearly stated that the Trade Zone was **not** a stand-by location.

The night of the operation I assigned each CPO a stand-by area that we had visited on the tour with none closer than one mile from the border. Sounds easy but sometimes people just don't listen. On that fateful night this was certainly the case.

Two of us from the CET team were doing the trade zone surveillance from the roof of the Mariposa POE. We did not even let the regular Inspectors know that we were in the area. At 9:00 PM we slipped into the commercial facility that had closed at 8:00 PM and we waited there for an hour until the Port closed at 10:00. After the last Inspector departed MAP we made our way to the MAP utility room where we could gain access to the roof. Just after the Port closed at 10:00 PM we observed spotters crossing the canyon heading to the trade zone. They had arrived in a convoy that was now staged in Mexico on the south side of Ephraim. A Ford LTD pulled up to a trench that Customs had cut in the canyon to prevent drive throughs. The trench was a good six feet deep and ten feet wide, but the dopers are creative; they bridged the trench in about ten seconds pulling what looked like runway mat out of a truck and making a temporary bridge.

The LTD was now staged at the ready just south of the 'bridge' and the spotters had entered the Trade Zone. Everything was going just great for an illegal crossing with us on the ready to intercept; until the shots rang out.

One of the spotters saw the CPO sitting in his vehicle in the *trade zone* and probably assumed he was a rival drug trafficker. The spotter pulled a rifle out from under his trench coat and as he began to bring it to bear on the CPO, the CPO fired his weapon through the windshield of his vehicle at the well-armed spotter. The spotter absconded back to Mexico and by the time the three spotters arrived at the staging point the bridge was gone as were all but one vehicle. The spotters jumped in the waiting vehicle and that was as close to a load as we got on Operation Shadow Wolf. Fortunately, the only two casualties were the windshield and the CPO's pride.

Over the years Kim and I used to reminisce about the "old days" and Kim must have thanked me a hundred times for that "wake-up". By the day after the trade zone incident everyone in the Port had heard about the *Trade Zone Shooting* as it became known. Kim referred to that unplanned educational event every time we reminisced and every time he would end that memory with "I get goose bumps every time I think about us in that parking lot with a well-armed and ready to shoot cartel if that had been the case."

Herman, well let's just say that when he resigned fifteen years later the going away party was a few days after his departure.

BILLION $ DOLLAR $ HIGHWAY

Operation Construction Hole
1991 to 1993

The Nogales Grand Avenue Port of Entry (POE) underwent a face lift from 1991 to 1993. During this period of time a temporary POE was established just west of the Port. The location of the temporary port was far enough from the permanent port to preclude visual observation of the area under construction. The construction site soon became a favorite avenue for all aspects of illegal activity crossing the border; it was a virtual open door to and from Mexico.

Smuggling organizations cut holes in the poorly maintained construction fence which now served as the International Boundary. The holes or gates were owned by Gatekeepers working for the smuggling organizations. Polleto's[4] or chickens in English worked the "holes" day and night for the gatekeepers. The Polleto's (also called coyotes) allowed passage through their "hole" for a price. The price depended on how much the Polleto "decided" the customer could pay. The Polleto's would then escort their fare through the hole and into the United States. If the customer did not come up with the money (no credit cards!), they could not use the "gate". If anyone used the hole without paying, the Polleto would simply stick a gun in the face of the hole jumper and take what he wanted. If the hole jumper did not have enough to satisfy the Gatekeeper the Polleto would pull the trigger. This was punishment and a message to other illegal crosser's that the hole was owned.

This practice was taking place at the bottom steps which led to the front doors of the U.S. Customs District Headquarters. I knew about this activity as did the other members of the Contraband Enforcement Team (CET) team. As senior member of the team I was elected to put pressure on the CET Supervisor, Vern Werth, to talk to the District Director (DD) about running an operation to try to curtail the blatant illegal activities. Werth was an 8 - 4, Monday through Friday type supervisor who would rather ignore these goings on than take a chance on an operation requiring his presence outside those parameters. With the entire team ready to resign over the construction site dilemma Werth finally agreed to approach the DD with our request.

I have often wondered if Werth actually approached the DD or if coincidence saved the team, at any rate the team was saved by an Office of Enforcement (OE) Customs Patrol Officer Lefty Unzer. Information was received by Lefty through an informant that Cocaine was being run through the hole in the construction fence by an organization using females who were body carrying. (Body carrying is a technique where contraband is secured to the body, usually by tape, under the clothing). Lefty had approached the DD with a request for a joint OE/I&C (Inspection and Control) operation with the CET team to intercept the mule train of cocaine. The DD agreed and as fate would have it Werth would not be required to break his 8 - 4, Monday through Friday routine. I would be acting supervisor for I&C on this joint operation.

A Concept of Operation (ConOps) was put together, an Operations Plan (OpsPlan) designed

---

[4]Polleto - term used for alien smugglers, the illegal aliens look like chicks following a mother hen.

and approved, and the wheels of Operation Construction Hole began to turn. The operation, due to its location, was fairly simple as far as logistics, planning and equipment went. Dress was civilian clothing. Vehicles, optical aids, radios and all related equipment were personally assigned and no special equipment would be needed. There were two surveillance points of the holes in the fence. The first, believe it or not, was the south window of the CET Office. The second would be the south and east windows of the Mission Support section of District Headquarters. As both positions were located within a protected area each position was manned by one Inspector. The plan called for three vehicles, two with one Inspector and one OE Special Agent and the third with one OE Special Agent solo. A total of three vehicles, four Inspectors and three Special Agents would be used. A fourth vehicle was on stand-by and would be used by the two Inspectors manning the surveillance points but would not be used in the tail away or the take down. The two Inspectors from the surveillance points would proceed to the stop only after it was initiated. We would not break cover until the convoy was several miles out of town. This was to ensure that spotters for the drug traffickers could not alert the convoy that they may have been compromised if we were observed by the bad guys. The operation would run from dusk to dawn over several days.

The planned response to a load or suspected load of narcotics entering through the hole was to have one of two veteran Inspectors (myself or Rogger Bivouac) ride with Agent Unzer. When notified by the surveillance team that a possible load had entered, the rider with Unzer would disembark and walk to within a few feet of the person or hopefully group of smugglers. At that point, close foot surveillance would be possible. Our two-way radios were equipped with an earpiece, a remote microphone which was pinned just under the collar and a push-to-talk switch that was secreted in our non-gun hand with the wire from the radio running down the shirt sleeve. If the Inspector performing the foot surveillance determined that the party was indeed carrying narcotics, he would notify the mobile units via radio that the group was carrying contraband. He would then keep the team apprised of the group's progress and follow the group to either a stash location or to a load-up point where a vehicle would then move the group north. OE would decide when and where to take the smugglers down. If they went to a stash house, we would probably take them down as they approached the house before entering. If they went mobile in a vehicle a tail away would be initiated and we would take them down further north. If we got far enough away from the hole in the fence, maybe it would not be burned and we might be able to get another load or two until they realized that we were working it.

On the first night I was with Lefty Unzer and would be the Inspector who would affect the foot surveillance on suspected loads. Inspectors Rogger Bivouac and Charles Browning were performing the surveillance and Inspector Archalo Brooks was with Special Agent Avers Friar; Agent Curly Ramble was riding solo.

Just after midnight Browning advised over the radio that three prospects, two males and one female were approaching from Mexico and that one of the males had his hand inside his jacket as if carrying something. As they came through the hole Rogger Bivouac picked them up and indicated that he was sure that the one subject had something small inside his jacket. Lefty Unzer and I talked it over as to whether or not we were willing to take the chance of burning the surveillance on the first day for one small package. The decision was made that on this one I would follow the subjects as far as possible and then try to take them down as if our encounter

162

were totally coincidental.

Our plans never materialized as Bivouac came back on the radio and advised that the subjects had returned to the area in front of District where they stopped to engage in a conversation, but it appeared that the trio was headed back to Mexico.

Bivouac came back on the radio, advised that the two males appeared to be arguing and the female had moved just behind one of the males. The two appeared to be a couple who were arguing with the other male.

It was also noted that the subject with the "package" in his coat still had his "GUN".

"He's got a gun, he's got a gun!" Bivouac yelled into the radio "and he is robbing a couple on the steps of District. I'm going down!"

I yelled to Lefty "Let's go, let's go!"

Lefty and I were set up no more than two blocks from the District steps. Bivouac had to cut through two rooms, go down a hallway about fifty feet, down two flights of stairs, back fifty feet and then another twenty-five feet to the steps. Bivouac beat us there by about fifteen seconds. He was standing there with a husband and wife combo crouching on the ground. The armed robber had absconded back to Mexico when Bivouac yelled *"Aduana"* (Customs). The Mexican couple said that the bandit had taken their money and jewelry just that quickly.

The female told us that they entered through the hole without paying the gatekeeper or guide because they did not have any money. She said that they did not know who the other guy was and that he was following them when they entered. As they were going north just a short distance from the border the bandit brandished his weapon and told them that they had to return to Mexico because they had not paid the toll. She said as they approached the hole there were several other males near the fence in Mexico. The bandit began talking to the group in Mexico, so the couple stopped. They could see that the guys in Mexico were very bad men obviously the gatekeepers of the hole and the couple refused to give themselves up to them.

The female broke down in tears and had to hold on to her husband for stability when she added that she clearly heard the bandits talking among themselves and it was obvious that they were going to shoot the male had we not arrived on scene. The bandits took everything those two had during the robbery and were still unhappy with the couple who didn't have enough money for their liking, therefore the male would pay with his life. This is a typical way the gatekeepers and their coyotes pissed on the fire hydrant (like a dog marking their territory) to send a message that crossing their territory without payment and permission would not be tolerated and the penalty is a death sentence as punishment.

Since this was not a Federal crime but fell under State and local jurisdiction, we notified the Nogales Police Department who responded and arrived with about six vehicles all running emergency equipment. When they arrived we turned the case over to them.

We had probably saved the male's life and probably saved the female from a brutal rape. That's reality and it sure gives you a good feeling. Still, we all felt as if the whole incident was a complete disaster for our operation. The bandits nabbed everything of value that the couple possessed and still got back to Mexico with their ill-gotten prize. Worse yet, it now seemed obvious that we were watching the construction site! Damn, the first night out and the operation seemed blown!

The next night we went out again only a little less optimistic due to the previous night's occurrences. Night two saw Bivouac partnered with Unzer, Browning partnered with Friar, Brooks in the CET office and me in the Mission Support office. The second hour of the surveillance I observed two males come through the hole, stroll north a little way and return to the hole and wait. I called on the radio and advised that it "looks like we have a couple of coyotes staging" (for a crossing). Sure enough, minutes later twelve females worked their way through the hole. All twelve appeared to be quite bulky under their coats. Just as the last female passed through the hole, a male on the Mexican side passed a sports type bag through the hole to one of the coyotes on the north side. As the group of twelve females and the two coyotes, one now carrying the sports bag, passed directly below me and directly under a light I could see the sports bag looked rectangular. Bags with cloths in them usually look oval and do not have well defined edges.

I radioed all units "This looks like it might be the ones we're waiting for".

Lefty Unzer radioed back and said, "You call it, are they loaded?"

"O.K., yes, I'll call it. The women look pretty good but I'm not sure because of their coats but, the bag the guy is carrying, I'm sure. I can see the outline of packages." I replied.

"Bivouac's out and on his way to intercept the group." Lefty Unzer advised and added "Everyone get moving. Rogger it's your show from here on keep us posted as often as you can without burning yourself."

Rogger whispered into his radio "They're cutting through between the Safeway and the bus station."

'Perfect' I thought, I can move to Mort O'Kennedy's office and get a perfect view from there. I moved to the office and went to the window and there they were, a nice little convoy, headed west with Bivouac no more than ten feet behind them. Now a little background, Rogger Bivouac is Hispanic and with his Oakland Raider jacket and ball cap on backward, carrying his small UDA (Undocumented Alien) bag he blended perfectly and was totally unnoticed by the group. He was just another fence jumper to them.

The group continued on across the street in the direction of the Burger King parking lot. I called to Brooks who was still in the CET office and said "This looks like a go Archalo. Let's head down to the vault (our car was stationed just outside the door near the vault). Looks like they will be doing a tail away and I want to be ready to respond if things break bad."

Just as Archalo Brooks and I got to the top of the stairs a voice on the radio screamed "He's got a gun! He's got a gun!" Déjà vu, it was Rogger Bivouac.

Then came the words you never want to hear; "Shots fired! We have shots fired, and he is headed back to the hole."

"I'm going out the front." I told Archalo "You head out the back here and get some of the Inspectors from the Port. If he gets by me maybe you guys can get him at the hole."

I ran to the front of the District building and slammed out the doors. Flew down the steps and waited where the shooter would have to pass me to get to the hole. Soon I heard running footsteps coming towards me. I waited with gun in hand for the runner to come into view. I would have about twenty feet from the time I saw him until he reached me, plenty of safe distance. Here he comes, got him!

I quickly leaned my upper body out from my cover position and extended my gun hand aiming the S&W auto into the runners' center mass some twenty feet away but closing quickly and yelled "Aduana." That was all managed to say before I saw my target and lowered the weapon. Damn if it wasn't Charles Browning.

"Where the hell is he Charles?" I said. "No way that he got by me here. He couldn't have beaten me here, no way."

"I don't know, I lost him in the Safeway parking lot." Charles said. Then after taking a few deep breaths he continued, "When he took off running from Rogger I jumped out of the car and when he saw me coming out of the car, he headed back through the Safeway lot."

I jumped on the radio and said, "He didn't make it to the hole; he must still be in the Safeway parking lot."

Bivouac came back "I'm on the west side. I'll be working my way to the east. Be careful, I recognize this guy. He's our armed robber from last night!"

"10-4. Charles Browning and I will be moving from east to west." I replied.

Charles Browning and I headed for the Safeway parking lot and started a sweep. There was a line of cars parked diagonally in the lot leaving a path about two feet wide between them and the north wall of the District building. I took the path and Charles Browning took the back side of the cars, thus eliminating any avenue of escape to the east.

We worked our way through the lot, car to car, knowing that our gunman was more than willing to kill. The area is very dark and only a nose under the bumper afforded a view under each car. The night was cold and as I peered under the cars, I remember holding my breath so the vapor would not hinder my visibility looking from dark to even darker. I knew that the shooter had the advantage as he would be looking from dark to lighter. Each time I dropped my face below a bumper I felt as if I were in a spotlight. As I peered into the darkness under the cars waiting eternally, the few tenths of a second, for my eyes to adjust to the pitch blackness, I expected to see a flash. The last thing I would ever see would by a muzzle flash at point blank range.

As I began crouching down under a car approximately one third of the length of the parking lot from where we began the search, I heard Rogger Bivouac yell "Aduana! Aduana de los Estatus Unitos!" (Translation: Customs! US Customs)

I came up and saw Rogger Bivouac crouching at the back tire of a car about four cars away. He had his gun pointed under the back of the car at the trunk area.

The last I saw of Charles Browning was him standing at the trunk portion of the car I was about to look under. Yes, I have heard of supernatural acts during Adrenalin rushes, lifting up cars and such, but I'd never seen one until that night. Charles Browning moved the four-car distance at light speed and without moving his feet. By the time I got to the scene Charles Browning was laying on his stomach with the barrel of his gun in the shooters ear. The shooter had his gun pointed at Bivouac, Mexican stand-off style.

Well, I guess looking down the barrel of Rogger Bivouac's gun and feeling the sub-freezing steel of Charles Browning's hardware playing rhythms on one's eardrum would be enough to convince even the hardiest assassins that this was a lose-lose situation. The loser very carefully placed the weapon on the pavement and when told carefully squirmed out from his position under the car.

I used the radio to advise the team that we had apprehended the subject in the Safeway parking lot. Within minutes all three OE agents arrived to take custody of our shooter. When they arrived, I asked them where they had secured the mule train of cocaine smugglers.

The three Agents looked at each other and Ramble said "Mule train? I guess that we got so involved in the shooting and the chase that we lost them."

'Got so *involved* in the shooting and chase', I thought. 'I was *involved* in the shooting and the chase but I sure as hell don't remember seeing any of these guys going car to car with us through that damn parking lot.'

I looked at Rogger Bivouac and said, "Well Rogger, tell me, everything was going so well what the hell happened over at the BK? Did that pile of dung make you?"

"Hell no!" he said emphatically "He made someone else. I just ended up in the middle again!"

Sometimes you just have to sit back, shake your head and say, "God smiled on you tonight." and that is my response to the events that took place on that night for sure.

As Rogger Bivouac relayed his incredible tale Charles Browning, Archalo Brooks, three U. S. Customs Special Agents and I sat in awe without uttering a word until the last detail was orated then, in unison, emitted a response, "God's alive and well." We said that as if it had been rehearsed and that is another one that goes in my *first and only time that happened* folder.

"And he was looking out for you tonight, Rogger." I added.

As Rogger Bivouac and the convoy crossed I-19 headed to the BK parking lot, the lead escort spotted another male hanging around outside of the BK. The escort apparently recognized the new player as one of a rival group. They exchanged words which Rogger Bivouac could not make out. Then our guy pulled a gun, the other player reacted faster than our guy and managed to side step the first shot. He then grabbed the shooters gun arm and brought the arm down to the ground at about a forty-five-degree angle. Shot's two and three went into the pavement during the struggle. In the meantime, Rogger Bivouac responded by pulling his weapon, bringing it to bear, and calling out "Aduana!" Both wrestlers, at that point, looked at Bivouac. Bivouac then has his déjà vu moment for the night and recognized the guy as the armed robber of the previous night. The shooter aimed his gun at Rogger and Rogger pulled the trigger on his semi-automatic. Nothing! The weapon malfunctioned! As the shooter came to bear on Rogger, he pulled the trigger on his revolver. Nothing! His weapon, which had just fired three shots with no problem, malfunctioned!

 Mr. Shooter elected to run and repair. Rogger elected to repair and chase. After Rogger cleared his weapon and made it functional he lit into his pursuit. Sometime during the scenario Rogger managed (subconsciously) to relay the pertinent details over his two-way radio.

Thanks to Bivouac's cool headiness, professionalism and instincts we all met in the Safeway parking lot with the successful apprehension of a would-be professional killer. Since this tied in to the previous night's robbery and probable botched murder, we turned this case over to Nogales, PD who was on scene after responding to numerous calls from the public regarding shots fired.

Now with a border thug in the custody of Nogales's finest and the OE folks moving out Code 3 to put out a BOLO (Be On the Look Out) to our law enforcement partners in hopes of intercepting the load vehicle before it made it to Tucson which is the probable next link in the distribution chain, I told the guys to write up witness statements and then call it a night. Rogger Bivouac saw a white 12 passenger van in the BK parking lot and the mule train appeared to be heading for it so there was still hope of taking down the load. I went up to the CET office to notify the District Director (DD) or the Assistant District Director (ADD) of the night's events. This was before personal cell phones and the only ones you saw were on TV and looked like a suitcase. Voice mail was an answering machine (tape recorder) connected to your telephone generally sitting right next to the phone and e-mail was only a concept at best.

As I arrived in the CET office the phone was ringing. Wow, I thought, the DD has already heard about the action. I hurried over to the phone and answered "Nogales CET, this line is not secure". The voice on the other end was not one that I wanted to hear, in fact quite the opposite.

"This is Houston Sector what's going on there, I heard shots fired?" It was USCS regional communications, a direct line to the Regional Commissioner, the DD's boss. Folks excuse the French, but this is definitely one of those "Oh Shit!!!" moments.

Oh no, oh hell on. No way in this world will I let the Regional Commissioner know what has occurred before I let the DD know. That no mind airport weenie would love nothing better than to blind side my DD. Oh hell no, that is not going to happen on my watch!

I calmly answer with the best thing that jumped into my head at the time; I said "Nothing." and promptly hung up.

I immediately placed a call to the DD and got his answering machine. I left him a message to call me at the CET office as soon as possible. I hung up and immediately placed a second call to the ADD and left the same message. Now for the hard part, waiting for a return call.

Within seconds of hanging up with the ADD's answering machine the phone rang. Now I am on the hook to answer just in case it is the DD or ADD. I answer and of course it is the same guy "This is Houston Sector what's going on there, I heard shots fired?" same question, same response "Nothing" followed by a quick mash of the hang-up button with a finger that was hovering over it.

Within a minute ring, ring a ding once again, same results. A few more minutes another call only this time his anger is beginning to become evident over the wonderfully clear phone lines and he is getting long winded: "I said, this is Houston Sector what's going on there, I heard shots fired?"

I saw no reason to entertain his extended conversation with additional dialogue, so I kept to my original response of "Nothing".

This goes on with the poor guy adding additional dialogue every couple of calls such as 'did you hear what I said? Do you understand me and who I am, I am speaking for the RC'.

I never changed my answer which seemed to just irritate him to no end. By the time I answered and heard "Hello Rick this is Mr. Fredericks" the poor guy was in such a state that I could just make out what he was actually trying to say through his hysterical screaming into the phone.

Hearing Mr. Fredericks voice not only was a wash of relief but gave me pause for thought. I almost chuckled as the thought went through my mind: *If the Houston Sector fellow got his hands on me, my body armor would not protect me from his bare knuckles.*

"Good morning Mr. Fredericks." I finally answered and I relayed the night's events to him including the conversation with the terribly irate fellow in Houston. Mr. Fredericks was quite pleased with the outcome of events.

"OE may or may not get their load. I cannot understand why they didn't either join in on the chase of the shooter or grab the mule train." he said and added "I would rather them grab the mule train than get in your way with apprehending the shooter."

He followed with "We took a criminal element off the street, an element that is willing to engage in a shootout in the parking lot of a busy fast food joint. He could have killed anyone of the innocent people in at that establishment. He proved himself two nights in a row to have no regard for human life."

I have to admit that I relaxed from the tension that I hadn't realized I was under when he spoke. Through all the years I had worked with the United States Customs Service and its successor Customs and Border Protection, Mr. Fredericks was by far the best manager I ever worked for in either agency.

Mr. Fredericks told me to go home and sleep well knowing we did the world a service. I asked him what he wanted me to tell Houston Sector and he told me that I had answered the phone for the last time that night. His last words were "Let it ring as you are walking out the door. I will handle the RC in the morning."

I hung-up, packed-up and headed out the door. Ah, yes, the phone was ringing!

Two days later we made the Nogales local newspaper as the team that took down the armed bandits "terrorizing" Nogales. As it turned out NPD knew the shooter well and he never got far from the border where he would abscond into Mexico to elude arrest. They even threw the term "Heroes" in there. We were heroes to the local community.

Unfortunately, the Regional Commissioner did not see us in the same light as those who live and die at the hands of these border thugs, but that is another chapter.

BILLION $ DOLLAR $ HIGHWAY

Knowledge Runs Down Leash
January 25, 1992
Two Hand Guns and 200 Rounds of Ammo

January is almost over and I am trying to get back into the grueling work on the southwest border. I had two details back to back, in fact they overlapped and I am way behind on my seizures compared to the other CET guys. The first detail was with Operation Alliance working the Douglas, AZ and Naco, AZ areas of operation (AOR). The concept of operations (CONOPS) had been worked out several months earlier and I had been involved from the beginning stages as the USCS Point of Contact (POC).

Shortly before the Alliance operation kicked off the USCS Houston, Texas District Director (DD) requested that our DD assist them with a ninety-day detail for special operations and training on the new portable contraband detector better known as Buster. At that time there were only two Busters in the Customs service and I had one of them. The operation was at the seaport, so it was entirely in the commercial environment. With these parameters that left only one person qualified to fulfill the detail. Yep, yours truly. The Inspector with the other Buster never worked cargo and refused to do so.

As luck would have it Houston wanted to start their series of operations a week before the Alliance operation ended. Our DD notified Houston that I would be one week late for their kick off so as it turned out one detail ended on Friday and I had to be in Houston on the following Monday. That gave me one day, Saturday, to reunite with my family, rest up from motel living and prepare for an extended detail with a departure date set for Sunday. Both details would turn out to be very exhausting with at least twelve-hour days and seven days per week.

The Alliance operation was set entirely between the Ports of Entry and required almost entirely a sun down to sun up time frame. We moved locations every night and the operations required hiking into a preselected area to lay in and observe known or suspected smuggling routes. When narcotics activity was observed those of us laying in would notify stand-by response units and vector them in to intercept the loads. All of the activity was targeting foot traffic. Foot traffic included human back-packers as well as four-legged pack trains. Human back packers would usually carry somewhere between fifty to eighty pounds of contraband. These packers would sometimes pack for days and it was common for them to pack fifty or more miles north of the border. Their pay would rarely go above a few hundred dollars for the journey.

The duration of this operation was four weeks and involved Federal, state and local law enforcement organizations. We were very successful which makes every agency working the detail unite as one entity hence the name *Alliance*. In line with the original CONOPS and mutual agreement of the final operation order (OPORD) the US Customs Office of Enforcement (USCS OE) was the lead agency therefore all seizures were recorded and processed by them. Essentially all enforcement activity was as Operation Alliance even though

Customs laid in and vectored Cochise County Sheriff's and Arizona DPS who actually made the take down. Technically and legally we were Operation Alliance officers as were USCS OE. Even though USCS OE may not have been present at the spotting and take down they processed the seizure as per rules of the game or the OPORD if you prefer. This being the case I have no pictures, nor can I discuss any of the seizures made during this operation.

As I rolled in to the house at the conclusion of the operation on Friday afternoon, I was already thinking about departing for Houston and a much longer detail to look forward to. I kept telling myself that it would be much warmer than laying in under a mesquite bush from dusk to dawn.

I am very much a home body who enjoys family time much more than most folks. I am not looking forward to three months of motel, hotel or any other whos-it-tel living. If I could bring my wife along it would be bearable but going there solo – not for me. I didn't drink, party nor enjoy restaurant dining. For me it was sitting alone in a small room on the 14th floor of a five-star hotel overlooking *The Galleria*. Sorry, *The Galleria* meant nothing to me, just another mall that was bigger and more expensive than most.

As it turned out a five-star hotel was a mega hindrance and after working the seaport all day dragging into the elite lodging facility filthy, smelly and in uniform I elicited some awful looks and I even had several high-class snoots, or guests as the establishment called them, jump off the elevator as I got on. On one occasion we had performed two LQV's (Landed Quantity Verification) on the same day. We met the first vessel as it docked in Galveston. We were waiting in hiding for the vessel, a banana boat, and as the gangway was being lowered at four in the morning, we broke cover and secured access to the gangway. No one on or no one off but CET members and OE Agents. I was one of two Inspectors who searched the very bottom of the hull or keel where the nastiness that got on my uniform NEVER washed off. It was an oil and who knows what mixture that resembled hot tar. I fully admit that that crap was *B A* flipping *D,* and smelled horrible.

From the hull up one level if memory serves me, to the engine room. I was a border rat working the Arizona border where we did no sea going vessels and in the military I was U.S. Army with a lot of experience with helicopters but no vessel experience there either. I am going strictly on just a few vessel searches some 25 plus years ago so if I can't distinguish keel from bow or get the exact locations wrong my sincere apologies to the mariners. I do remember the engine room was spotless and when my seaport experienced partner walked in he said "They have a German engineer. Look how clean this place is." He was correct and I spoke enough German for a greeting and friendly chat. I also remember checking up, down, behind and everywhere in the engine room and it was about 200 degrees Fahrenheit behind the engines that were themselves about a million degrees. You did not want to touch any part of them. Oh man, it was hot around them bad boys. Then to the refrigerators where it was about 35 degrees and lastly up the smoke or exhaust stacks that brought us back to 200 degrees. I did not get the galley, the cargo holds or sleeping quarters on the banana boat; that would have been too easy. The vessel had picked up in Colombia thus the LQV.

From there we went to Texas City and did a chemical vessel in 'dry dock'. When we arrived they were pulling up the gangway. All the seaport weenies went nuts and after a bit we were heading up the gangway that had been returned to its boarding position. The vessel was preparing to depart so that warranted penalty number one. By law Customs must clear the vessel and all cargo for departure. Shippers Export Declarations must be filed and even if there are no export goods on board Customs can perform an outbound exam to verify that they are in compliance with export laws. The vessel had not been cleared to depart by Customs therefore was not authorized to depart.

On this one I did get the sleeping quarters as my first assignment and my seaport partner was still guiding me though. I learned much on this first seaport trip including my second hick-up on this trip. I learned that at times the cargo vessels took on paying passengers. I learned this when we found two marijuana cigarettes in one of the rooms. Since the guy was a paying customer not associated with the shipping line, we made him flush the evil weed rather than try to prosecute a 75 year old guy from Belgium. Yep 75, dopers come in all sizes, sexes and ages. We did, of course, notify our supervisor who responded to the room and he agreed to flush rather than prosecute. He left my partner to finish the rooms since it was getting late and informed me that I was with him for the next section of the vessel. The supervisor and I headed to one of the holds that, since the vessel was in dry dock, should be empty making it a perfect place to test the Buster on a seagoing vessel. Since this was a chemical transport ship it had what I would call hoppers rather than open cargo holds. As we arrived atop the bulk cargo hold, I looked into a pitch-black void with a ladder to enter the hold. I started down the ladder first into darkness and about ten feet down I did not hit a ladder rung but rather something that felt like sand. My foot sunk in to the sandy feeling material and I stopped. Just above me was the supervisor descending down the ladder. I said, "Hold on I just stepped into something." I retrieved my flashlight hanging from my Sam Browne (gun belt) and punched the on button. The whole damn cargo hold lit up from the extremely reflective 'sand' I had hit.

The supervisor yelped and was heading back up at light speed. I have to be honest I was moving out as fast as he was. Just a slight panic. No, a bit more than a slight panic, maybe closer to a full-blown panic. To this day I do not know what that was, but it had a paint odor, so my thought is that it was probably something they put in paint for reflective signs such as stop or yield, possibly the paint for roadways such as lane markers or traffic yellow curbs. I suppose I will never know but I know that it was being exported illegally and when I left Houston there was a major investigation for SED violations. SED being Shippers Export Declaration. This of course warranted a second penalty. I believe the penalties were well over a million dollars.

When I entered the hotel that day, I fully expected it to be my last one in that plush place but they didn't evict me, so all was well I suppose. This new detail was something else. It actually started very well with my fellow inspectors who met me at the door of the aircraft as I arrived at the airport. We exited at the Jetway door and my luggage was already in the Customs vehicle at the bottom of the ladder. I never entered the terminal. That was the one and only time that had ever happened.

I felt like a VIP until I met the Houston District Director. I can't remember her name now, but I sure remember how pissed off she was. Her greeting was what I would call hostile. She was all over me about being a week late for their kick off and she let it be known that Houston was much more important than an Operation Alliance operation. She also informed me that all the transportation had already been assigned so I would have to find my own way back and forth from down town Houston to the Seaport where I was to report by eight every morning. I don't remember if I even said a word during the meeting but left the District office with the feeling that I was not exactly welcome. Fortunately, this LQV day out was early on and the supervisor who had entered the chemical laden chamber with me ended up being my ride back to Houston from Texas City. We stayed behind in Texas City to give witness statements and such to the folks investigating the not so empty, not so dry dock vessel. I asked him if he could drop me off at the hotel since I did not have a ride and he was shocked. We had a very good discussion about the DD and when we pulled in at the Port of Houston, I drove back to the hotel in a spare Customs canine vehicle that I used until the detail terminated.

As it turned out I really enjoyed my detail in Houston and met and worked with some outstanding Inspectors. Best of all I met one of the most incredible people I ever had the honor to make his acquaintance. Being a U.S. Army Vietnam era vet, I was completely humbled to be assigned to a team at the Barbours Cut Container Terminal. There I met and worked with a true hero and one of the most outstanding human beings you could ever imagine. May he never be forgotten. He was a First Sergeant (1SG) in the in the US Army during Vietnam.

> *1SG was awarded the Congressional Medal of Honor, our nation's highest honor, for his heroic actions during battle in Polei Doc Vietnam. On March 22, 1967 the First Sergeant was with the 1st Battalion, 6th Infantry and his Company was ambushed by the North Vietnamese Army. The First Sergeant's Company took many casualties and the 1SG's heroic actions and disregard for his own safety over those of his soldiers earned him this great honor.*
>
> *The First Sergeant put his life on the line many times as he moved from position to position for his Soldiers welfare and more importantly their survival. He eventually took charge of the Company when the Commissioned Officers were killed or severely wounded. The First Sergeant refused medical extraction until replacements had arrived despite injuries he had received during the battle.*
>
> *1SG is a true Hero and I am truly honored to have known and worked with him.*

My first day at the Cut we were assigned to examine a container shipment of coffee. The beans arrived in 150 or so pound bags (not palatalized) and we did the entire devan. In Nogales we used stevedores so loading bags on pallets and operating the fork lift was alien to me. The First Sergeant was first on the fork lift and after 30 minutes he joined me throwing the bags, after all throwing 150-pound bags is a two-man job. Another 30 minutes and another fork lift swap. The First Sergeant asked me if I could operate a fork lift and I answered truthfully that no I had never driven one. After a couple of hours, I asked the First Sergeant if I could take a break and he answered, "The break is manning the fork lift". He then asked again if I could operate a fork lift and suddenly, I realized I could and answered, "sure thing, you bet I can". At the next swap I was teaching myself how to operate a fork lift and when the next pallet was ready, I looked like a pro on that darn thing. 1SG had a way of making you, make you.

By the way, a few days after the banana boat LQV I learned that the team had seized sixty pounds of cocaine concealed in a water cooler. The cooler was in the crew quarters but since it was in a common area no arrests were made. At the end of the detail as far as I know the water cooler cocaine was the only seizure made during the detail, but who knows obviously I was not in the inner circle.

Even though I ended up enjoying the Houston detail I was happy and relieved to see Houston shrinking as I watched out the window seat of the aircraft. Happy to be going home and relieved that the Houston DD never found out that I had been assigned one of her dog team vehicles. I thought it was fitting that it was a dog vehicle, it made me think of her each time I drove it.

I took Monday as my day off so I could have three days with my family and when I reported in on Tuesday I almost felt out of place. Nothing had changed except that my name was nowhere to be found on the seizure board. When I left, I was all over it and now it was nowhere to be found.

When I hit the line and began roving, I felt like I was not hitting on all cylinders, I felt like I was starting all over again. I had to completely change my mindset from a seaport weenie to a border rat. I felt like I was missing things, not seeing the little glitches left when smugglers conceal their handiwork. The bottom line was, I felt lost.

Five days later on Saturday and I am just beginning to feel like old times. Earlier in the day I received high Buster readings on the quarter panels of a T-bird. The readings were right there with marijuana. I told the Immigration Inspector (II) that I would walk the car to secondary for an exam. The II, Aurtalla Ferdez, was one of the best at reading people. If Aurtalla told me that the driver and/or occupants of a vehicle were concealing something I would look until I found their reason for discomfort. There was always something, be it Customs, Agriculture or Immigration but there was always something. When I told her I was going to walk the vehicle down she said "I was just going to ask you to take it. This guy is falling apart."

I took one look at the guy and had to agree, his demeanor was screaming 'Guilty, I am guilty. Put the handcuffs on.'

I took his amnesty card and said "Thanks Aurtalla, I will let you know how much and where it is at."

When we got to secondary, I took a secondary declaration and the guy could hardly speak. Neither Spanish or English worked. When I had him get out of the car and walked him to the secondary holding area his legs made jello look stable. When doing a pat down the suspect is made to put his hands behind his back and interlock the fingers. Once in this position you hold his interlocked fingers thus immobilizing his hands. Should he have a weapon he can't get to it or should he try to abscond he is going nowhere. When I secured his hands, they were so sweaty it was again reminiscent of jello. It was impossible to make a firm grip on those jello hands, another sure sign of extreme nervousness.

As I secured him in the secondary holding cell, combining the high Buster readings and the suspects demeanor, I was sure that I had a load. I headed straight to the car and took a good look at the screws securing the interior wall of the quarter panel. They had been tampered with recently, very recently. I began removing the interior wall for access to the natural void in the quarter panel. As I removed the last screw, I knew that I was going to find something. I am thinking cocaine or marijuana? At this point I will take either, I am back!

When I pulled the cover off, I almost passed out. I was looking at a quarter panel loaded with sugarcane. Sugarcane!!! Sitting on top of the sugarcane were two small cages each containing one parrot. Yes, a parrot, a bird or *pájaro* when taking a declaration in Spanish. ¿Que trae? (What are you bringing) then ¿Trae *pájaros*? (Are you bringing birds). Yep, I asked him the money question, plant question, bird question and others all with a negative response. Not much of a negative but as much as I was going to get from this bundle of nerves. No wonder he was nervous, he had plants and birds. By the way if you really want to get PO'd they tape the bird's beaks closed so they can't utter a sound. I don't know about you but that always just flat pissed me off. I can't tolerate cruelty.

The disappointment of finding sugarcane rather than dope and the poor birds with their beaks taped closed combined to put me at a point that I called the Aggies (birds and plants fell under the Department of Agriculture) and turned the "load" over to them. The Aggie asked me why I was giving the seizure to him when we could fine the guy more for general smuggling than the Aggies could for illegally importing plants and birds. I told him the truth; I probably should not see that individual again – period. He understood and took the seizure. It added to his seizure count and was a big catch for him whereas for Customs it would be overlooked by the upper echelon anyhow.

So, there I am roving on my Friday after a disappointing week topped off by the earlier Aggie caper when a vehicle rolls up that looks pretty good. I stroll over still thinking about how nice it will be to just go home and relax from my roving workout that I haven't been keeping up on with the extended details. My body was telling me that I was out of shape for missing several months of crawling around in, on and under automobiles. There are no fork lifts here to take that sit-down break for thirty minutes.

I strolled over and using a mirror looked at the back bumper, gas tank then drive shaft. Nothing there. I checked the back seat, front seat, dash and still nothing. Using the mirror, I check for a hood load negative and then the front bumper. Foil. Aluminum foil. A package wrapped in aluminum foil visible in the drain holes of the front bumper.

I walked over to the primary inspector and asked for the passport telling her that I was going to walk the vehicle to secondary for an exam. The primary inspector then told me that the driver seemed a bit nervous and that he had told her that he was on his way to Guadalajara, Jalisco, Mexico. She said that he was an amnesty resident alien and Mexican Customs denied him entry into Mexico. That was quite common as many Mexicans considered the amnesty recipients as traitors for illegally departing or fleeing Mexico. Since it was well known by the cartels that the turnarounds were common and many times were just waved through because they never legally entered Mexico, this phenomenon was exploited to get a free pass for their illegal drugs. The cartels almost always used Immigration Inspectors since their primary area of concern was people rather than what they were carrying. Just reality and by the same token the ASO's or alien smuggling organizations would use Customs lanes. That is just the nature of the beast. What I did know was that there were packages wrapped in foil in the bumper and I had never seen marijuana or cocaine wrapped in foil. Heroin on the other hand, well the foil fit.

I walked to the driver door and took one look at the driver. He was definitely nervous and had that 'I am not going to secondary' look about him, so I told him to open the trunk. I wanted to send him away from the front bumper to limit the possibility he might just put the pedal to the metal, run the Port and head back to Mexico. He looked relieved and let out a sigh of relief which confirmed in my mind that there was a load in the front bumper. Once out of the car I put him in an arm lock and escorted him to the office where I put him in the holding cell. I had one of the other Inspectors move the vehicle to secondary while I searched and secured the suspect.

By the time I made it to secondary there was a dog team (K-9) running the vehicle. I had not told anyone where the load was, so I watched until the K-9 did his thing. The handler looked up and said "Nothing".

Standing next to me was an Immigration K-9 handler and the handler asked me if I would wait until they (he and his dog) ran the vehicle. I told him to have at it. That run was also negative.

I took out my probe and went over to the car, crawled under the bumper and using my flashlight took a closer look. There it was, aluminum foil shining in the bright light of my three-cell rechargeable Maglite. I inserted the probe and met resistance. I force the probe in and the feel was gritty. When I retrieved the probe there was nothing on it. I had probed Mexican Brown heroin before and since it is crystal it breaks up when you force a probe through it resulting in a gritty feeling, but nothing sticks to a probe. Yep, everything says heroin.

There was now an audience and they were anxiously waiting so I said, "It feels like crystal, so I think it is Mexican Brown."

The Customs dog handler said, "Now that you probed it there should be odor, let me run it again."

I said, "Have at it, I can wait."

He ran to his vehicle, got his dog and began at the rear bumper. As he came up the side of the car his dog was already getting excited. When they got to the front bumper the dog nailed it. Great alert! The handler threw the dog his reward and the handler said "There is certainly odor there now. He is all over it."

Next in line was the Immigration team. "I know it has already been confirmed but let me run it also for training." Off they went and another great alert.

Back in those days' heroin was a rarity on the Mexican border and out of the blue a third team was there. Another Customs team and also going to run it for training. Great training session and another aggressive alert. Three out of three alerts now that the package had been violated and odor could escape.

Three is a charm and there were no more dog teams mysteriously appearing. The K-9 supervisor however did arrive bragging on his dogs as he looked at the scratches on the bumper put there by the alerting dogs. It was finally time to drop the bumper and retrieve the prize. As I went to work on the bumper the audience grew. It was amazing at times how quickly word traveled. I had told no one, in fact I didn't even request the K-9 runs. I already knew that no matter what the dogs did I was going to drop the bumper. Heroin however really drew a crowd. As the bumper hit the ground, there they were, packages wrapped in foil.

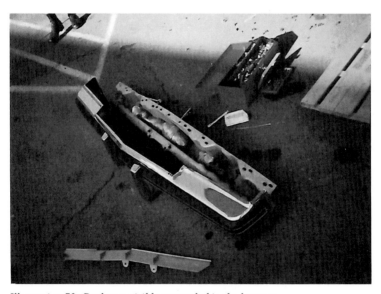

Illustration 72: Packages visible concealed in the bumper.

Now time to see the contents and call the Office of Enforcement. Donning plastic gloves I plucked the packages out of the bumper and immediately I knew that the heroin load was not happening. I didn't know exactly what was secreted in the foil packages but it sure as heck was not drugs.

I transported the packages in to the office where I opened the load of guns and bullets. Two pistols and some ammunition. When a bad day is a *really* bad day it just figures that it would continue right on to the end.

I made the required call to the Office of Enforcement who declined to participate in a two-gun weapon seizure that would now be handled administratively. Since there is no law against importing the weapons, I had to seize the wares on general smuggling and failure to declare charges. What a killer, and to think that I could have been on my way home to enjoy a couple of days off with my family. Ouch that hurts.

The most revealing consequence of this seizure was the K-9's. The only explanation for the aggressive alerts was that on the second run the handlers knew where the "load" was and that knowledge was picked up on by the dogs. Knowledge definitely ran down leash.

Illustration 73: The audience still thinking heroin

Illustration 74: The great catch

Illustration 75: The author staring in disbelief at the K-9 confirmed load

Addendum: As mentioned above there was no law on importing the weapons into the United States unless they are foreign made, had been commercially exported or are being imported as a commercial product. These guns did not fall into any of these categories. Mexico on the other hand has very strict gun laws and importing guns into Mexico is very difficult and very expensive. The driver was probably telling the truth about being denied entry into Mexico. More than likely Mexican Customs turned him around and sent him back to us. Either way he engaged in an illegal activity at the border with a resulting penalty ($5,000) for general smuggling/failure to declare and loss of the guns and ammunition as well as the seizure of his car under Title 18 Section 1595 a(c): *Except as specified in subsection (b) or (c) of section 1594 of this title, every vessel, vehicle, animal, aircraft, or other thing used in, to aid in, or to facilitate, by obtaining information or in any other way, the importation, bringing in, unlading, landing, removal, concealing, harboring, or subsequent transportation of any article which is being or has been introduced, or attempted to be introduced, into the United States contrary to law, whether upon such vessel, vehicle, animal, aircraft, or other thing or otherwise, may be seized and forfeited together with its tackle, apparel, furniture, harness, or equipment.*

Thought you might want to sample some of the legal jargon that law enforcement must follow to perform our duties.

* * *

Authors Addendum:

If you would like to view more in honor of the First Sergeant and his Soldiers I recommend the documentary *Honor In The Valley Of Tears*.

The military is family. There are different branches that sometimes bicker and bump heads like all families, but in the end, like all families we are brothers and sisters. Never forget my brothers and sisters who gave all for us:

JIMMY R MURRELL · FREDDIE TURNER · PHILLIP R BERGFIELD · DONALD L EVANS
GERRY A HARR · RUSSELL C MANN · TERRY JACK MARTELL · RICHARD SALLEE Jr
GARY P TOMLINSON · STEVEN G WILLIAMS · MANOLO BRIONES AGNES · VICTOR W LEW
RD M PURCELL · NAPOLEON JOHNSON · GILBERT LEDGER · PAUL LOPEZ · ISRAEL MEDINA
Jr · WINDOL W McNUTT · LAWRENCE WILKERSON · DONALD G CARR · ROBERT F DAVIS
HARD S PATTERSON · RUBEN RUBIO · FREDERICK B SUMMERVILLE · DANIEL W THOMAS
OW · MICHAEL J KNOX · RAYMOND R MAYS · CHARLES P PANQUERNE · CHARLES E BEALS
MARION T GRIFFIN · SAMUEL W McDANIEL II · WAYNE C PISCIOTTA · JOHN H MORRIS Jr
D J KRIEG · ROBERT J MANIAS · BRYAN L WILKEN · THOMAS W BICKFORD · ROBERT L KING
THOMAS T COLLINS · MICHAEL E LUKOW · LANCE D WORKMAN · CURTIS G VAN WINKLE
KINS · ROY D RUSSELL · WILLIAM R ROBISON · HOWARD J BECKER Jr · STEPHEN A BEDNAR
COOK · JAMES M DICKEY · ALEXANDER W DUPLESSIE · ROBERT M LARSON · TED J TAYLOR
DYER · JOHN H LOPOCHONSKY Jr · ALLEN E NOBLE · GREGORY I SAHLBERG · JAY S ASTON
EK · JAMES A JOHNSON · STEVEN J MINKLER · CHARLES W ROBERTS Jr · RUDOLPH STEVENS
BERT · NORMAN MAXIE · ALBERT E PETERSON Jr · JOHN L FETHEROLF · GERRY DON COULT
VID B BEGLAU · LUIS J MONROIG · MARGARITO RODRIQUEZ GOMEZ · TONY ANGUIANO
RANDALL D DALTON · RONALD N GOODWIN · STEPHEN E SLOCUM · CHARLES R HARRIS
ND · WILLIAM J DONOVAN · JOHN C HALSEY · DANNY LEE LIGHTSEY · LINWOOD L BAKER
HARRIS Jr · RALPH E McELRATH · CLIFFORD F DOWLING · RANDALL H GEIS · JOHN A GROSS
W SCHEU · ROBERT E SCHULZE · DOMENIC SMIGLIANI · KEN H TAKETA · CHARLES CLARK
RPHY · DONALD E SCOTT · ROBERT L WILLARD · EDWARD J CAVANAUGH · ALLEN H CLARK
D · HOWARD L JONES · SAMUEL L McAPHEE · NEIL ADAMS Jr · MANUEL GOMEZ GUTIERREZ
IG · RICHARD J DU PLESSIS · RANDY A FLESHMAN · RANDY LEE CAYLOR · ROBERT A PIPER
ES · WILLIAM J BRADFORD · CLINTON H EPPS · WILLIAM C HINES · TOMMY MIKE McCLEER
ROBERTS · WALTER K CAPPS · JOHNNY W FREE · ROBERT MIRANDA · THOMAS E KEIMILLER
LAFERRIO · EDWIN N TROXEL · ROBERT A PULASKI · MARK L HAMILTON · RAYMOND A ROSE
CK III · DAVID E CINKOSKY · ROBERT B CURRAN · DAVID L GARCILLE · ROBERT D SEVERSON
AMER · MARSHALL E NAFFZIGER · RODRICK TROUP · MARK J EKLUND · WILLIE McCLOUD Jr
J VICHOSKY Jr · BRUCE A BERG · ORAN E BINGHAM · LOREN D HAGEN · ALFRED F POSPISIL
WILLIAMS · JAMES R BROWN · THOMAS M HANKINS · HAROLD B FLYNN · ARNOLD LOVINS
ERT B RANDALL · THOMAS A DOLAN · SANTOS CASTELLANOS Jr · DIETER H DISCHHAUSER
ES Jr · WILLIAM J LOGAN · NATHANIAL C MATTHEWS · WILLARD F PAYNE · PETER J GAUVIN
NCLE · DU ANDERUM · GARY L HOLIAN · ERIC S KELLY · LAWRENCE L KELLY · LARRY McCOY
SON · JOHN M RYDLEWICZ · GAIL L STRICKLAND · JOHN C THOMPSON Jr · JAMES WRIGHT
JAMES MARK HEATON · JOHN F PEPIN · FLOYD W KOTEWA Jr · HAYWOOD RODGERS
OW B CHASTAIN · SCOTT GRABER · VERNON HART · LEROY REID Jr · JOHN W KENNEDY
CH ANTONIO T TOSA · ARTHUR G DENTON · WILLIE C KUYKENDALL · JOHN L BRANNON
GOODIN · CHRISTOPHER G MORBITZER · BRUCE MORGAN

KENNETH C WILLIAMS · CARL
RICHARD J HOCK · PATRI
RONALD A LONGFELLOW · HAROL
WALTER C B MORAN · FE
MARK E ALLEN · MELVIN
GREGORY C DAVIS · KURT INT HOUT
DONALD G BAILEY · GARY W YORK
CHARLES E GREENE · DONALD W LOWE
JAMES E MAXWELL · GEORGE H TOL
JAMES W KIEHNE · ROBERT M GRID · LUTHER
ROBERT E PRYOR · CHRISTOPHER H T
PAUL D KREGER · BRUCE P ROWE
DON H WARE · BERNARD L JOHNSON
MARK J FITZGERALD · ROBERT G GALBREATH
DAVID N JOHNSTON · ROMAN L JONES
ROBERT L DAUGHERTY · SCOTT N JACOBSON
REGEN A MONETTE · ROBERT MONTOLVE DELGAD
RAYMOND F ANTHONY Jr · BRUCE D JO
GEORGE W SEVIGNY · RICHARD A CROCKE
JOHN M MINOR · JOHN J MOYNAHAN · JAMES J
COLUMBUS WATSON Jr · JAMES C WILLIAMSON
LARRY W HARVEY · JAMES G TAYLOR · MIGUEL ANG
BILLY JOE HAMMOND · DENNIS S PE
JAMES MANOR · DAVID E PANNA BECKER
LARRY BATTS · HENRY P BRAUNE
RICHARD C HALPIN · CURTIS D MILLER
KENNETH R VOS · DAVID P SHELTON · ROBERT S
WILLIAM A TODD · IRVING B RAMSOWER II
BRUCE A CROSBY Jr · MELVIN W FINCH
DALE W FARRIS · JAMES M McCRACKEN
JAMES F WORTH · WAYNE L BOLTE · JOHN
ROBIN F CATWOOD Jr · CHARLES A LEVIS · VER
THOMAS R MUREN · DOUGLAS L ONELL · VE
CHARLES C WINDELER Jr · JAMES H A
ROBERT H ALDRICH · THOMAS E DUNLOP · ROY D PA
WILLIAM R PEARSON · HOWARD B LULL
BRUCE C WALKER · FRANK E BRUGHE
JAMES M BARRY · SCOTT D KETO
JOSEPH C SZEKELY · EDWARD C RIETSCHY · STAN L
DAVID J LEE · RONALD A MALL

Illustration 76: Vietnam Veterans Memorial Washington, DC

180

Moment of Silence Please

Thank You

BILLION $ DOLLAR $ HIGHWAY

The Carne Asada Load
March 28, 1992
461 Pounds Marijuana

As a lead inspector on the District CET team one of my assignments was to plan and lead our regular meetings with Mr. Fredericks the District Director (DD). The meetings included briefings on seizures and other significant activities that had occurred since the previous meeting. Also tossed in were any CONOPS (concept of operations) for planned operations as well as recommendations for future operations and/or activities. The DD would fill us in on the latest from Headquarters and of course relay his guidance and objectives.

In early February of 1992 the DD ended the meeting with "Oh by the way I want a CET presence at the truck dock." I remember my surprise and ridiculous reply "You want us at the truck dock?" The DD responded with "Yes, HQ mentioned it at our last briefing. It is a new national CET mandate."

My reply was something like 'OK sir, will do.'

That direction went right to the bottom of my to do list somewhere below 'meeting closed'. The truck dock or Commercial Facility as it is officially designated was the last place anyone of us on CET wanted to be. There had been only one drug seizure at that facility in over 9 years and according to all the intelligence from our side officially Inspection and Control (I&C) and the investigations side officially the Office of Enforcement (OE), there was no narcotics smuggling taking place at the truck dock. The one seizure was an attempt to use a visit by the Commissioner of Customs as a distraction to get a load through. The truck dock was not a place for a CET weenie.

I am well aware of the importance of trade enforcement. Believe me it was without a doubt one of the most important missions of the US Customs Service. Trade enforcement protects American commerce and generates billions of dollars in revenue for the US Government in areas such as duties, penalties and user fees. One of the most important areas of trade enforcement is intellectual property rights (IPR). IPR violations alone can cost American business millions of dollars every year and US Customs is the front runner in battling these crimes. Still, our mission on CET was anti-narcotics, working the truck dock was not high on our list. We left counterfeit Mickey Mouse items to the trade specialists and our efforts were focused on the drug war.

Since I had somewhat dismissed the truck dock by dropping the priority to somewhere slightly below zero the DD's direction was not fulfilled as it should have been. At the next few meetings the DD again pointed us to the truck dock and I am embarrassed to admit that each time it was dismissed. Finally, the DD had had enough and at the third or fourth meeting he once again said "I want a CET presence at the truck dock." I once again said something like 'OK sir, will do'.

182

Then the DD reiterated his desire when he leaned over the table and emphasizing his point with his finger bouncing about a quarter inch from my nose he simply said "you don't understand obviously, (bounce, bounce, bounce) I said I want a CET presence at the truck dock" (bouncing stopped with his finger now about a quarter inch from my left eye). I was a bit in shock and I said "You *are* serious Mr. Fredericks. I will have someone there tomorrow sir. Guaranteed!" As the DD got up and left the conference room, we all looked at each other. I said, "OK who is going to be the first to volunteer for the truck dock?" All fingers pointed to the poor soul who was elected by finger vote and it was final. CET would be present at the no mind truck dock.

The next day as I sat in the office talking to the Chief Inspector of the Commercial Facility, I told him that I would be working in his facility as the DD had established a CET position for commercial operations. The Chief, far from happy, grumbled that he was well aware of the District Directors position and he had already prepared an office for me. The "office" was actually one of four booths. The booths are on the four corners of the dock itself, isolated from the main building. Perfect for my CET secret squirrel operational planning and covert missions. Well maybe that is pushing it a bit for the early stage of my eventual nine years at the dock, but in reality, that is exactly what it did become. The other three booths housed six work stations. Somehow, I became the resident of the largest *office* at the Commercial Facility. Within an hour of my arrival at the dreaded truck dock I was sitting in my climate-controlled office with my feet up on the desk thinking I had made it to heaven. I went from a rover where I seldom had the opportunity to sit down and where I was normally first in the line of fire when things broke bad; to total relaxation. My first day as the CET representative at the "hell hole" went by so fast I almost dreaded leaving, and I thought you had to be a braindead no mind to work there.

On day two I walked into my booth and it wasn't a dream. I was actually in my kingdom. I sat there and kicked back for my second day in heaven, adjusted the thermostat to correspond to my most comfortable environment and relished my new-found paradise. Man was this great or what! I went inside the facilities main office and acquired some of the needed reading material for commercial operations and began to educate myself on my new abode. My first day went by so fast that I was concerned that I might not get through all the material I had acquired to "fit in" as a cargo guy. I worked at educating myself until I thought 'well it must be time to go home', judging on the previous days quick close, so when I looked at the time I thought 'what the hell, I have only been here two hours!' So much for paradise, the new-found paradise was over. I had to get to work! All that sitting around goofing off sure made for a long day.

I went down to one of the booths where commercial entries were being worked. I had two weeks training at the facility when I first arrived as a new Inspector many years ago, so I knew the process. I grabbed some entry paperwork and began scrutinizing it. It all looked a bit like Greek to me. I sort of, maybe remembered some of the *gobbledygook* but, no mostly Greek. I looked at the actual commercial Inspectors and they were all reading and **WORKING** the dad gum entry paperwork. I thought to myself 'what are you doing? Go look for DOPE!!!' At that thought I carefully replaced the paperwork and high tailed it out of there post haste.

Back on the dock I thought OK, again I am point man on this Commercial Facility venture so there is no guidance, history, rules or hints as to what I should be doing. This is another "make it up as I go" assignment. I thought about it and everyone at the dock is looking at paperwork so that is NOT the way to go. What do I do in the passenger lanes? I look for anomalies on the conveyance and use my issued tools. That is what I must do here. Yep, get the portable contraband detector nicknamed Buster and hit the conveyances. It is produce season and the dock is completely full with a line of trucks waiting to enter the completely full facility. The line of trucks is literally miles long. Every space on the dock has a truck in it and only empty trucks are allowed to proceed through the facility without backing up to the dock for at least a "tailgate" inspection. This is not a bunch of cars and pick-up trucks, these are monsters compared to what I am used to.

Well, I thought, I have to start somewhere so let me start on the empties that do not have to report to the dock. I learned that the empties were examined visually only by National Guard (NG) personnel assigned to assist at the facility. More unsettling was that the route they took completely bypassed Customs personnel (other than the entry gate where no exams took place). The factor that led to this wide-open door was a mandate to expedite legitimate traffic. For the NG to accomplish this mandate they were directed to set-up at the far north end of the compound. This allowed the trucks an avenue to exit through the unmanned north gate whereas trucks laden with cargo departed through the exit gate where the entry paperwork was finalized. I have heard the terms "expedite legitimate traffic" and "expedite legitimate cargo" used extensively in my career by HQ nimrods who don't remember life outside the beltway. What life they do remember upon occasion are airports or seaports – no Mexican border experience. They don't realize that the only way to determine if a person, conveyance or thing is legitimate is to examine it.

Illustration 77: Empties-red path; Laden-green path; purple circle-scale

I headed up to the location where the NG had established their "inspection" area just east of the north gate. When I arrived at the inspection station there were about half a dozen soldiers at that location and when a truck drove by, they would tap the trailer on the side with wooden batons. As I stood there watching their operation the sergeant came over to say hello and introduce himself. I asked what they were doing with the batons and he said, "I don't know, that is what they told us to do". I told him, "You can put those sticks away, we won't be needing them. I will be working with you folks here."

Much to my surprise they were elated. When I broke out the PCD Buster, they went from elation to total awe. One of the soldiers walked over and gleaming almost whispered "That's one of those Buster devices isn't it? I heard you got some new ones."

"Yes ma'am" I replied. "We will be using it instead of those sticks."

At that time there were only four or five Busters in the Port. Only one other CET inspector and I had a personal Buster assigned to us whereas the new arrivals had been assigned to a team.

Illustration 78: Unmanned North Gate

I worked the empties for the next couple of days and I kept one eye on the cargo laden trucks departing the exit gate just to our south. Empties were intermittent and there were times when there were no empties. When this occurred, I would head to the dock and check some trucks as well as observe the exams being performed at the dock on the laden vehicles. The conveyance exams essentially were somewhere between nil and zero.

One more caveat, since my arrival at the Truck Dock I became aware that the Cargo Chief had established a special team to work counter-narcotics. The team was officially called C-NET (Cargo Narcotics Enforcement Team). I didn't know much about their mission except that the mission was actually a Counter-CET Team. They were there to make sure I did not get a load of dope. I had danced this dance for years in the passenger lanes. Therefore, my next move was going to be tricky with tact and diplomacy the foundation as well as the framework of my proposed restructuring for the traffic flow through the compound. My ace in the hole was knowing that the DD would back me and knowing also that the Cargo Chief knew that as well.

I had been at the facility for less than a week and here I am sitting in my booth waiting for my second meeting with the Chief of the Nogales Commercial Facility. It was getting close to me presenting my proposal not for just an alteration of the traffic flow but a complete restructuring of the traffic flow through *his* area of operation. This was a concern, but a much bigger concern was my next meeting with the DD. That meeting was right around the corner and I know what the main topic of the meeting will be. I will surely be briefing him on truck dock CET counter-drug operations so Chief Battle here I am, you have been trumped by my knowledge that the DD will want something that he can relay to HQ if that animal raises its ugly head.

As I am sitting there going through my approach to the re-routing request there is a knock at the door. Wow, my first visitor. I went over and answered the door and there stands a K9 team (a dog handler with his dog on leash).

"What can I do for you Chuck?" I asked.

"Hey, I just heard that you were out here now, so I will be looking for you. I hate this place. You call these truck dock folks when the dog alerts and it takes them an hour to show up, first thing they do is they bitch that I am causing a back-up and the dope exam is over in 30 seconds." Chuck continued in an excited whisper. "We all know there ain't no dope here but if I am here, they could at least go through the motions. I mean maybe ZT or something. I bet half these drivers smoke a little weed in that long ass line."

"Well I ain't here to look for ZT Chuck but I will sure as hell give you a good narcotics exam." I corrected him. ZT is of course zero tolerance or personal use drugs. It was ushered in with the *just say no* campaign.

"Well I will be calling you even though the Chief just informed me that I am to call the C-NET team, not you." he went on "Did you know they started that team because they knew you were coming out here?"

"So I have heard but I have no idea what their mandate is. I really could care less, I am here to do a job and I am going to do it no matter what. If they want to shadow me that is fine." I responded. Then added "I don't even know who is on their team."

"Oh, they aren't going to shadow you; they have them at the entry gate with a Buster, almost like rovers. The thing is, only one knows anything about finding dope and that is Pelon. The other two are Rita and Lambion and they don't know nothing." As he relayed this tidbit of information his voice again went to a whisper as though he thought we were being watched. Who knows, maybe he was right.

"Well I am here if you need me." I finished.

As Chuck and his K9 partner Charge departed I sat back down putting the finishing touches on my upcoming meeting with the Chief. Chuck had perfect timing with the information on C-NET. It sure as the dickens confirmed my first thoughts about the new cargo team. It certainly put a "confirmed" check mark on their mandate as a Counter-CET Team. One thing was for sure, Chuck had it right, only one of the three C-NET folks was a worker. The other two wouldn't know which end of the Buster is the working end.

As I headed to the Chief's office, I thought it also confirmed the reasoning behind our upcoming meeting. In my few days at the *dope free* facility I had become convinced that the lack of counter-drug enforcement left the facility anything but *dope free*. If the cartels had not seen what I saw; their spotters would lose their heads – literally!

When I arrived at the Chief's office the door was open, the secretary was nowhere to be seen and I could see Mr. Battle through his open door sitting behind his desk. He looked up as I approached his door and before I could knock, he said in his always pleasant tone "Hi Rick, come on in and grab a chair." Mr. Battle and I were very well acquainted and one commonality that put us in the 'friends' category was baseball. My son and his son both played baseball for their respective high schools. When the two schools played one another Mr. Battle and I would always meet and sit together for the game. I have always respected Mr. Battle as one of the best managers I have ever had the pleasure to work with.

After a little chat or small talk if you prefer, we got down to business. "Well Rick tell me what is on your mind. I know you are itching to get something going or you would be talking to Werth, not me (Werth was the CET supervisor but was strictly hands off)."

"Yes sir" I replied "I have spent some time with the NG working empties and watching the laden vehicles heading out the exit gate unchecked by CET. To accomplish my mission as per the DD's instructions I actually have to Buster all trucks empty and laden."

"OK and just how do you propose to do that? Do you plan on doing pre-primary exams?" he queried with a bit of concern is his voice. I knew the reason behind the concern. He did not want me having access to the conveyances before his C-NET folks.

"Sir I would like to run all vehicles that enter the compound through one point where I can set-up and check each one. In fact, every vehicle with border nexus will be checked." I replied.

The Chief thought about it and I know he was thinking that Mr. Fredericks will be all over this, so he would have to make it happen, but on his terms. "Good idea" he responded, "but you absolutely cannot impede the flow of traffic."

'Damn he is good!' I thought. How the hell am I going to do that? How can I check an eighteen-wheeler while it is moving? That would be like, well suicide!!!

"10-4 Mr. Battle. Thank you. I will start tomorrow." was my reply. I had formed a plan as he spoke. I knew just the place and it was exactly where I had planned to set-up my inspection point all along. Pure dumb luck but sometimes luck pans out.

My initial plan was to set up my operation on the north side of the dock where I could not be observed from Mexico and as luck would have it that is where the old truck scale was already in place with the most horrible speed bump in the history of speed bumps. A passenger car could hardly manipulate the over-sized road hazard and the trucks had to come to a brief stop on top of the speed bump to keep from upsetting their cargo. Then they would slowly roll off the other side thus keeping the cargo from shifting. Perfect for me to do my thing.

The next day I was out there at the truck scale and sure enough it was workable. I had rerouted traffic using cones, sent the NG to my booth to help with devans at the dock and now every vehicle that entered the dock was mine. I would walk down to meet the trucks and walk along with the trucks placing the Buster on the tractor then the nose of the trailer, side, floor and finally the back doors. Not ideal or anywhere near perfect, but workable. On day two it seemed that everyone in Customs had heard about the idiot Bustering moving tractor trailers at the old weigh scale. As I was performing this ridiculous inspection, I heard laughter behind me. I turned around and there stood the District Ombudsman Ms. Delayno. Now there stood a person, also a Chief, without a job. The position she held was established for her mainly because she was on first name basis with the Assistant Commissioner for Inspection and Control. There stood the eyes and ears of Customs Headquarters getting a good laugh out of me tempting fate with rolling death.

Illustration 79: Trucks backed up to dock with one approaching the scale

"You don't really think you can get a load off a moving vehicle, do you?" she jeered from her high perch leaning on the handrail at the end of the dock.

"Well ma'am, that remains to be seen." I replied. "I sure won't know until I try and ma'am, I feel pretty good about the odds."

"Does Mr. Fredericks know what you are doing?" the Ombudsman queried.

"Ma'am, he knows I am here doing narcotics exams." I answered "And that is exactly what I am doing. Just like roving the passenger lanes. On a bigger scale but really no different."

As she turned to leave she said, "Well, that is between you and Mr. Fredericks I suppose."

As she walked away laughing, I thought 'Damn good thing the CET meeting is this afternoon because HQ will be enlightened as soon as *she* can get in contact with them. Hopefully they are on the Hill (testifying to Congress) or somewhere untouchable'.

I continued on with my mission as the main attraction at the dock. The perch was a well visited area that day and if I sold soda and popcorn, I could have retired much sooner. I believe every employee stationed at the Commercial Facility with just a couple of four exceptions managed to find their way to my location with some chuckling and others just watching in silence then wandering away back to the dark depths of oblivion. Chuck the K9 handler stopped by a couple of times and assisted by walking his K9 along the other side of the truck as I worked but that was short lived and he eventually came over and said his dog couldn't work the moving trucks because they scared the poor critter. Smart dog, what can I say.

I have to admit that it was cold in the morning, very noisy, quite dirty, stunk of diesel fumes and all in all was a bit intimidating. At one point I had the brilliant idea of using the old scale house as shelter but that was nixed about two seconds after I entered the extremely small confines and realized that nothing but spiders and other vermin had entered that shack in years. I don't think the drivers were too thrilled either as many of them would put the pedal to the metal as soon as their rear tires cleared the speed hump on their way to the exit gate not fifty yards away.

Day two at the scale ended early when it came time to head back to the District building for our regular meeting with the DD. I must admit I had some very mixed as well as unsure feelings about the meeting. Unless Ms. Delayno had managed to notify HQ and HQ notified the DD, he was unaware of the scale operation. I would find out when I got there but I was somewhat uneasy with today's meeting. I was fairly certain that no one from the truck dock had mentioned it mainly because I had not heard a peep from the rest of the CET team including the Chief Enforcement Officer Chief Crow or the CET supervisor.

When I arrived back at District, I headed straight to the conference room where the meeting was to take place. The only person I saw was the CET secretary, Carley, who was just leaving the conference room as I entered. She had just finished preparing it for the meeting and other than a quick hug and a "you are early", she just hurried on out. That led me to believe that the DD more than likely did not know what was going on, so I would be briefing him from my point of view.

I sat there in the conference room relaxing and realized that I was pretty damn tired, in fact I was worn out. A little over a day and a half and I was beat. I was used to hard work, but this was different, fast walking, stretching up and walking backwards to buster the nose of the trailer, walking sideways to get the side, then still walking sideways but stooping to get the floor and finally climbing and hanging on to the back doors to buster them. When finished rushing back to catch the next truck before it made it to the speed bump. As I was pondering how miserable I felt, in walked Mr. Fredericks.

"Hey Rick" he started "Carley told me you were here already and she said you looked haggard and that you smelled and tasted like diesel so I surmised that you are operational at the Commercial Facility."

"Yes sir, my apologies again for my oversight in not making this happen the first time you directed it." I said, and I was very sincere. Mr. Fredericks was and still is the absolute best District Director I ever worked for. He was very enforcement minded and had a pair that would make a bull jealous. He backed us up and stood-up to HQ, IA, OE and others on many occasions where other DD's would have caved in and left us hanging. No, I should have acted the first time and it still bothers me to this day that I did not.

He just waved his hand and said "I know you guys replaced the 'tr' with an 'f' long ago when it came to the truck dock. I really expected more opposition, but I will tell you here and now between us, you jumped in and obviously made something work out there, where Crow and Werth were actually given this guidance weeks ago and they still haven't mentioned anything about it to me. If you told them, they have distanced themselves from the operation. Again, between us, that is why we have this CET operators meeting and they are NOT allowed to attend. DO NOT repeat this but that is the gist of it."

Wow, talk about a pep talk. I don't know if that is what it was meant to be but, damn I felt like I was king shit. Then he continued almost completely off the subject "by the way and do not answer, I can smell the diesel and you do look a bit haggard but 'tasted like diesel'. Oh never mind, my mind was wandering."

Hell, it was just a teeny tiny kiss between old friends – really!!!

Anyhow the team arrived and that was that for that!

Much to my surprise Mr. Fredericks did not start with the truck dock but with some other business. I thought 'someone has already briefed him on the truck dock', I was not sure if that was good or bad. He went on and brought up the Port seizures or lack thereof. It was a bit of an ass chewing in a way since we were still in the heavy drug season. Mexico has thousands of produce shipments daily during the winter months. Thousands of tons of produce also brings thousands of pounds of illicit cargo commingled with legitimate cargo. The excessive number of conveyances to ship all these goods makes it much harder to pick the one truck out of a thousand that is loaded with dope secreted somewhere in these giant beasts. Many of the trucks do not cross the border but unload their cargo in warehouses in Mexico where it is repacked into trailers that then cross into the United States and those trailers go to warehouses on the US side to be unloaded in the border towns where the cargo is reloaded into US trucks for final destinations in the US. Yep, you guessed it, the drugs that come up commingled with legitimate cargo is also re-packed for cross border shipment. It may come in commercial trucks, passenger vehicles, through the fence, through tunnels – you name it. The one method of smuggling that I think should be made more public starts with a DUMB detention resulting in a seizure of usually heroin or cocaine. DUMB – detention until movement of bowels. Yep, we wait until these internal body carriers defecate (shit to most folks) then we retrieve the packages and arrest the carrier also known as "swallowers" because they swallow the packages in order to poop it out. Then some drug user snorts this up their nose or shoots it in their veins. It is called "shit" for a reason, shooting or snorting the shit. Before you put that in your veins or up your nose, think about how it got here. Don't just say no, say Hell No!

Anyhow, back to our meeting. Mr. Fredericks was concerned about the lack of recent seizures and then turned to me and asked, "Should we shut down the truck dock operation and get you back to the line?"

Without thinking I said, "No sir, if you give me two weeks, I will have you a load at the truck dock." Wow I couldn't believe I just said that! The rest of the team looked at me like I was out of my mind and I almost agreed with them. The thing was I was now convinced that dope had

191

to be moving through that wide-open facility.

Mr. Fredericks was completely taken aback. "Are you serious Inspector Davis? Do you think everyone is wrong and there really is dope moving through the truck dock?"

"Yes sir I do. In fact, I do not see how any drug organization would miss the opportunity." I said. "It will be a well-organized cartel I think but if I were moving tons of dope, I would certainly seize the opportunity. I don't think you will see a mom and pop load but well organized, yes sir. Just give me two weeks."

"Well you have two weeks. Tell me about the operation. The first day you arrived I know Chief Battle established a drug team and that was the last I heard of that. I know you were given the southeast booth, but I haven't heard anything else. Fill me in." This said he kicked back, put his hands behind his head and was obviously waiting for an in-depth briefing.

I started with day one and ended with the mornings scale operation. "So, you are using the buster on moving trucks? Is it safe?" he asked.

"Yes sir." I might have exceeded the truth just a bit there.

"Will the buster work on a moving vehicle?" he asked. My response was "I believe it will. I have used it all morning and I am getting readings that make me believe it will."

"I have a conference call next week with HQ and I will tell them we have a CET presence there, but I think I will go light on using the Buster on moving vehicles." he said thinking out loud.

I felt a twinge of panic and was not quite sure how to broach my concern. I decided to jump right in even though I was not sure how Mr. Fredericks felt about Ms. Delayno. "Uh Mr. Fredericks just FYI, Ms. Delayno stopped by this morning and, well she got a good laugh out of my operation. Just thought you might want to know she was there kind of observing from the handrail at the end of the dock. I don't know how long she was there."

Mr. Fredericks looked at me and his face had instantly changed. His look at me was quite chilling. I wasn't sure if he was infuriated with me or concerned about her. I thought maybe I had overstepped my bounds with a borderline accusation directed at a Chief and the Ombudsman at that.

"Thanks guys, meeting over. Go get some dope." Mr. Fredericks said with a not so convincing smile. Convincing or not I was suddenly very relieved and eager to be on the other side of the conference room door. "Not you Rick, I need you to stay."

The rest of the team got up and moving quite deliberately but extremely cautious to be silent departed without a look or gesture to me. As they escaped Mr. Fredericks broke the silence when he said matter of factually "Close the door please."

Silence for a few seconds as we both concentrated on the now closed door then Mr. Fredericks broke the uneasiness with "Well Fuck!"

That was the first and one of the few times I ever heard that word cross his lips. "That changes things. I will have to brief HQ on our Commercial Operation extensively."

"Sorry sir, do you want me to alter the moving vehicle exam?" I asked.

"Hell no! You said it is the best way and it will work therefore you just keep doing what you are doing. I know exactly why you are working with moving vehicles – Battle!" I could tell his mind was racing and to my great relief I knew I was not his target.

"Battle called *her* too I am sure (referring to Ms. Delayno). He is scared shitless that you are going to get a load, so he brought her in. Obviously you know she is a direct link to HQ or you wouldn't have mentioned her and you are right." His mind was still racing.

Damn I hate politics, but this is the government and the Commissioner is a political appointee nominated by the President. That is deep politics at the highest level.

"Hopefully you are right about a load in two weeks. That will make things much easier. Either way this is my District and I will run it my way. Tell me exactly what you are doing and how you are doing it." he said looking deep into my mind through my eyes.

I spilled every detail of my assignment to the truck dock including my first day of sitting with my feet on the desk enjoying the climate-controlled office. I wanted to make sure that he knew how and why I ended up on my suicide mission. When I left that conference room, I think we both felt at ease. I also felt that it was not so much a suicide mission as a be smart operation since that is the way I relayed it to the boss. Yep I felt pretty good and was also given latitude on hours worked, overtime, you name it, I had it. This had become a political battle between a couple of Chiefs with ties to HQ and the best District Director the US Customs Service ever had. Me, I was just a pawn but a pawn that could Check Mate the other side.

For the next several days I worked my ass off. Obviously something had been passed to the rest of the Customs world because the only visitor I had was Chuck and his K9 and then only when he had a dog alert. He wanted me to check the conveyances that his dog hit on, so I obliged. Who knows, I might even get a load that way – not.

March 28th still a couple of weeks from the last snow. In Tucson I always say we haven't had our last snow until Easter. It always snows on or about Easter so right in line with that it is a cold, rainy Saturday. I am working Saturday because Saturdays at the truck dock are very, very lax and the cold and rain today is driving the Inspectors even deeper into the climate-controlled booths. As luck would have it my Buster malfunctioned so I entered the main offices of the Commercial Facility. Being Saturday there was no management to be found so I approached Glory Floater, the Acting Supervisor and asked him if he had a Buster I could borrow.

"Hey Glory, do you have a Buster I can borrow, mine just went on the blink." I asked. Glory was an old friend and always bitter, so I expected some resistance.

"Oh, you want to borrow one of *our* Busters? Hell, we don't have Busters here anymore, they both went to C-NET. I guess we don't rate as regular Inspectors. Go ask them and if they give you any shit tell them I, as the acting honcho here told them to lend you one. I don't need Mr. Fredericks calling me to the carpet for not supporting his District CET Team." Yep that was Glory, bitter as usual but quite helpful to me by default.

"Thanks Glory, uh where is their office?" I asked.

"You don't know, now that is funny. They have the northeast booth. Straight north of the CET booth." he sarcastically replied and then mumbled as he walked away "Northeast, southeast and the blue room all on the east side. We now call it the 'enforcement' side. I am not even sure if we can look that direction."

Job well done Glory, I walked up to the C-NET booth and knocked at the door. One of the C-NET Inspectors answered the door just opening it about three inches and peeked out. "Oh, it is you Rick, what's up?" she asked.

"My Buster is 10-7 (out of service) and I was wondering if I could borrow one of yours." I replied.

"Hang on." she replied and about three seconds later opened the door just wide enough to pass the Buster through and then she closed the door before I could even thank her.

'Secret squirrel stuff going on in there' I thought, but none of my business. I know they don't want me to know anything about their operation and that is fine with me. I was just happy I had a working Buster (new and unused from the looks of it) and didn't even have to pull the "acting honcho" trump card. Off to my work site I went just glad to be back in business.

It was now close to 2:00 PM and I had been at the dock since 8:00 AM. Rather than warming up as the day dragged on it kept getting colder and wetter. Now there is some sleet mixing in with the rain and miserable is an understatement for my wet, half frozen body. I was almost to the point of taking refuge in that nightmare of the scale house, but the spiders and other vermin wouldn't open the door. It was so cold that I was having trouble manipulating the Buster and along came Chuck with his K9 sitting in the nice warm vehicle.

Just as Chuck was parking a truck was approaching. I headed for the truck and began my now routine exam. I hit the nose of the trailer with Buster and checked the readings. Wow, that is a high reading. By the time I checked the reading the nose had passed me, so I put the Buster on the side. High readings for the entire length. I jogged up to the driver door and stopped the truck. I asked for the paperwork and checked for a release. It was a general exam which is just a document review and it was signed off, a proper release. In this weather it probably did not even get a tailgate exam since under a general exam one is not required.

Chuck came over and said, "When you finish this one could you come to the south dock and check a cab that my dog hit on?"

"Sure but let me get this one set-up for an intensive exam first, I got some interesting readings." I replied.

"Let me run Charge first, OK." was his reply.

"Have at it, I will hold it right here." Why not, a dog alert would go a long way for the override to Intensive.

I waited as he ran back to his van and got Charge out. I watched as he ran the entire tractor and trailer with no response from the dog. Chuck put his dog back in the van and walked over and said "Nada". Then he asked again if I would check his suspect vehicle. I agreed again and told him I would meet him at the suspect vehicle. It was parked on the south side of the dock, on the opposite side from our location.

Well that dog run was a bit of a disappointment. Oh well I have seen dogs miss many times, so I told the driver to return to the dock and park in one of the slots at the *blue room*. The blue room was actually the far northeast end of the dock where an eight-foot-high fence had been erected to isolate the section for narcotics exams. I escorted the truck to the area and when the driver had backed up to the dock, I escorted him to a bench seat outside the blue room and told him to wait there. Ironically the bench was just outside the booth where C-NET had set-up their office.

I went over to the stevedore's office and told them to give me a 50% devan (there were two rows of pallets in the trailer so a 50% devan will be one entire row of pallets removed from doors to nose). Now that I had that going, I headed to the opposite side of the dock to comply with Chuck's request. When I got there he told me Charge had hit in the drivers compartment, close to the ashtray. 'Great' I thought ZT at best. I checked the drivers compartment and found nothing but an ashtray that reeked of Marijuana. Not even ashes much less a roach, this driver wasn't stupid. ZT does not include odor.

"Nothing but an ashtray that reeks of MJ." I said. "It was a good alert though so make sure Charge gets his reward."

I headed back to the Blue Room to see what progress the stevedores had made on my truck and when I entered I almost went into a cardiac stoppage or heart attack if you prefer. My truck was gone. I hightailed it to the stevedores' office and asked the supervisor "Where the hell is my truck."

"It is at slot 81, Lambion made me move it. He said he couldn't cook with us unloading the truck." he said almost in a panic. I believe he may have seen his life flash before his eyes.

I had seen a grill there in the Blue Room but paid no attention to it. I went to slot 81 and sure enough there sat my truck with about two thirds of the pallets off the truck and the stevedores working on the other third. I went looking for Lambion and found him carrying a large tray covered with aluminum foil.

"What the hell did you move my truck out of the Blue Room for?" I unceremoniously asked him.

"We are having a promotion ceremony for Rita and Ira. We had this planned and we planned it for the Blue Room. The carne asada is my specialty and we are about half an hour from *our* celebration. I am the C-NET Senior Inspector and this is my dock." he said.

I was so mad that I just walked away. C-NET is there to do what? One is in the booth hiding and the other is cooking (his specialty). I wonder if number three is there or on day off. Oh well I could care less and frankly none of my business. Not only that but now I wanted to keep an eye on my truck and move the driver from the bench where I had placed him. Slot 81 is directly across from that damn bench and he can see everything going on in the trailer. I went over to the driver and told him it was too cold to be sitting there and that I was moving him inside where it was warm. I brought him in and put him in a holding cell. That was the only way I could leave him in the main building without an escort. Yep it required a pat down, weapons check – the works. I also informed Glory he had a guest in the holding cell.

I went back out to the truck and the stevedores had almost finished. I sat there on the bench now and waited. I have to admit, the damn carne asada smelled pretty good from where I was sitting but I didn't think I was invited.

The stevedores finally finished and departed. I walked into the trailer and ran the buster up and down the wall. Normal, then abnormal as I went from top to bottom. At the bottom there are pallet jack guards that are placed to protect the walls from the pallet jacks that are used to load and unload pallets. This is where the abnormal readings were. The guards have very large screws that held them in place. I went back to my vehicle and retrieved the biggest screw driver I had. Back to the trailer and I started removing the screws that held the guards in place. I took out about a dozen, enough that I could pry the guard out and take a look behind it. Bigger than life there they were, packages. I stood there in awe and one of the cargo weenies walked in and joined me in the trailer. The plate had already popped back into place concealing the packages. Nick is one of the nicest people you will ever meet. He came over with a paper plate with three burritos on it. "Hi Rick, you want some burritos? We are having a carne asada."

"No thanks Nick, I will pass." I said.

Somewhat less than two weeks. In fact, less than a week since I had made my promise to Mr. Fredericks and the pawn had Check Mated the big dogs. Laugh now Ms. Delayno. Actually, this did not cross my mind at the time. I actually went into Law Enforcement mode.

Illustration 80: Packages of Marijuana

I put the screws back in the guard and entered the main building and headed over to Acting Supervisor Floater. "Glory" I began "I got a load out there in space 81. I am calling OE to see if they are going to do a CCD (controlled delivery)."

"You got a load." Glory went ashen "What kind of load, ZT?"

Obviously Glory was not thinking clearly, CCD for a ZT – never. My response made him almost puke I would say from his reaction "No it is going to be several hundred pounds. Let me call OE, you might want to call Battle."

I called the OE duty agent and to my surprise they told me that they were going to do a controlled delivery. I informed Glory and again I thought he was going to upchuck.

I headed back out and told the stevedores to reload the trailer as casual as possible in an attempt to conceal our knowledge. The less people that know, the better.

I stood there watching them reload and just as they were finishing, I saw Battle walking down the dock heading my way. He came over and asked, "Is this the load?"

"Yes sir, OE is going to attempt a controlled delivery." I advised him.

"Where is the C-NET team?" he asked "And why didn't you do this in the blue room? All narcotics exams are to be done in the blue room."

"Yes sir I know and I put it there but the truck was moved out for the carne asada." I assumed he was aware of the promotion party.

197

"Carne asada, I told them it had to be *after* the compound closed." he almost blew a gasket.

He then walked over to the C-NET office and ripped out his key, opened the door and there were two Inspectors in quite a compromising position. Yes, sexually compromising! Battle stood there in shock for a moment and closed the door (way to quickly in my opinion) with my last vision of that scene being one person sitting in a chair with her legs over each arm and her partner the C-NET Inspector who had loaned me the Buster kneeling on the floor in front of the chair. Both in their birthday suit. At least now I know what secret squirrel stuff was going on and why I was given the Buster so quickly and without an argument. I guess when I upset the glass the whole damn water cooler falls. Chief Battle looked back at me, shrugged his shoulders and headed to the Blue Room. I did not follow him, nor did I want to follow him. I guess Acting Supervisor Floater failed to notify the troops that there was a load and that the Chief was coming in.

The OE agents arrived about an hour later and attempted a delivery but it was unsuccessful, so the truck was brought back to the dock where I seized 134 packages of Marijuana with a total weight of 461 pounds.

This was the first time that I used watermelon bins as containers for illicit drugs, but it won't be the last time watermelon bins are used. I sealed my fate as this was the beginning of my nine-year tour at the dreaded truck dock.

Illustration 81: 134 packages concealed behind pallet jack guards

Sometime later Ira told me about the rest of the story. Apparently Acting Supervisor Floater did notify C-NET but well after he had notified Mr. Battle. Ira said that he was in the blue room eating burritos and enjoying his ill-advised promotion party. Lambion came running in carrying an extremely large round serving tray and told Ira that the Chief was on his way and they had to get all the carne asada evidence out of there. He told Ira to load everything on the tray and put it into Lambion's truck. Lambion was going to take care of the grill. Ira said he stacked all the tortillas, meat, salsa, beans, everything on the tray and picked it up. He said it was so heavy that he could barely carry it. When he got to the sliding gate at the entrance to the blue room, he had no way of opening the gate. He said he shouted for someone to open the gate and moments later the gate rolled open. Ira said he stood there looking at his accomplice who had freed him from the scene of the illicit carne asada and said, "Hello Mr. Battle, would you like a burrito."

When it rains it pours, what can I say?

The load became known as the carne asada load and as far as I know it is still talked about at the Commercial Facility usually during the do's and don'ts portion of new guy training. The day after the load the NG reported to the scale to assist. CNN turned up at some point and made some file footage that I was totally unaware of until I saw it on TV. In the picture you can see the scale house, the rail on the dock where Chief Delayno was observing the operation and a truck on the scale with a NG waving him forward.

Illustration 82: Day one or two post seizure.

The operation that started with one Inspector working solo instantly turned into a major CET operation with all CET Inspectors moved to the Commercial Facility for several months. We acquired a cherry picker, additional K9's, drills and other tools. As far as HQ reaction, they began using the whole fiasco as a must for all commercial ports along the Mexican border. Less the two ladies in the in the C-NET booth as I recall. I don't believe that HQ included that as part of the protocol.

The operation also changed at the direction of Mr. Fredericks. We no longer had to worry quite as much about "impeding the flow of traffic", so thereafter we could stop traffic for a proper and much safer exam when we deemed it was necessary. We still had to do our best to keep things moving so we all used the walk and Buster as we go approach, but we did have much more leeway. With the entire team out there, we opened a second lane of traffic that offset our stop and examine approach in compliance with expediting traffic.

Illustration 83: Post seizure scale operation. Over-sized speed bump is visible on left side. A K9 team is also seen in front of the cherry picker.

Illustration 84: Cherry picker in use

Illustration 85: The author using a probe on bulk cargo.

By the end of my two-week period we had a second load of dope at 880 pounds of weed. I had promised Mr. Fredericks a load so I missed my target on the plus side. I will take that any day. Other changes included the C-NET team being disbanded which was neither here nor there for me but the change that bothered me happened to Mr. Battle. As I stated earlier, I liked Mr. Battle and as a result of my operation he was re-assigned to passenger processing. The Ombudsman position was abolished and Ms. Delayno was re-assigned as the Chief of the Commercial Facility. The first two loads were Marijuana and then as if to prove me right again we began intercepting cocaine loads. In a 1997 power point presentation covering a time frame from June 1995 to February 1997 we had seized 24.5 pounds of Methamphetamine, 3,719 pounds of Marijuana and 8,826 pounds of cocaine. I remember getting so many cocaine loads that when I drilled a compartment and came out with Marijuana I said, "Wow this is weed, we can relax a little." With cocaine we would break out our Mini 14's, access control was tightened to the point of nausea and the stress levels went through the roof. Cocaine in those days was highly controlled by Mexican drug cartels such as Amado Carrillo Fuentes (Juarez Cartel) who operated in Nogales and like I said above proved me right again – 8,826 pounds of cocaine are not mom and pop runs.

Illustration 86: Two lanes approaching the scale. The cones block off the route to the north gate previously used by empties.

The scale operation was renamed Secondary Express by the new Cargo Chief. Where she came up with that name is anyone's guess and why she was allowed to rename it is anyone's guess. Eventually two or three DD's later Nogales abolished the CET team and I went back to Passenger Operations. This lasted a few months until the Port re-established the CET team with a new Supervisor, a Chief no less, and a bunch of fairly new Inspectors. Their operation was established at the scale only they were given an office on the end of the dock. That lasted until they missed 3,000 pounds of cocaine that was nabbed in an empty trailer with a very large nose compartment. One of our old CET guys was working the exit gate and got it. I was sent back to the dock on a new team of three with a new name, the Mobil Response Team. We again started nabbing numerous big loads and I worked there until I couldn't stand the politics anymore. I asked to be sent back to passenger processing where an injury received on the job sent me to the Customs Command Center in Tucson. I never worked Nogales again.

Illustration 87: Roof inspection on refrigerated trailer just a bit spooky with all the moving trucks in the area but sure made access easy.

Illustration 88: We also nabbed a scissor lift to accommodate the K-9's.

BILLION $ DOLLAR $ HIGHWAY

Help Wanted: New OB-GYN for Tubatama, MX
July 14, 1992
58 Pounds Cocaine

Today I get to sleep in just a bit, a day that I will head in just a tad late and work only eight hours – a rarity in the old Customs Service. Today I will be working a surprise special operation in Sasabe, Arizona. I am sure that many of you, even many Arizonians are saying "Sasabe, where the dickens is Sasabe?" Well the short and long of it is that Sasabe is in the middle of *NOWHERE*. Yep, just my kind-a place! Sasabe is a United States Port of Entry (POE) 77 miles by vehicle from Tucson (where I reside) and Nogales (my home port) is 65 miles from Tucson. The journey to Sasabe adds about ten miles on my commute but it is well worth it.

I love Sasabe and enjoy not only the change of pace, but the drive to and from this little POE that is historically a cattle crossing. Take a look at the map below and you can see both the US and Mexican Ports of Entry and to the west of the POE's you can see the cattle pens or *corrals* where, in another era, thousands of head of cattle crossed from Mexico to the many ranches in Arizona. Some of the ranches are still operational and can be seen on the drive from highway 86 (also known as the Ajo highway) then down highway 286 or South Sasabe Hwy.

Illustration 89: Port of Sasabe, the border fence is running diagonal in the center of the photo. Imagery courtesy of the U.S. Geological Survey. Visit the USGS at https://usgs.gov.

There was a time when this area of Arizona from Sasabe through Arivaca, into Amado and on to Nogales was a popular hangout for the Hollywood elite like John Wayne, Elizabeth Taylor, Robert Wagner and others. Now it is one section along the "Billion Dollar Corridor".

Back in the day Sasabe was known as a RIP port, that's a Retired in Place port. For the most part that is exactly what it was, a kicked back port fueled by apathy and a belief that "nothing illegal comes through the port, it all goes around". There is no doubt that tons of Marijuana went around the port. So much so that less than a mile from the Port there were two illegitimate crossing points into Mexico that had improved dirt roads going to them. These crossings were commonly referred to as the "East Gate" with very easy access to any vehicle and the "West Gate", not as easy as the East Gate and virtually impassable after a good Monsoon rain. This being said, I must add one caveat - almost ALL illegal crossings from Mexico into the US are "owned" by what are known as "Gate Keepers". The Gate Keepers control their territory viciously and do not hesitate to use deadly force. Facing this reality there are many mom and pop smuggling operations that must use the POE's or face lethal retaliation. The gatekeepers even had "employees" that sat in court at drug hearings to pick out smugglers that had used their corridors without paying. They would then collect from failed attempts including those who went to jail. This reality opens the door for corruption on both sides at the border. Facing this reality and the fact that the town of Sasabe itself had more than its share of "spotters" reporting for the criminal organizations, when I worked a detail in Sasabe I would literally sneak in with an automobile I had not used previously. When I approached the Port I would hold off entering and watch for a vehicle that looked promising then, just as it entered the Port, I would proceed to the Port where I would perform my inspection.

Illustration 90: Town of Sasabe, a dozen or so homes and the all in one gas station / store / payphone. Imagery courtesy of the U.S. Geological Survey. Visit the USGS at https://usgs.gov.

This was the case today; I sat in my vehicle just out of sight of the town folk and the POE waiting for a good target. At just after noon a likely looking vehicle approached the primary lanes. I cranked up my vehicle and headed to the port. The suspect vehicle arrived just before me and I noticed the primary Inspector was already manning the lane. This was unusual for Sasabe back then as the Inspectors normally waited inside until the inbound vehicle ran over a trip that rang a bell inside announcing their approach. Only then would they exit the Customs House. I noticed that the individual manning the lane was an Immigration Inspector (II) and she was renowned for her thorough immigration inspections including scrutinizing documents and performing a thorough interview to verify their admissibility. As I approached the Port the vehicle was released and had started to head north into the U.S. just as I pulled up. I stopped the vehicle and told the inspector Ceya Pataria to hold it there until I checked it out. I proceeded to the vehicle, a 1985 Chevrolet pick-up truck; a favorite smuggling instrument used by drug smugglers for its duel gas tanks. During the examination I noticed that the fuel tanks had recently been tampered with and there was dried mud artificially concentrated on the tanks. I escorted the vehicle to secondary where I took a secondary declaration, checked the driver's passport (with a *permisso*[5] tucked in it) and placed it under the seat belt which was my normal routine. I then escorted the driver and lone occupant into the "headhouse" where he was patted down and secured. On entering I advised the two US Customs Inspectors, the two US Immigration Inspectors and the Port Director (PD) on duty that I was there for a CET detail and would be inspecting the vehicle in secondary. During this process the driver, wearing a full cast on his right leg, stated that he was the OB/GYN doctor for Tubatama Mexico. I returned to the suspect vehicle in secondary and began my inspection. I crawled under the truck and using a mirror noticed bondo[6] on top of the tanks. Bondo is used by body shops to fill non-repairable body damage on vehicles. Sanded and painted it is almost impossible to detect visibly. Drug smugglers on the other hand, use it to seal trap doors cut into the gas tanks for accessing non-factory compartments.

Once I detected the access point into the compartment, I was fairly certain that there was contraband concealed in the tanks. I also knew where I could drill to access the compartment so out came the drill and *voilà* Cocaine on the drill bit. Cocaine in Sasabe, you have got to be kidding me!!! Cocaine was extremely rare on the Southwest border back then. I went inside and advised the PD that we had a cocaine load and then used the phone to call US Customs Sector Radio to notify the Office of Enforcement (OE - the investigative branch of Customs) that we had a cocaine load in Sasabe. I held as Sector made the notification and when the radio operator returned, he advised me that the two nearest OE personnel were at San Miguel Gate approximately two hours away and they would be responding. He also told me that one is a Special Agent the other is a Customs Patrol Officer, a member of the Shadow Wolves (a specialized force staffed entirely by Native Americans). Sector advised me their names were Edmond Klink and Pierre Eagle. So now we wait.

Inspector Greggor Elight one of the two Customs inspectors asked me if I would show him how I was able to detect the compartment and also how I knew where to drill into the cocaine

---

[5]A permiso was issued by the Immigration and Naturalization Service for Mexican passport holders going more than 25 miles from the border but only for Border States.
[6]Bondo is a compound used as a filler for making automobile repairs

without hitting the gasoline. I told him to bring the car jack and I would certainly oblige. We jacked up the passenger's side of the truck to make crawling under the vehicle much easier. As we were under the truck, I noticed the II from primary walk to her car and begin backing up coming very close to the load vehicle we were under. As she came closer and closer, we suspended the impromptu training session and rapidly got the heck out from under the truck.

I watched her not believing that in her haste, she had almost hit the vehicle we were under. She paid no attention to us whatsoever and down the road into Sasabe she went. I went to my car and grabbed my binoculars to see where this II was headed in such a hurry and as I watched she proceeded directly to the only pay phone I know of in Sasabe. She was on the phone about a minute, hung up, got back in her car and headed back up the hill to the Port. Greggor had already entered the headhouse and I joined those inside to wait for OE out of the desert heat. Ceya came in a few minutes later and headed straight to the Immigration side and disappeared into the back office.

About 10 minutes later I heard in the distance many car doors closing. I went out and looked south and there, just across the line in Mexico, were several black Suburban's with numerous guys all carrying assault rifles – and they were looking at *me*. I went to my car and broke out my Mini 14 tactical rifle, walked over to the load vehicle and set-up at the front wheel with the Mini 14 looking across the hood at *them*. I then placed three fully loaded magazines on the hood overacting as I smacked them down so the gun welders down south would know that I meant business. If they wanted to make it interesting, I was ready.

After about 5 minutes the PD came out looked at me using cover and concealment at ready arms, then he looked into Mexico at the opposing force armed to the teeth and he uttered two words "Oh Shit" Then just that quick he was gone, back into the Customs House he went. Upon occasion an Inspector would take a peek out and promptly retreat back into the depths. One more phenomenon, not one vehicle even approached the border crossing during this stand-off. None from the north and none from the south.

A looooooooooooong and extremely hot two hours or so later I heard vehicles coming up the hill behind me. As they approached, all the guys on the south side got back into their vehicles and headed south. I turned around and there were two vehicles with both drivers now out and walking toward me. One gringo (white guy) and one very large Native American. The gringo was in the lead, so I walked over to him and said "Am I glad to see you! You must be Edmond Klink".

"No" he said, "actually I am Pierre Eagle".

The giant Native American then corrected me and said "I am Edmond L. Klink the third. Were you making the assumption that Pierre Eagle was the Indian and Edmond Klink must be the gringo?"

I answered, "yep you got me, us Choctaws always jump to conclusions".

Edmond said "Oh, so you are Indian too. Well Brother, looks like you were prepared for battle there, but we scared them off".

I did not reply with the first thing that jumped into my mind. After all Edmond is about 6'5" and somewhere between 250 and 300 lbs. I just let it go and instead said with my crackly voice "I have to get a shot of water, I have been cooking on the hood of this damn vehicle for a couple of hours".

The middle of July in the Sonora Desert is NOT the place to spend time with both arms holding a rifle at ready aim, resting on a frying pan in 110° heat. Yep I was pretty well done and possibly just a bit dehydrated.

After a trip inside where I re-hydrated Special Agent Eagle looked at the guy handcuffed to a bench and asked, "Is that your driver?"

I replied, "Yep that is him, Doctor Vasquez".

Now I have to admit that the Special Agents that worked the West Desert are a different breed than those working metro areas. Pierre, not missing a thing, just had to slap me down. He looked at me then at the driver again pointing at his broken leg in a cast from ankle to hip and asked "I guess you cuffed him to the bench because there is no holding cell and you didn't want him to abscond? Watching that foot pursuit would have been the highlight of my day".

"Protocol, just following protocol" was my response. I didn't want to elaborate on my main concern. The same concern that had me waiting and watching rather than just driving up to the port when I arrived. One just had to be aware of possible inside assistance from an employee or two at the dinky little port.

Now that I was back to full strength, re-hydrated and body temperature at 98.6°, Pierre, Edmond and I walked out to the load vehicle. On the way Pierre asked where it was loaded. I told him the gas tanks. When we got to the vehicle, he just stood there looking at it for a few minutes and asked again where the cocaine was located. Again, I told him the gas tanks. He looked at me and asked, "Why did you put the tanks back on?"

"Put them back on? I never dropped them, I drilled them. I tested the cocaine that the drill bit brought out" I explained.

He looked at me and then said to Edmond "I told you those Nogales CET guys were out of flipping their mind." then to me incredulously "You drilled into the gas tank?"

I shrugged my shoulders and said, "It worked."

After returning to the headhouse from the vehicle the Special Agents began their interview of the driver and asked Inspector Greggor to translate since he is a certified Spanish instructor and that expertise can be helpful in court.

The driver claimed no knowledge of course. The only noteworthy detail out of the interview was that he claimed to be the OB/GYN in Tubatama, not *an* OB/GYN but the *only* OB/GYN in Tubatama.

When the interview was terminated Pierre asked me for the Doctor's passport. I told him that it was still in the truck and that I would get it. I proceeded back to the truck, opened the door and there was the seat belt with no passport under it. WTF!

I thought about it and the only people near the vehicle were the two investigators, me and Inspector Greggor. I walked back to the headhouse and Greggor was standing on the porch. I asked him if he had seen the passport and he said "Yes, Il Pataria asked me if the doctor's passport was over on the Customs side of the port and I told her I saw it in the vehicle. She asked if I would bring it to her so she could start processing his parole into the United States if they were going to arrest him. I went and got it and gave it to her."

I said "Greggor you just removed evidence from a crime scene. You need to write a witness statement now detailing that."

I went to the Immigration side and asked Ceya if she had the passport. She replied in the negative. I asked her "who's passport is that then" pointing at a Mexican passport on the desk behind her.

She turned and looked at the desk. When she turned back to face me her eyes never met mine and she said "Oh yea, I forgot. I was going to parole him in."

She turned around, picked up the passport and said, "Here do you need it?"

I took the passport and flipped through it. "Ceya" I said looking her intently in the eyes that still refused to meet mine "where is the permisso?"

I believe at that point she soiled herself "Permisso, uh what permisso? He didn't have a permisso."

I said to her "When I took his passport there was a permisso in it. Obviously you had to have given him one since you released him. I stopped him on his way to Tucson. Tucson is quite a bit further than 25 miles so obviously you issued him a permisso. Where is it?"

Her eyes dropped straight down now, and she said "Oh yes, I did but he will be paroled so he won't need it. I shredded it for when he is paroled."

I did not say another word just turned and walked away thinking to myself 'I will let Internal Affairs continue this'.

I brought the passport to Pierre and closed the door to the office. "Here is the fine doctor's passport and I am going to throw a whole new chapter into your investigation. There was a permisso in this damn passport when I took it from Vasquez, Pataria had Greggor retrieve the passport from the truck where I had left it and when I first asked her about it, she denied issuing one. When I pushed, she admitted that she issued it but said she had shredded it so she could parole him in."

"Well I know Pataria pretty well and she is by the book period" Pierre had a concerned look on his face as he spoke then he added "What you are telling me is a bit troubling."

"You think" I replied, "Let me fill you in on a chunk more that pushes it beyond troubling and since you are the case agent you need to know."

I relayed her run to the pay phone and added "I watched the truck enter from Mexico and pull up to the primary terminal where Pataria was waiting for it. Her entire inspection took less than a minute. Totally out of character for her. She obviously didn't check his *comprovantes* (receipts and other paperwork used to establish residency in Mexico) or give him her traditional grueling verbal interview. Lastly but most important, she had to have the permisso in her possession and completely filled out before he got here. Obviously, she knew the crossing time, vehicle and occupant before they arrived."

"Holy shit!" now Pierre's mind was racing "and then the MFJP show up in force but something held them back. My thought is they didn't fancy looking down the barrel of your Mini 14."

"Yes, and like Edmond said, you scared them off. None of the port folks knew you guys were at San Miguel Gate so none had any idea when you would arrive. Come to think of it, they probably thought with this being coke you guys would be coming in force via Back Hawk helicopters." I then added "I am going to talk to Fran Mercury when I get back to the office tomorrow." Fran was a Special Agent with Internal Affairs who was part of the CET team. His office was right next to mine.

"Yes, definitely do that. I will call him later and will let him know to expect you tomorrow and also that I am aware there may be an IA lateral investigation in connection with my dope smuggling one." he said and added "Don't put anything out over the radio or phone from here! Do it in person tomorrow. I will go through *our* channels to make sure he knows you are coming."

It wasn't long before more OE guys and some Border Patrol Agents arrived and things became a bit more comfortable. Now with plenty of firepower and plain old man power we dropped the gas tanks and retrieved the secreted packages of cocaine with a total weight of 58 pounds. OE took custody of the load and all the extra enforcement departed in a convoy to secure the dope in their seizure room.

Illustration 91: Load vehicle with Pataria's vehicle just visible on the left of the photo.

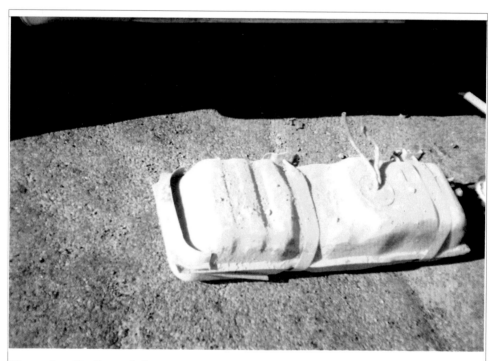

Illustration 92: Grounded gas tank

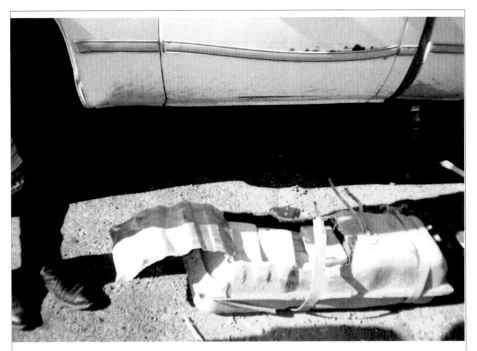

Illustration 93: Open tank compartment revealing cocaine packages

Illustration 94: Oro written on packages: translation - gold

Illustration 95: Empty compartment

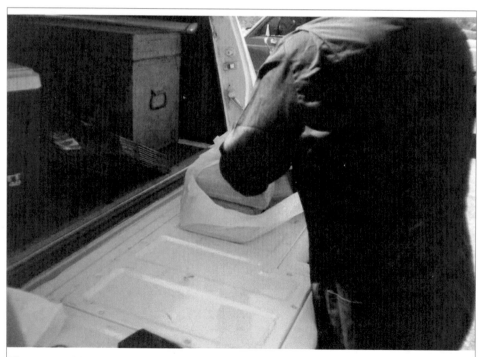

Illustration 96: Bag it and tag it.

Illustration 97: This charm will be going to auction. A trusted vehicle. Any takers?

The following day I was in Fran's office relaying the events as described. Fran was pulsating and his side of the conversation was mostly "WTF" and "that is amazing". I never found out the outcome of Fran's case. I know he was working it and prior to its conclusion Pataria retired and relocated somewhere in the northeast. Far, far from the Mexican border.

This could be the end, but this case has an epilogue:

Several months later we are all meeting again at pretrial. Well almost all; it is Greggor Elight, Edmond Klink, Pierre Eagle and me. Yep this is where I found out that Ceya Pataria had retired and had relocated back east therefore she would not be testifying. Anyhow, there we sit with the AUSA (Assistant United States Attorney) going through pretrial. During pretrial the AUSA laid out her case and how she is going to present it. She also asked a few questions and gave us a few "look out for's". I have been to many pretrials and this was no different than the others. Greggor Elight however was in a panic from the time we walked in the door. As I said earlier, he was a Spanish instructor for many years at the Federal Law Enforcement Training Center but had never been to court. The poor AUSA was doing her best to help him but there is only so much that can be done at pretrial.

When we left, he was still going on and on about his testimony and he wasn't sure he would come in for the trial the next day.

Well Elight made it to trial. The following day he was there bright and early. If you have never been a witness in court it is a bit spooky. The defense attorney will do and say anything to discredit you. They will ask the same question three or four different ways in hopes that you give a slightly different answer and if you do, he or she will point it out to the jury and claim that you have no credibility, therefore they shouldn't believe anything you say.

As a witness you can't hear the other witnesses' testimony, so I can only relay what I was told about Elight's testimony.

I was the first witness called so I went and did my thing and after being dismissed from the stand but not the trial I headed to the witness room. What that means is that you are on stand-by for possible recall; therefore, it is off to a witness room to wait. I was there by myself until Pierre came in and announced that they were nearing lunch break. He asked how well I knew Elight and I told him that I had never even met him before the day of the seizure. Pierre shook his head and relayed Elight's testimony, not the content but the delivery. He said that every time a question was asked Elight would pull out his portfolio and look through it before he answered. About four questions in the defense attorney pointed this oddity out to the judge and asked to see the portfolio. The judge and both attorneys met at the bench with the AUSA carrying the portfolio. The judge asked the AUSA what was in it and she admitted that she had no idea (we had cautioned him not to bring any notes, witness statements or such to court). In the portfolio were notes from the pretrial, witness statements, a copy of the Search, Arrest and Seizure report and a multitude of other notes he had made to himself the previous night after the pretrial. There was nothing really out of line and for the most part the defense had everything anyhow. What he obviously did not have were the notes from pretrial. According to Pierre he went off about the AUSA counseling the witness and a few other accusations some of which were serious enough to get the AUSA disbarred. Pierre said that the judge scrutinized everything in that portfolio and determined there were no legal issues. The trial would resume after lunch. Pierre said that Elight and Edmond would be along soon. When they arrived we all headed out to lunch. Pierre and Edmond never said a word about the mess to Elight and after a very quiet lunch back to court we went. Court was dismissed that afternoon with no more drama. The defense was based on no knowledge, a borrowed vehicle and this trip being the first time he had crossed in it. I was quite surprised when I heard that because during the search and inventory of the vehicle numerous credit card receipts were found in the glove box from gas stations and a motel (always the same one in Tucson). All the receipts were in the defendant's name with his signature on them. The not so good doctor was found guilty.

I was not present at the sentencing, but Pierre told me about it several days later. He said the defense attorney had a sob story appeal for leniency because Dr. Vasquez was the only OB/GYN in town and there were many expectant mothers who needed him. The judge, being one of my favorite judges, had a great come back as he issued the sentence. According to Pierre he looked at the defense attorney and said, "Well those expectant mothers had better find some mid-wives because their OB/GYN in going to jail for smuggling cocaine."

Again, this could conclude the story but there is one more addition. A few days after the sentencing I ran into Pierre again, this time in Nogales and I took one look at him and asked, "Are you O.K.?"

He answered '"Well I am here in Nogales to let Mr. Fredericks (the District Director) know that I am on my way to arrest Greggor."

I was shocked "Arrest Greggor, what in the world for?"

He answered, "Do you remember Greggor's portfolio that almost got the AUSA disbarred?" I nodded in the affirmative. "Well remember when we went to lunch." Again, I nodded yes. "Apparently he left it in the cafe, and someone found it and turned it in to the court. The judge presented it to the ASUA and now she issued a warrant for his arrest on evidence tampering and failure to control sensitive court documents. I am supposed to go arrest him. I came down here to see if the DD can change her mind before I get to Sasabe."

Pierre won this one; the DD was able to quash the flames that were burning out of control with the AUSA. Not that she didn't have good reason to explode. I will say one thing; I would bet she never takes another case from Sasabe. Not much has changed there since this seizure. Not even the sign regarding the law to report. It is the only place where you will see the Customs sign now that it is all CBP under the Department of Homeland Security.

BILLION $ DOLLAR $ HIGHWAY
Authors Note

Many thanks for to all who have contributed to this book. Those who have contributed the most to this work are you the readers. Without you Billion Dollar Highway would never have been written. I had many people from Law Enforcement to HVAC folks installing my heat pump push me to put my stories down in writing. When I retired I listened and followed their lead.

These pages chronicle my first few years with an organization that was dedicated to keeping our countries borders secure. As with all law enforcement some of my fellow Inspectors, Agents and Patrol Officers were lost in the line of duty. Please remember them in your thoughts and prayers.

I reiterate that these were actual events with real people. The only deviations from the true facts are the names of my colleagues. The names are quite fictitious and if one of the names matches an actual person that person is not the subject of this work.

This concludes the first of three photo albums. I will be starting on the second photo album soon and if God is willing there will be a Billion Dollar Highway – Otra Vez.

As an encore I have added one of my favorite seizures, so we jump ahead a few years to 1996. Please read on and enjoy the final chapter of Billion Dollar Highway Arizona Interstate 19.

BILLION $ DOLLAR $ HIGHWAY

Transformed Transformer
February 6, 1996
1,246 Pounds Cocaine

Today is an unusually warm day at the truck dock drug screening area. The traffic is very heavy with the produce season still in full swing. In the morning I used my light jacket and now in the early afternoon I have already shed it. The truck dock operation has now come full cycle and I am now right back to where I was four years earlier for the *carne asada* load, solo at the scale. At least I have a roof and it is not raining. Also, today is Tuesday, rather than Saturday.

Speaking of Tuesday, as I just mentioned the traffic is very heavy and generally speaking Tuesday's are normally a bit lighter than the other six days. Monday's are usually super busy because only a small portion of the importers and exporters work on Sunday, however during produce season the trucks with their perishable goods that were harvested during the week must keep coming from the growing areas further south in Mexico and end-up backing up on the Mexican side. Come Monday the importers and exporters are back at it so the spigot flows and trucks are backed up at the border sometimes until midnight.

Tuesdays are light because the trip to the border from the growing areas of Mexico takes two days. Just like the importers and exporters at the border, many of the facilities down south in Mexico are closed on Sunday so the trucks start rolling again on Monday. Two days later on Wednesday the toilet is flushed and here come all the trucks that left Monday. This leaves Tuesday as a slow day – *normally*, but not today. This solo day is crazy busy.

Just as I am thinking that it would be a darn good time for the traffic to break before the traffic breaks me, I see Sam Luis heading my way. Sam is a very good inspector who I recruited for Customs. He has turned out to be even better than I bragged him up to District Director when he submitted his application with me as a reference. The DD was not high on hiring people from his previous agency, but he made an exception on my recommendation. Sometimes you get lucky and one of your recommendations out performs your appraisal which sure makes you look good. Sam definitely tops the list in this category. To this day he is just a ball of fire out there, older and somewhat gray but like the battery bunny, he keeps on going and going.

As he approaches, I am thinking 'coffee!' and a sit-down break. "Hey Sam, it is about time they sent someone to give am a relief, I am beat."

Sam looked at me like I was out of my mind and said "Oh no, I am not here to relieve you. I was wondering if you can come and look at something for us."

Well, he sure busted that bubble. "Sure, I can use a break from here." I said just a bit disappointed "What do you have?"

"Well Kaolin Stephens found some discrepancies on an entry for a transformer, so we checked it but didn't find anything." he reported "Kaolin said he had seen these before so he was going to sign it off, but I told him we should get you to look at it first."

Kaolin was a true truck dock weenie. He knew that entry paperwork inside and out, so Sam had my interest. I had become quite familiar with the paperwork myself since my arrival in the commercial world four years prior and in fact was now performing as our DAU (Document Analysis Unit). Like everything else, it was a DAU of three – me, myself and I. Yep it was one of my collateral duties. I now knew the ins and outs of those Greek documents better than most of the cargo folks.

There had never been a drug seizure in Nogales from criteria that was generated through the entry paperwork, but I did put a smuggling organization out of business using said paperwork as a basis for my research. I was able to come up with a Mexican exporter and a US importer that I was sure were running drugs.

I put criteria against the two entities as well as lookouts on the principal players. The criteria called for a 100% narcotics exam. After the third entry all with negative exams the Chief, Ms. Delayno, asked if I would consider removing the criteria since it was putting a large burden on the staff. I refused telling her that I was sure these entities were smuggling hard narcotics. I had been either on day off or off site when my previous three lookouts had made entry. Since the commodity was perishable it was out of the question to hold a shipment until my return therefore, I had not seen them myself. I told her one would eventually make entry on a day when I was present and then I would examine it myself and depending on the outcome I would then re-think the lookout.

When we parted that day, it was not exactly on the greatest of terms. She was quite furious and to be honest, she had reason to be. The thing was, I was not as confident in the truck dock weenies doing a narcotics exam as she was. Fortunately, there would not be a fourth shipment.

Two days later I was paged to the office for a phone call. As I walked in to the office Klug Lancelot said "It is an Officer Pain from Shelby County Tennessee. He says it is about your lookout on Mango Town and they got your guy Andy Kong."

Now I am excited but scratching my head just a bit. Mango Town is the importer of record, a business name such as Ford, Dodge and Walmart. Kong is the owner of Mango Town. From my research I pegged him as a drug King Pin; not one of the players; but the big dog himself. I couldn't see him transporting a load of dope cross country so what is he doing in the Deep South when his area of operation is California?

I looked at the phone with only one blinking light on line 2 and surmised that must be Officer Pain. I picked up the phone, punched line 2 and answered, "Inspector Davis."

The voice on the other end was a male about mid-thirties I would guess and a distinct Tennessee drawl "Hello Inspector Davis my name is Officer Pain and we have your boy Andy Kong with a lot of drugs. Your lookout was instrumental in getting him." ('gitin im' in southern drawl)

"That is great, how did it go down?" I asked.

"Well I was out there in the middle of nowhere in partikler just a toodlin along and I see this vehicle hauling bunns straight at me. Afor I knew it he blew right on bi." he said in that distinctive but very pleasant drawl. He then said, and I will do my best to interpret to English "I whirled around and lit him up. There was Kong sitting there irritated, big guy named Fausto in the passenger seat and Kong's wife Juanita in the back. They were all hinky and nervous, so I asked them if I they would consent to a search of the vehicle. Kong declined. I really didn't have anything but reckless driving and that was pretty weak, so I called for a dog."

He hesitated so I chimed in "I believe Fausto is his body guard and Juanita is his girlfriend. His wife lives in Mexico and as far as I can tell she hasn't crossed in years. Juanita is about twenty years younger than his wife and a Mexican citizen. His wife is a Mexican citizen but she, like Kong, is very Chinese."

"Oh, well that is good to know, and it explains a lot." he uttered obviously writing and also deep in thought. "We may be able to use that information. Hmm, yes, they are not cooperating. They are claiming ignorance of the drugs."

"So, you said you got a load of drugs?" I asked. "How did my hit come into play?"

"Oh yea, well when I asked for a dog they came back and said the nearest one was more than an hour away and the Captain would not authorize a detention for that long." He said this with almost a snarl. "I told dispatch that there was more to this than bad driving. Three Mexican citizens in a California plated van registered to a Chinese named person who is not present and to complicate the stop, all three occupants are evasive and quite nervous." He continued and I detected a bit of pride in his voice "I asked Dispatch to call every Law Enforcement Organization they could find to see if there was anything out there. They called (an unnamed Customs intelligence center) and the center came back with your narcotics hits on Kong and his business. By the way he kept going on that he was a respected importer and businessman in California where he owned a multi-million dollar produce business. He even gave us his business card. That is where we got the name of his business, Mango Town."

"Well he certainly is the owner of Mango Town." I said. "He lives in Mexico but owns a business on this side. My research tells me that his Mango sales are not where the multi-million dollars are generated."

"Well when the Captain saw your lookout indicating Kong's suspected involvement in drug smuggling and distribution, he authorized the detention for the drug dog. When the dog finally arrived and ran the vehicle he pointed to the console between the front seats." Officer Pain sounded quite proud now and the irritation for his Captain was a distant memory.

As I listened, I knew exactly where the dog had alerted or pointed as the Officer put it, but it is a small area. I waited as I am sure he lit a cigarette, I recognize the Zippo. After taking a drag he continued "We got a kilo of heroin and a kilo of meth."

I was shocked. I had expected "a lot of drugs" to be somewhat more. I sometimes forget that when I worked as a patrolman a kilo was enormous. I said, "A kilo of heroin and how much meth?"

He answered "Yes sir, a kilo of heroin and a kilo of meth. That will get him a good long stay in one our fine Tennessee prisons."

At this point my mind was racing, I had been looking at Kong very closely and one thing I saw that I could not comprehend was now clear. Kong had just leased a warehouse in Miami Florida.

"Prison is precisely where he belongs, but I will tell you something else. Kong is not a mule that transports drugs, he is the big dog, the king pin of this operation." I replied "The only reason he has that dope is because he is expanding his operation to the east coast. Those two packages are samples, I am sure of it."

"Damn, damn do you think so?" he was definitely interested now. "Can you tell me what brought you to that conclusion, so I can let the detectives know?"

I explained the Florida connection and Officer Pain hurried off the phone to give the information to the detectives. He said he would call me back with an update. To my surprise the return call was in no more than an hour.

"Well I'll tell you what; them detectives took your information and went back in the interview room with it in hand, literally. They scribbled it on a sheet of typing paper, took about a hundred more blank sheets and stuck them under it." his Tennessee drawl was now full of pride **and** satisfaction "They walked in that room with one of them looking at a blank page near the bottom of the stack. Then as he was flipping through the pages, they told Kong they had just talked to Customs who knows about his east coast connection as well as the warehouse in Miami. When they told him that I thought he was going to die right then and there. Instead he offered his help because he wants to clear his good Chinese name."

"So he admitted to his operation?" I asked.

"Yes sir and before they ran me out of the viewing room I heard them setting up a meet with his New Jersey conspirators." the Zippo again clicks open . . . then shut and a deep inhale. "We got them, we sure did."

This was back when research and analysis funding was on the bubble as a waste of funds. The Government Accounting Office was asking what bang we were getting for the research and analysis buck. This case made it to Washington, DC and I was asked to put this case into a presentation for GAO executives who were visiting Nogales. Back then computer presentation programs were in their infancy and cartoonish, but they worked.

So now I am a believer in research and analysis making seizures and cases out of paperwork discrepancies. This being the case I feel like the discrepancies Kaolin detected surely warrant a good examination for this suspicious entry.

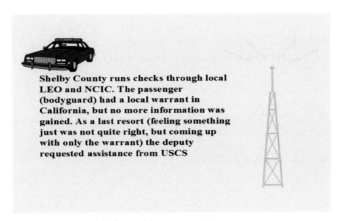

Illustration 98: Slide from GAO presentation

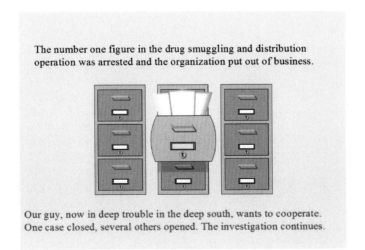

Illustration 99: Final page of GAO presentation with paperwork depicted as the foundation that dismantled a drug smuggling organization.

"What does Kaolin have on the paperwork?" I asked Sam.

"Well he said that he thinks the importer address is fictitious." he replied.

"Well that is pretty good reason to suspect someone either doesn't want a paper trail leading to them or they don't want the actual importer to see a counterfeit shipment using their name and importer number." I said "That is good enough for me. What is the commodity?"

We were dead in the middle of produce season, so I was expecting tomatoes, cucumbers, mangoes or some other produce. The last thing I was expecting was his answer "A transformer."

That one stopped me dead in my tracks. I had seen entries where transformers were the commodity but the biggest one would go in a four-inch square box. "A transformer?" I repeated, "Not a shipment of transformers?"

"No one big transformer on a stake bed truck." he assured me.

We continued on and when we got to the transformer there it was, over five feet tall and it filled the entire bed of the truck. This was a first for me. Even though I had seen many of these transformers supplying entire buildings I had never really paid much attention to them.

"This is US goods being returned for repair" Sam informed me "and Kaolin said that he has seen them cross but not very often."

"Well this is a first for me, but it is no different than any other inspection. We just have to look for something that doesn't belong. Something out of place." I said, probably more to me than to Sam. I was running this beast through my head trying to conceive a plan of attack on this new challenge.

"I notice that it has a new paint job. Why paint a transformer that is on its way to a repair facility? Seems to me the repair facility would paint it *after* repairs not the other way around." I was again talking to myself. Sam must have known it because he stood there in silence.

Thinking to myself now I concluded that the only reason to paint a broken piece of equipment was to disguise something. I began looking for that something and sure enough found it. Even today I will not disclose what I found but as soon as I saw it, I was sure we had a load of dope.

I opened the only access point and low and behold it looked just like a transformer should look, at least it seemed right. Wires, cables, switches and cooling oil. It sure looked legitimate from that vantage point. Sam stood there staring at the same thing and said, "Well so much for that."

I went back and double checked the discrepancies that I had used to conclude that this high dollar value item was indeed loaded and after a second look I was even more convinced that there was dope there. Utilizing a portable contraband detector, I located an area where I could use a drill with minimal damage. I told Sam to go to my booth and bring me a hand-held drill. He headed to my booth and ran into supervisor Elmer Linex and Kaolin.

SCI Linex stopped Sam and asked, "Where are you heading Sam? Have you guys released the transformer? The broker is asking when it is going to be released."

I am thinking 'Damn I didn't need this'. Supervisor Linex is a good supervisor but is extremely skittish. I wouldn't say paranoid, but the word does jump into my mind.

I could hear the conversation from my perch atop the suspected Trojan Horse and I heard poor Sam reply very defensively "Rick sent me to his booth to get a drill."

Elmer looked at me sitting there on top of the transformer and the look on his face was, the best I can describe it is actually, well paranoid jumps into my mind. He abruptly ended Sam's drill run and he went into a quickstep march, eyes trained on me. "You are not going to drill that thing are you?" he asked.

"Yes, I am sure I can go in right here with no problem." I said.

"Did you find bondo?" the same 'old guard' question that dinosaur Custom Inspectors would always ask just before they told you not to get that intrusive. Intrusive is another term they loved. We even have an acronym for certain pieces of inspection tools: NII for non-intrusive inspection devices.

"No, I didn't find bondo but I am sure there has been tampering with this transformer." I admitted "Someone has been working inside it."

"Well unless you find bondo there will be no drilling." exactly opposite of his brother, also a Customs supervisor.

Elmer's brother Cosmos Linex said on numerous occasions "Ricko if you say it is there, it is there. Do what you have to do." Cosmos was diagnosed with cancer and passed away from it on a time line with my brother. Both were diagnosed with it within weeks of each other and both passed away within weeks of each other. Cosmos was and still is one of the most respected people I ever knew. I can never say enough about him, just a great person and an even better supervisor. He is greatly missed.

Elmer however was not willing to go out on a limb. He was, like many other supervisors, scared to death of a tort claim. In my opinion, tort claims are there for a reason and this scenario is a perfect example of that reason.

"10-4 let me give it another look and see if I can find some bondo." I said, "I will let you know if I find some."

"OK, perfect." With that Elmer strolled off back toward his office. Kaolin stayed behind and said "I will wait here until you are satisfied. I have already signed off the entry and I will drop it off with the broker, so we can expedite the release."

I thought 'release my ass' and took about two minutes looking for bondo never leaving the top of the transformer, just enough time for Elmer to enter the building, then I looked at Sam and said, "Sam go to my booth and bring me that drill."

Sam looked shocked and said, "Did you find bondo?"

"Nope but I am the Senior here and I am directing you to retrieve the drill. You are only doing as directed." I replied.

Kaolin, also a Senior, said "I will be no part of this. Elmer is going to be furious. That is insubordination. You told him you would look for bondo."

My reply to this idiot was simple and very truthful: "Yep that is what I told him and yep, I did look for bondo. I also told him I would let him know if I found some which I did not. He agreed to my terms, in fact said they were perfect if I recall. I have complied with his perfect terms. I said nothing about *not* finding bondo, so the only thing left to do is drill."

"I am out of here; don't even mention my name when that tort claim comes in." With that Kaolin was history.

Sam made a bee line to my booth and returned carrying the drill. "Are you sure you want to drill without finding bondo?" he asked.

"Absolutely, what are they going to do, send me back to passenger processing. Hell, I wish but I am sure Mr. Fredericks will back me." I said and added "He is a bull, not a steer like a couple of other folks around here."

"Yea, well and he is the District Director so who is going to say anything to him anyway." Sam said then added "It sure would have been nice to have found bondo." Just as he finished speaking, he smacked the edge of the transformer with an open-end wrench he was holding and voilà there was some bondo. "Look, look Rick bondo. There is some bondo. I am going to get Elmer and let him know."

Off he went at a dead run. I said to myself, 'Oh well I suppose I might as well wait'. I sat on top of the transformer and waited. I was thinking 'This is a high dollar item. Some folks are steers and would rather not be part of a high dollar tort claim. There is no need in waiting; I might as well start drilling because like Kaolin, Linix will be history deep in his office.'

I stood up and no sooner did I pull the trigger on the drill when I saw Sam running solo toward me. Moments later he was on top of the transformer. I stopped drilling and, knowing the answer, asked if Elmer was on his way. "No, but he said if there is bondo go ahead and drill." he was pointing at the area where I was drilling "Can I finish drilling? It is almost there."

I handed him the drill and said, "Have at it."

He carefully placed the drill bit in the indentation I had started. Sam looked at me and hesitated, just a bit of fear etched on his face. "Go ahead, Sam. I am an eleven you are a nine. It is my call and *my* ass."

In less than a minute the eight-inch bit disappeared as the bit breached the remainder of the metal roof. Sam looked up again with almost a panic expression etched on his face. He pulled the bit out and looked at it as if it would magically speak to him. Nice shiny groves from top to bottom. He re-inserted the bit and withdrew it a couple of times each time staring at the bare bit. He put it back in again and pulled the trigger on the drill running it in and partially out a couple of times then extracted it still spinning and released the trigger. Still just a nice clean drill bit. "It is empty." he said looking at the offending bit. "Nothing, nothing. Are we in trouble?"

"No, not really, but do me a favor." I said "Step back and let me probe the damn thing. You are eight inches deep in a five-foot-high container. When we opened the access panel there was oil less than an inch from the top. I see no oil on that damn bit."

At the truck dock, just like passenger processing, I always carried a probe. In passenger processing I used an old screw driver with a three and a half inch shaft, four inches at the most. I retired that for a broken car antenna the same length with a sharpened end containing a notch.

Illustration 100: Small antenna probe with notch visible
at the sharpened end. The handle is fuel line (hose).

At the truck dock I carried a full-length car antenna also sharpened with a bigger notch. Sam abandoned his position blocking the drill hole and I inserted the antenna. At about ten inches I hit a package. Sam saw me stop and I pushed it on through the first package and hit a second one. I looked at Sam and smiled. "Well there are at least two layers and it sure feels like coke."

228

His face lit up like the Fourth of July at the National Mall in Washington, DC. I pulled the probe out and the notch was loaded with shiny white powder. As soon as Sam saw it, he started jumping up and down, with us precariously perched on top of an unstable transformer sitting in the back of a stake bed truck. To top it off he was yelling at the top of his lungs "Its coke. Its coke." That kinda blew any covert delivery; that was a given.

For me I suddenly became aware of everyone and everything around us. One of the first things that jumped out at me was a yellow fixed wing aircraft flying around. It dawned on me that I had subconsciously been hearing it during most of the inspection. There were so many other distractions that it was definitely on a back burner. By now half the population at the truck dock were watching including several inspectors.

I said, "This is now a crime scene, clear those folks out of here." indicating the civilians to include Customs office personnel. In less than five minutes only Inspectors were present, and the yellow aircraft was still making passes.

I pointed it out to the other Inspectors and asked, "Have any of you ever seen that airplane before?"

No one had but now everyone was looking at it. "Try to get the tail number on its next pass." I said. I don't know if it was the pilot's sixth sense, he saw us all looking or if it was just coincidence that it had been there at all, but he made one more pass and was gone. As far as any of us could tell it had no tail number. That airplane is still a mystery to this day.

We notified the Office of Enforcement of the find and within half an hour every OE Special Agent had visited. They talked about doing a delivery but when it was revealed that Sam's exuberance had probably been noted by everyone in Nogales and maybe even Tucson, the idea was abandoned. It was now time to open the beast and retrieve the spoils.

This was not going to be like cutting a rocker panel or an aluminum gas tank. This was new territory for all of us. I started with the kick butt air chisel.

Illustration 101: The author using an air chisel in vain.

After five minutes and a whopping two inches I was absolutely certain that the air chisel was not an option. But we still had another cutting tool in our arsenal. Our secret weapon was none other than an air driven, hand held grinder. The only issue was, it was the size of a can of soda.

Illustration 102: Hand held grinder. Strike two.

Again, after several minutes of noise and sparks the only real damage was to the grinding wheel. Apparently all the sparks were emitted as the grinding wheel ground down to nothing. The transformer lost maybe an inch. That brought on option three. We borrowed a reciprocating saw from another agency, if memory serves me it was the US Border Patrol.

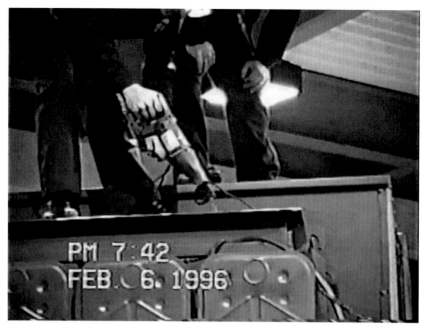

Illustration 103: Just may be the answer.

The tide had finally turned in this conflict and we had the enemy moving out. Yep you could actually see the saw cutting and moving along. I still had to use the small grinding wheel at the corners to change direction, but we could see and smell victory (cutting painted metal emits a nauseous odor).

Sam and I were doing all the work, but we had many gun toting looky-loos and a few know-it-alls with their two cents worth of nothing to toss in. Elmer came by with Ms. Delayno and she was beaming. "So, Kaolin finally got a load!" she said as Sam and I were struggling with the inadequate cutting tools prior to the arrival of the reciprocating saw.

Elmer corrected her and said "Well no, he already signed the release, but Rick found the discrepancies and" at that point Delayno interrupted Elmer and said "He referred it to Rick, but it is Kaolin's seizure. This is a truck dock seizure period."

I thought 'been there done that. Delayno must have taken a page from Thorny's book.' She continued "I told him to get a seizure number, so he is tied up for now."

Well that is definitely a Thorny move and it was orchestrated by the Chief of the Commercial Facility. There was a reason for her violation of protocol that will become obvious later. The only way to get a seizure number is by opening a Search, Arrest and Seizure report. The way to steal a seizure is by cutting the SAS while the real Inspectors are still tied up working the load.

By design the SAS is to be filled out by the seizing Inspector and has fields for other personnel involved in a seizure. The seizing Inspector can be anyone involved in the seizure. This is more for legal grounds than doling out credit, but it does give credit by default. The fields include referring officer, discovering officer, personal search performed by, case agent, District Director, supervisor and witnesses. Pretty much everyone involved. Kaolin, like other seizureless Inspectors who never discovered a load, had his name in every Inspector slot including discovering officer. The guy who said *"I will be no part of this. Elmer is going to be furious."* and disappeared after his final remarks *"You told him you would look for bondo. I am out of here, **don't even mention my name** when that tort claim comes in."* This deception or false reporting would come back to bite him on his back side.

Once opened we could see the magnitude of the seizure. It was now dark and the commercial facility was pretty isolated. Worst yet it was not very well lit with the only lighting at the dock thus spotlighting us. We literally could not see our perimeter fence. Several things were obvious: this amount of hard narcotics is not a mom and pop operation; we were looking at a very big chunk of some very bad people's money (obviously a drug cartel operation); we are very close to Mexico where those bad people live; the cartels controlled many of the law enforcement organizations as well as some of the military units in Mexico and we are going to be here for a while.

Illustration 104: Victory at last. Seeing is believing.

232

We decided to do the unpacking at the Mariposa POE (MAP) where we had more Law Enforcement Officers, much better lighting and a better defensive postilion should that need arise. As we arrived at MAP we were met by a slew of Inspectors one of them being an old seasoned Senior Inspector Kindrick Pauls. Pauls was small in stature and perfect for assisting with unloading the numerous bricks of cocaine from the confined space. We used secondary examination tables to hold the bricks and set up an assembly line to expedite the process.

Illustration 105: First brick removed

Illustration 106: Digging in.

Illustration 107: No, he is not shrinking.

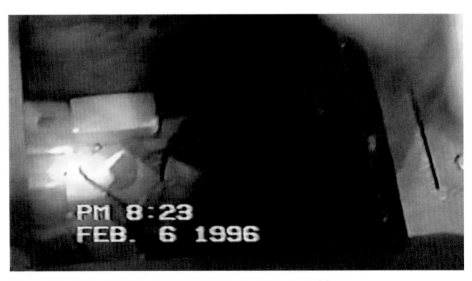

Illustration 108: Still digging, yep that is Pauls just visible.

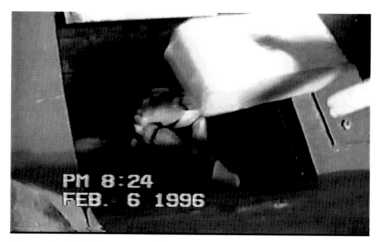

Illustration 109: Toss me another one.

At some point during this process Kaolin appeared bragging about his seizure taking cocaine off the streets. I suspect that he was sent over to get in front of the camera. He started with thanking Sam and me for our help. He said he couldn't have done it without us. That statement brought about a round of laughter from the other Inspectors who knew him. He then made another statement you would expect from a rookie "I don't think they will run any more of these through here." He thinks he is that good? Some people will never cease to amaze me.

Illustration 110: Kaolin was not camera shy.

When all was done a total of 297 packages were removed with a total weight of 1,246 pounds. The load filled two inspection tables.

Illustration 111: 1st table.

Illustration 112: 2nd table

The packages were unlike any I had seen before or have seen since in that they were in two sizes: regular kilo size and most were jumbo two kilo size. The one kilo sizes were wrapped with brown, beige, gray and white heavy plastic tape and the two-kilo jumbo size were all yellow. If you noticed in illustration 111 there are five packages lying on the pavement in front of the table. There is one of each color starting from the bottom up just above the 8 in *PM 8:29* – gray, white, brown and beige with a two-kilo yellow on top. For those who noticed and are wondering why they are there, we sampled and tested each to ensure they were all cocaine.

236

Those packages would also go to the lab for scientific confirmation, purity, etc.

Markings are always a challenge to decipher and this seizure was no different. Most had no markings; however, some were marked with ΔLCΔ the others with a picture of the Stars and Bars or officially the *flag* of the Confederate States of America during the United States Civil War in the 1860's. We seldom determined the exact meaning of the markings, but one would venture a guess that this load was headed to the southeastern United States.

Illustration 113: A mixed batch in both size and wrapping.

The Case Agent on this load was none other than an agent that I am reminded of every time I watch the Bruce Willis movie *The Fifth Element*. The Fifth Element (with the interesting name of Leeloo in the movie) was molded after the agent, perfect in every way. This case should have been an escalator to the top for her but because the AUSA wanted an open and shut case (or at least that was the excuse) and her management wanted a prosecution our Leeloo ended up in between a rock and a hard place.

I helped her put together a Power Point presentation for the Grand Jury. It would have been a first. It had numerous pictures, documents and explanations that were damning for the principals. It tracked the organizations movements step by step back and forth to their destination in the US (not the South by the way). The evidence was overwhelming and arranged so a 5th grader could see the obvious. Like everything about the Fifth Element, her work was perfect. None of it ever made it to a Grand Jury. Makes one wonder which side the AUSA was on.

OE management should have backed our Leeloo instead of an incompetent, or worse, US Attorney. They were "Investigators" after all and saw the same evidence I saw as well as the evidence graphically represented in the presentation. Maybe that bunch of arrogant male chauvinists should have dropped the denigration of the few female agents in the OE office and done a little investigating in their own back yard. In a country built on laws that include a judge and jury, a record-breaking cocaine seizure was decided by one AUSA unquestioned by OE brass.

As we say in the Government – This page intentionally left blank.

About the Author

The author retired after more than 40 years of federal service a GS-15 Supervisory Customs and Border Protection Officer assigned to the Joint Task Force – West, Arizona as the Director, Joint Intelligence and Operations Center. In his forty plus years of government service which includes time in the military during the Vietnam Era, he performed a wide range of functions and duties at varying levels of complexity.

The author began his Customs career in Nogales, AZ in 1987 as an Inspector. In 1990 the Chief, Passenger Operations created a new drug interdiction team (TROLL Team). As the District leader in drug seizures he was assigned as one of the first members of the team. In less than three months, his success on the TROLL Team, including one of the largest cocaine seizures on the Southwest border at the time and the largest in the Nogales District (607 pounds of Cocaine being smuggled by an INS Inspector returning from Church in Mexico), led the District Director to reassign him to the District Contraband Enforcement Team (CET). One of his first loads on CET broke his previous cocaine record with a 644 pound cocaine seizure. In 1992 he was assigned to establish a CET presence at the Nogales Commercial Facility. Upon arrival at the Commercial Facility, he established the CET office, assessed the operation of the facility and determined the best use of CET assets at the facility. Within three weeks CET had the first two cold hit narcotics loads at the facility (880 and 461 pounds) in over nine years. The operation quickly went from a one-man operation to a full CET deployment at what became known as Secondary Express. At the Commercial Facility he began electronic targeting when a new Chief Enforcement Officer assigned him to use the computer to target rail. Using a 286 computer that required a boot disk at startup he taught himself dBase and wrote programs for not only rail but other entities including propane tankers as well as a tool issue and accountability data base. The targeting programs were based on specific criteria for rail, and specific criteria that of course was completely different for the propane tankers. The author began using Customs data bases and targeting programs to target commercial shipments which resulted in the first criteria generated cocaine seizure in Nogales (more than 1,200 pounds) and in another case the dismantling of a drug smuggling operation through a traffic stop in Shelby County, Tennessee. The author was deeply engaged in anti-drug technology from testing the first PCD Busters to working with Research & Development on the prototype VACIS (an x-ray type imaging system). After working with R&D on the development of the prototype VACIS he ran the first field test of the system after it was deployed in Nogales. The author was also assigned the full Truck X-ray system when it was built and was considered a subject matter expert on both systems. These systems required special instruction and the author developed and instructed all training for Nogales on both the VACIS and TXR including radiation safety training that required concurrence from the Radiation Safety Officer at headquarters as well as the Nuclear Regulatory Commission. The author was recognized as a subject matter expert in compartment and concealment detection as well as other law enforcement technique's including interview techniques, use of law enforcement technology, arrest procedures and court testimony. He was one of two Inspectors selected to establish, develop lesson plans and instruct the first compartment and concealment training for Customs. The training was so successful that outside law enforcement partners requested the training which led to an expansion of the training to outside State, local and other federal agencies including the Illinois State Police at their academy in Springfield, Oklahoma State Police, the Maricopa County Sheriff Office and several National Guard units. In line with this came his selection to assist in the creation of the Federal Law Enforcement Training Center's Southwest Border Interdiction Training in Laredo, Texas that included the development and instruction of two training sessions, Portable Contraband Detector (PCD Buster) and Secondary Express. An additional duty was the Port Enforcement Command Center upon its establishment at the Truck X-ray and the author was eventually moved to the District Enforcement Command Center (DECC) at the Customs Management Center where he established the Post Seizure Analysis Team at the DECC utilizing Customs data bases and targeting programs as well as a locally created analytical tool. On 9/11/2001the anti-drug operation at the DECC became anti-terrorism and the author coordinated the Level 1 procedures in the Arizona CMC regarding the September 11 attacks to include working closely with the FBI Command Center and other Federal, State and local entities. Anti-terrorism was the main focus for the author at the DECC from the day of the attacks until his volunteer or more accurately, voluntold departure to the new Office of Border Security at Headquarters in Washington DC working strictly anti-terrorism. That began his ten-year tour at Customs Headquarters; but that is another book.

55106961R00137

Made in the USA
Columbia, SC
10 April 2019